THE **ECKE**
POINSETTIA
MANUAL

THE **ECKE**
POINSETTIA
MANUAL

Paul Ecke III, James E. Faust, Ph.D., Jack Williams, Andy Higgins

Ball Publishing | Batavia, Illinois

Ball Publishing
P.O. Box 9
335 N. River St.
Batavia, IL 60510
www.ballpublishing.com

Library of Congress Cataloging-in-Publication Data

The Ecke poinsettia manual / Paul Ecke III ... [et al.].
      p. cm.
   Includes index.
   ISBN 1-883052-41-6 (hardcover : alk. paper)
   1. Poinsettias. I. Ecke, Paul, 1955-

   SB413.P63E34 2004
   635.9'3369--dc22
                              2004008565

Printed and bound in Singapore by Imago.
10 09 08 07 06 05 04   1 2 3 4 5 6 7 8 9

DEDICATION

Many people knew my father as a businessman, an employer, a friend, a fellow board member, or were perhaps interviewed by him while taking his order at a restaurant. I am sure that the people he encountered on a daily basis formed very different impressions of him.

I'd like to share a little of what Paul Ecke Jr. was like as a father. It is my way of dedicating this book to him and a way to share the impact he had on all three of his children: myself and my sisters, Liz and Sara.

A good place to start is with our family motto: "We never give up." This was posted on our kitchen bulletin board for maximum impact, but it was put into practice daily as the three of us were encouraged to keep trying. Whether it was perfecting our second-grade handwriting, training one of our 4-H animals, or learning to ride a bike, Dad was always offering words of encouragement. My guess is that many people besides us were encouraged by him and inspired to do their best.

Paul Ecke Jr.

"Good start" was the operative phrase. Traveling, always an adventure in our family, started with packing the luggage in the car. We kids would often take a crack at loading it up, only to have Dad come out and say "Good start!" and then proceed to take everything out and repack it the "Navy way!"

Dad joined the U.S. Navy at seventeen and loved to tell this story, which we believe sums up the way he approached most things in life. During the Korean Conflict, his ship, the USS *Perkins* was anchored off the coast of Korea. After some heavy shelling, the dirt was knocked out of the planter boxes he had installed in the officer's mess. During the confusion of clean up, the dirt was thrown out. Without soil, the plants would die. So, what did Paul Ecke Jr. do? He convinced the captain of the destroyer to let him go ashore with a small crew of armed men in the dark of night to get dirt from the coast of North Korea for his planter boxes! Anyone who knew my father knows he was not making this up.

My dad liked things neat and tidy, not to mention freshly painted. After years of observing him do this, many of us here at the Ranch now automatically pick up trash or remove dead leaves from plants in airports or hotel lobbies, wherever we happen to be.

He was a wonderful grandfather and made our children feel as special as he did everyone else. Prior to his death, he bought a Model A Ford just to take them for rides. In fact, he was so excited the day his first grandchild, Corinne May, was born, he flew to San Francisco to see her and had the cab wait at the curb so he could go right back home on the next flight. He really didn't have time to be there, but not much stopped our dad.

But here is what we think he was best at: Dad was a man keenly interested in other people. While he certainly liked to tell a story or two about himself, one of his greatest gifts was asking questions about *you* and making *you* feel important. As kids, this tended to embarrass us because instead of just melting into the background as parents *should* do, Dad immersed himself in our friends' lives and insisted on getting the nitty-gritty details. He paid a lot of attention to our friends, and although it was somewhat annoying at the time, we appreciated the fact that he was interested, and I believe our friends benefited from his interest in them.

When we would all be out at a family dinner, he would ask the wait staff, "Are you in school?" and "What are you studying? Have you considered the benefits of a career in agriculture?" This would elicit groans of "Oh, Dad" from us kids, but little did we know that he was teaching us how to be interested in others.

Dad absolutely loved to communicate with people and was a prolific letter writer. All his letters, even the ones with just one line, were typed on letterhead and signed with his trademark flourish in pink or green highlighter. While we were at college, we each got an average of one letter a day, often with a newspaper or magazine article enclosed for our review and comment. I have to confess, after the advent of electronic mail, I did not encourage him to learn to use e-mail himself. Can you imagine?

We learned from him that it was not *what* we had, but rather the friends and relationships we had in life that were most important. He was a very generous man with the community and the industry, but never at our expense. He taught us the value of integrity, and we were expected to honor all promises we made.

Truly, we feel blessed to have had such a father as Paul Ecke Jr. As we now raise our own children, we often remember his example: to lead with absolute integrity and undying persistence. We never give up, and that's a wonderful legacy.

We can take from his life as an example that we should:

- Have high standards in all we do.
- Love our friends and family, and tell them so.
- Enjoy each day as it comes.

We know that he did, and he would want the same for each of us.

This book is dedicated to you, Dad, in your loving memory.

Paul Ecke III

CONTENTS

ACKNOWLEDGEMENTS

A project of this magnitude cannot be successfully undertaken without the support of good friends and talented colleagues. We are grateful for the opportunity to thank the following people for the gift of their time, expertise, and commitment:

Paul Ecke Jr., O. A. Matkin, and Dr. David Hartley for the portions of their collaborative work on *The Poinsettia Manual* that were used, and to Jack Williams, Jan Hall, David Hartley, John Biernbaum, Bill Fonteno, and Heiner Lieth for their articles published in *The Poinsettia* (journal of the Poinsettia Growers Association).

Bill Argo, Jim Barrett, Carolyn Bartuska, Rob Berghage, John Dole, Hans Ragnar Gislerod, P. Allen Hammer, Royal Heins, Bin Liu, Joe Moore, and Brian Weesis for photographs, technical help, and ideas that undoubtedly improved our final product, and to John Dole, Paul Fisher, and Geoffrey Njue for contributing chapter 13, Cut Poinsettias.

Jan Hall, Roger Kehoe, and Ruth Kobayashi for their technical skills and guidance throughout the writing and editing process.

Ball Publishing Managing Editor Rick Blanchette for his encouragement and advice.

We offer our special thanks to Carey Kramer, Product Integration Manager at the Ecke Ranch, who organized and led the daily effort required to keep us focused and on schedule, Joyce Mizock for help with editing and rewrites, and Bob Bretell for his magnificent photographs.

For past and continuing contributions, we thank the commercial greenhouse growers and university floriculture researchers from around the world who continue to provide valuable information based on their evaluations of new poinsettia cultivars and cultural research.

The greatest asset of any company is usually its people. The list of dedicated employees who get the day-to-day work done and offer their expertise and ideas to bring forward greater efficiencies is long. Even though they are sometimes behind the scenes, they are the true heart and soul of our company. Accordingly, we must acknowledge our product development and production teams who consistently challenge why and how we produce our crops, often forcing us to adapt with new techniques; our plant pathologist and pesticide manager for the development and implementation of protocols for commercial application of insect exclusion screening programs before other companies adopted these practices, enabling us to become a model in the area of pest exclusion and clean stock programs for more than just poinsettias; and our management and marketing teams, who ensure our survival by keeping pace with the demands of the economy and the needs of the marketplace.

ABOUT THE AUTHORS

PAUL ECKE III

With a passion for efficiency and doing things right the first time, Paul Ecke III has been instrumental in leading the Ecke Ranch since 1990. Combining a B.S. in horticulture from Colorado State, an MBA from Duke University and three years of offshore production management experience with Hewlett-Packard, Paul has brought a progressive business perspective to all Ranch operations and has led the way in implementing high-tech growing processes and procedures. Under his watchful eye, the Ranch shifted business focus into three primary strategies: to offer lower cost options for grower customers, to diversify the product offering, and to get a better match of company offerings with the needs of customers. Using the knowledge and technical expertise associated with vegetative cutting production from poinsettias, he dramatically expanded the product line to include vegetative spring annuals and the formation of The Flower

Fields brand. Today about half of the Ranch business results from the vegetative spring annuals. Paul drove process and efficiency changes internally, working to provide customers with the right quality at the right price. Paul's knack for viewing obstacles as opportunities provides fresh motivation to those who work closely with him.

JAMES E. FAUST

Jim grew his first poinsettia crop in 1987 and readily admits having absolutely no clue what he was doing until Dr. David Hartley, research director at the Paul Ecke Ranch at the time, visited the greenhouse that season. He was amazed that someone understood every little detail about the poinsettia, and at that point decided that he, too, wanted to have that degree of expertise someday. So after spending a couple of years as a grower, Jim decided to go to graduate school at Michigan State in order to learn more about the physiology of floriculture crops, especially the poinsettia.

Over the past 15 years, Jim has conducted important research on a num-

ber of poinsettia issues including: stem breakage, branching issues, photomorphogenesis, stock plant production techniques, and plant growth regulators. Jim is currently on the horticulture faculty at Clemson University (which is, coincidentally, near the South Carolina home of Joel Robert Poinsett).

ANDY HIGGINS

With a background in both finance and horticulture, Andy Higgins has been a key figure in the Ecke Ranch's growth and development as an international company. Andy and his team were responsible for the founding and integrating our offshore facilities into the business, which allowed for a drastic expansion of Ranch crops and programs in North America. Without the combined focus of good horticulture and good business, expansion of that size and scale had the potential to put the Ecke Ranch at risk both

financially and as a supplier of high-quality cuttings to our customers. Key to this success is Andy's belief in an integrated production system that can meet ever-increasing customer expectations. Through Andy's leadership, the organization is stronger and positioned to continue its role as a reliable, quality supplier for the years to come.

JACK E. WILLIAMS

Poinsettias are an important crop in virtually every country of the world. Regardless if they are used for the traditional Christmas season or as a specialty crop for the Chinese New Year, the beauty of poinsettias has made them a favorite with consumers everywhere. But producing poinsettias in the heat of summer in Australia or the bitter cold of winter in Mongolia can be a challenge for growers located in these regions. And just like in North America, these growers can count on support from Ecke. As a technical specialist for Ecke, Jack works with our agents and growers

 worldwide to troubleshoot crop problems and help growers do a better job producing quality crops, regardless of where they are growing. To this end, Jack's boundless enthusiasm and commitment to high service standards earns him great respect throughout the industry.

HISTORY OF POINSETTIA CULTIVARS

Euphorbia pulcherrima Willd. ex Klotzsch, the poinsettia, is a member of the botanical family Euphorbiaceae, or spurge family. The genus was named for Euphorbius, a first-century Greek physician to King Juba II of Mauritania who used the milky sap (latex) for medicinal purposes. The genus *Euphorbia* is large, containing 1,600 to 2,000 species. All species are characterized by a single female (pistillate) flower, without petals and usually without sepals, surrounded by individual male (staminate) flowers that are enclosed in a cup-shaped structure called a cyathium (*pl.* cyathia).

Figure 1-1. The true flower of the poinsettia

One or more glands are borne on the cyathium. The showy red portion of the plant, popularly referred to as the flower, consists of modified leaves, or bracts. *E. pulcherrima* is a deciduous shrub reaching 15 feet in its native habitat in Mexico. Other members of the *Euphorbia* genus include: *E. fulgens,* scarlet plume; *E. marginata,* snow-on-the-mountain; *E. splendens,* crown-of-thorns; and several herbaceous perennials.

1

DISCOVERY AND EARLY USE

The poinsettia, a contemporary symbol of Christmas in many parts of the world, was cultivated by the Aztecs in Mexico. Called *cuetlaxochitl* by the Native Americans, poinsettias are native to the area near present-day Taxco. Because of the brilliant color, the flowers were a symbol of purity. It was highly prized by both King Netzahualcoyotl and Montezuma, but because of the climate, the poinsettia could not be grown in their capital, which is now Mexico City. The Aztecs also had practical uses for the plant. A reddish dye was made from the bracts, and a medicinal preparation was made from the latex and used to counteract fever.

During the seventeenth century, a group of Franciscan priests settled near Taxco, Mexico, and began to use the flower in the Fiesta of Santa Pesebre, a nativity procession. This custom was described by Don Hernando Ruiz de Alarcon, a resident of Taxco, in a letter to his brother, Spanish playwright Don Jean Ruiz de Alarcon. Juan Balme, a botanist of the same period, mentioned the poinsettia in his writings. He described it as having large green leaves and a small flower surrounded by bracts, almost as if for protection. The bracts, he said, turned a brilliant red. Balme found the plant flourishing on the slopes and valleys near Cuernavaca, Mexico.

Poinsettias were first introduced in the United States in 1825 by Joel Robert Poinsett. While serving as the first United States Ambassador to Mexico, he had occasion to visit Taxco and found the flowers growing on

Figure 1-2. Joel Poinsett, the first U.S. ambassador to Mexico and the botanist who brought the poinsettia to the United States.

the adjacent hillsides. Poinsett, a botanist of great ability, had some plants sent to his home in Greenville, South Carolina. He also distributed plants to botanical gardens and to horticultural friends, including John Bartram of Philadelphia. Bartram, in turn, supplied plants to Robert Buist, a nurseryman who first sold the plant as *Euphorbia pulcherrima* Willd. ex Klotzsch. of the Euphorbiaceae family. The name poinsettia, however, has remained the accepted common name in English-speaking countries.

CULTIVATION

In 1902, Albert Ecke, newly arrived in the United States from Germany via Switzerland, began farming in the Eagle Rock Valley, now a part of Los Angeles, California. In 1906, he sold his farm and moved his family to Hollywood. With the help of his son Hans he began raising field-grown flowers for the local fresh cut-flower market. Their initial crops were gladioli, chrysanthemums, and poinsettias. The exact date when the Ecke family started specializing in poinsettia production is unknown, but is believed to be around 1909. The family gradually directed its efforts toward producing field-grown poinsettias for the local fresh cut-flower market, though there was a limited quantity of stock being grown for dormant plant purposes. In 1919, after the death of Albert Ecke and his son Hans the second son, Paul, assumed management of the family business.

In 1919, the principal poinsettia cultivars being grown were 'True Red' and an early-blooming cultivar known as 'Early Red'. 'Early Red' held its foliage much better than 'True Red' and was grown as a cut flower and as a potted plant. Albert Ecke acquired these original cultivars from Southern California neighbors who were using the plants for landscaping around their homes. Around 1924, Louis Bourdet of St. Louis, Missouri, began advertising a cultivar called 'St. Louis'. This cultivar can still be found in Southern California landscapes today. In 1920, a sport of 'Early Red' was found that had wider, more compact bracts. This sport was named 'Hollywood' and was sold to Eastern U.S. greenhouse operators for many years for flowering potted plant production.

The modern era of poinsettia culture began with the introduction of the seedling 'Oak Leaf'. This cultivar was reported to been grown originally in Jersey City, New Jersey, by a Mrs. Enteman in 1923. From 1923 until the 1960s, all of the principle cultivars of any commercial importance were selections or sports from this original 'Oak Leaf' seedling. Most of these cultivars were selected and developed by Paul Ecke Sr. of Encinitas, California, and many were named after Ecke family members, such as 'Henriette Ecke' (1927), 'Mrs. Paul Ecke' (1929), 'Ruth Ecke' (1931), 'Albert Ecke' (1938), 'Ecke White' (1945), 'Barbara Ecke Supreme' (1949), and 'Elisabeth Ecke' (1960).

Figure 1-3. 'Oak Leaf', a cultivar introduced in 1923, began the modern era of poinsettia culture. 'Ruth Ecke' (pictured) was a cultivar derived from 'Oak Leaf'.

Figure 1-4. "Curly" bracts were first observed in 1927 on a cultivar named 'Henriette Ecke' and then in 1950 with 'Ecke's Flaming Sphere' (pictured).

In 1929, one of the first distinctive sports of 'Oak Leaf' was selected and named 'Mrs. Paul Ecke'. This shorter-growing type with wide bracts was welcomed to the newly emerging greenhouse flowering potted plant business. The cultivar 'Indianapolis Red' sported from 'Mrs. Paul Ecke' in 1932 in the greenhouse of Bauer & Steinkamp in Indianapolis, Indiana. This relatively short-growing cultivar produced two improved selections that were found in the Ecke field plants, 'Improved Indianapolis Red' in 1950 and 'Dark Indianapolis Red' in 1951.

In 1927, a plant with "double" incurved bracts, named 'Henriette Ecke', was found in a field planting in Hollywood, California. Twenty-three years later (1950), a very unusual sport of 'Henriette Ecke' was introduced that had all incurved bracts and no horizontal bracts, thus giving it an appearance similar to dahlia. This novelty was named 'Ecke's Flaming Sphere', but it did not prove to be a satisfactory greenhouse potted plant because the overall bract presentation was considered to be too small. It was not until the 1990s that the novelty market exploded and 'Winter Rose Dark Red' was introduced. 'Winter Rose Dark Red' has dark green leaves and an upright habit that allows for high-density planting. In 2004, the 'Winter Rose' series included seven different colors. The curly bract types have always had particularly good cut flower performance. In 2003, the 'Renaissance' series ('Red', 'White', 'Pink', and 'Peppermint') was introduced specifically for the cut flower market.

MODERN BREEDING & PRODUCTION

During the mid-1950s, poinsettia breeding programs were initiated at several institutions, including Pennsylvania State University, the University of Maryland, the USDA Research Center at Beltsville, Maryland, and by a number of commercial horticulture firms including: Azalealand, Lincoln, Nebraska; Paul Ecke Poinsettias, Encinitas, California; Mikkelsen's, Ashtabula, Ohio; Earl J. Small, Pinnellas Park, Florida; Yoder Brothers, Barberton, Ohio; Zieger Brothers, Hamburg, Germany; and Thormod Hegg & Son, Reistad, Norway. Dr. Robert N. Stewart, of the Agriculture Research Service in Beltsville, Maryland, used his genetic training to segregate desirable characteristics such as stiff stems, larger bracts, new colors, and lasting qualities. His contribution greatly helped to identify the character of mutation forms in poinsettias, and his cooperative efforts have been extremely helpful to the commercial hybridizers.

'Barbara Ecke Supreme' was the first tetraploid to be introduced to the trade (1949). Tetraploids have a higher number of chromosomes than the typical poinsettia, which result in thicker stems and bracts. Only a couple of tetraploid cultivars have had an impact in the marketplace, namely Gross 'Supjibi' (1988), introduced by Eduard Gross of France, and Peter

Jacobsen's 'Petoy' (1994), introduced by Peter Jacobsen of Denmark.

Poinsettias entered a new era with the introduction of the 'Paul Mikkelsen' cultivar in 1963. Until this time, the available poinsettia cultivars were primarily cut flower types and had a habit not conducive for container production. This cultivar had stiff stems and good foliage retention characteristics that provided the industry with the first longer-lasting cultivar of any commercial importance.

In 1968, an attractive, long-lasting red cultivar was introduced named Eckespoint 'C-1 Red'. This cultivar had very large bracts and an extremely showy presentation. 'C-1' provided the grower with the opportunity to produce a predictable multiflowered plant of high quality. 'C-1' also introduced the concept of a color series, in which additional colors with similar growth habits were offered. Cultivars within the series included: 'C-1 Red' (1968), 'C-1 Pink' (1968), 'C-1 Marble' (1969), 'C-1 White' (1970), 'C-1 Hot Pink' (1973), and 'C-1 Jingle Bells' (1973).

Figure 1-5. 'C-1', a long-lasting cultivar introduced in 1968, provided the grower with the opportunity to produce a predictable, high-quality multiflowered plant.

This color series concept brought mutation breeding to the forefront of poinsettia breeding techniques. Traditionally, new cultivars were developed through making numerous crosses to produce genetically unique seedlings. Mutation breeding focuses on taking a desirable cultivar, usually with red bracts, and intentionally causing genetic mutations to alter bract color while maintaining growth characteristics similar to the original red cultivar.

Very few poinsettias were grown in Europe before 1960. The poinsettia business consisted primarily of growing fresh-cut flowers in greenhouses. There had been a limited amount of potted plant business consisting mostly of plants with single blooms grown in 4" (10 cm) pots. The most common cultivars were 'Barbara Ecke Supreme', 'Indianapolis Red', 'Gloria', and 'Impromptu'. It was in the early 1960s that European growers began showing a great deal of interest in poinsettias.

In 1964, the first 'Annette Hegg Red' was grown in Norway. 'Annette Hegg Red' was the first truly free-branching poinsettia. The Hegg cultivars reliably produced five to eight stems from a pinch, thus creating an ideal plant for potted plant production. The Hegg cultivars have also proven to be among the most commercially successful modern cultivars, not being taken out of production until 2002. The 'Annette Hegg' family of cultivars epitomized the concept of the color series with more than fourteen culti-vars introduced from 1969 to 1987, including: 'Dark Red', 'Hot Pink', 'Diva', and 'Topwhite'.

Figure 1-6. 'Annette Hegg Red'

Figure 1-7. Approach grafting is used to improve the free-branching characteristics of poinsettias.

JOHN DOLE

The color series concept continued with the introduction of Gutbier 'V-14 Glory' in 1979 by Gregor Gutbier of Linz, Germany. 'V-14 Glory' had wide bracts, good branching, and did not require as high a night tem-perature in forcing as 'C-1' required. The Gutbier 'V-17 Angelika' series was very popular in Europe for several years before being introduced to North America in 1988. Many modern cultivars have 'V-17 Angelika' in their lineage, including the Peter Jacobsen's 'Peterstar' series (seven colors) and RAI Beckmann's 'Maren'. Medium green leaves, bright red bracts, and even branching are standard characteristics of 'V-17' cultivars.

Gregor Gutbier was one of the first breeders to experiment with grafting to improve plant performance. He discovered that the branching habit of plants he had grafted was better and more uniform than his ungrafted plants. It was later discovered that the free-branching characteristic was induced by transmission of a phytoplasma through the grafting process. Grafting poor-branching cultivars, such as 'C-1', onto free-branching rootstock, such as 'Annette Hegg', would cause 'C-1' to become free-branching. Approach grafting became a commonly used breeding technique in the 1980s.

Figure 1-8. The free-branching trait can be introduced into a poor-branching cultivar by grafting the poor-branching cultivar onto free-branching rootstock. Left: 'C-1' grafted onto 'C-1' rootstock results in restricted branching. Right: 'C-1' grafted onto 'Annette Hegg' rootstock results in free-branching.

Figure 1-9. Franz Fruehwirth was the breeder for the Paul Ecke Ranch who introduced 'Lilo' in 1988, named for his wife.

In 1988, Franz Fruehwirth, the breeder at the Paul Ecke Ranch, Encinitas, California, introduced Eckespoint 'Lilo', which started the new trend of dark green foliage that continues to be popular in the twenty-first century. 'Lilo' had exceptional resistance to epinasty, a wilted appearance resulting from exposure to ethylene in the postharvest environment; therefore, it performed exceptionally well in retail stores after being transported in sleeves and boxes for a couple of days.

Prior to 1990, few poinsettias were sold before the American Thanksgiving holiday (celebrated the fourth Thursday of November). The introduction of Eckespoint 'Freedom Red' in 1991 coincided with the advent of earlier market dates (early to mid-November), resulting from the earlier start of the Christmas shopping season. 'Freedom' quickly became the leading cultivar in the market. Dark green leaves and extremely large, deep-red bracts created a beautiful, easy-to-grow cultivar that worked well for the large, mass-market grower as well as the small, independent garden center grower. A series of similar performing 'Freedom' colors reached twelve cultivars in 2004.

Figure 1-10. The 'Freedom' family consists of twelve colors. 'Freedom' is an easy-to-grow cultivar that has been the grower's choice for over a decade.

The novelty cultivar market exploded in the 1990s. Previously, unique cultivars were available, but the customer primarily demanded red bracts. As the novelty market opened up, many unique colors and forms were released. Eckespoint 'Pink Peppermint' (pink flecks on light peach-pink), Eckespoint 'Monet' (dark pink on light pink), and Eckespoint 'Jingle Bell' (pink flecks on red) are just a few of the many examples of cultivars that gained an increased market share in the 1990s.

CURRENT TRENDS IN CULTIVAR DEVELOPMENT

The main trends that direct current breeding efforts can be categorized into grower traits and market traits. Grower traits focus on greenhouse performance and crop timing. Eckespoint 'Prestige Red' (2002) continues the trend in identifying high-performance cultivars. 'Prestige Red' is exceptionally well branched, with extremely sturdy stems that resist stem breakage during shipping and handling. Eckespoint 'Autumn Red' provides an earlier flowering date (November 10) for markets demanding color prior to 'Freedom'.

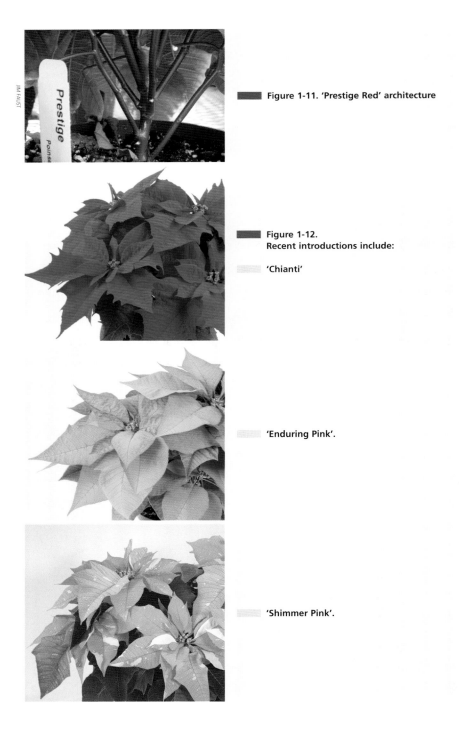

Figure 1-11. 'Prestige Red' architecture

Figure 1-12.
Recent introductions include:

'Chianti'

'Enduring Pink'.

'Shimmer Pink'.

Market traits focus on consumer appeal, recognition, and long shelf life. This trend fuels the continuing introduction of unique colors such as Eckespoint 'Plum Pudding' (purple), Eckespoint 'Chianti' (wine red bracts with showy cyathia that possess a large number of glands), and Eckespoint 'Shimmer Pink' (white flecks on pink bracts). Diverse forms also continue to be introduced, such as the 'Winter Rose' series (curly bracts), Eckespoint 'Holly Point' (variegated foliage), the Eckespoint 'Punch' series (smaller, erect bracts with high shoot counts), and the Eckespoint 'Jester' series (narrow, upright bracts that resemble a court jester's hat). Large, showy bracts and cleaner colors are always highly valued traits. Recent color improvements include 'Eckespoint Snowcap' (white) and Eckespoint 'Enduring Pink' (pink).

NEW *EUPHORBIA* SPECIES AND HYBRIDS

Breeding efforts at the Ecke Ranch are currently expanding to include other species within the *Euphorbia* genus. One of these species is *E. fulgens,* which has been produced and sold as a cut flower for many years. The tall, slender stems, delicate leaves, and colorful flowers that develop in the leaf axil of *E. fulgens* are ideal for fall and winter color, but until recently the plant habit has not been suitable for use in potted plant produc-

RUTH KOBAYASHI

Ruth Kobayashi

Ask Dr. Ruth Kobayashi about the future of poinsettias, and she will most likely tell you to look at our past to understand where we are headed.

All significant introductions bred at the Ecke Ranch have a distinct *wow* factor. The 'C-1' was known for its' impressive "dinner-plate-size bracts". 'Lilo' had the first dark leaves and a long shelf life, unlike anything else in the market. 'Freedom' was the first poinsettia that could be grown and sold in mid-November without blackcloth. And, of course, today 'Prestige' brings a new standard of strength and upright branch position, making it genetically resistant to stem breakage.

So what is the next *wow?* Is it another red poinsettia, or does it have a new combination of color patterns or unique foliage and bracts? According to Ruth, "It will be whatever brings that feeling of happiness we feel during the holidays! I am looking to expand the range of color and plant form in poinsettias beyond what we know is possible today. I am always looking for that next wow." It's a mix of science and serendipity, and according to Ruth, "that's what being a flower breeder is all about!"

tion. Through breeding and selection programs in Europe and North America, new hybrids are being developed that are shorter and better suited for flowering pot plant production. Production trials are currently in progress to develop the growing protocols required for this crop to enter the market.

The effort to develop truly unique new products has challenged our scientists to take advantage of new breeding techniques and create interspecific hybrids. Interspecific hybrids are new plants created through hybridizing different species within the same genus (in this case, *Euphorbia*). The different characteristics found in each species usually result in genetic or chromosomal incompatibilities that prevent the development of viable seed when cross-pollination occurs. New breeding techniques are allowing breeders to successfully accomplish these unique pairings and develop new ornamental crops for the greenhouse industry. The first new hybrid introduction offered from the Ecke Ranch is Eckespoint 'Dulce Rosa'. While this plant has some characteristics of its parent plants, the hybrid offers a completely new style of product unlike anything else available today.

Figure 1-13. A new interspecific hybrid called Eckespoint 'Dulce Rosa'

With similar photoperiodic requirements for flowering as the poinsettia, 'Dulce Rosa' can be grown for fall or blackclothed for flowering during spring or summer. The soft pink bracts and striking cyathia of 'Dulce Rosa' make this a nice alternative crop for early spring Easter and Mother's Day markets, provided it can be grown with other short-day crops programmed for these holidays. The introduction of new crops through innovative breeding programs will bring exciting new flowering crops for future generations of growers and retailers. For the Ecke Ranch, it's great that one of the first has its roots in poinsettias!

STOCK PLANTS

The production of poinsettia stock plants has been a significant program for many years. However, each year fewer growers produce poinsettia stock plants since most growers find that purchasing unrooted, callused, or rooted cuttings is more cost effective. By freeing up greenhouse space during the spring, it is possible to produce and sell some of the popular new bedding plant crops that can help growers improve their overall profitability and build a more loyal customer base throughout the year. As a result, the majority of cutting production now occurs offshore (Mexico and Central America) due to the milder climates, lower labor costs, and effective transportation systems that assure high-quality cuttings can be delivered for the propagation season.

PAUL ECKE DE GUATEMALA

The Ecke Ranch began growing poinsettia stock plants in Guatemala in 1997 and today it is the largest poinsettia stock production facility in the Americas. Over 700 people are employed, including over 40 college-degreed professionals.

Cuttings are harvested early in the day Saturday through Monday for Monday-through-Wednesday delivery in the United States and Canada. The cuttings are packed in trays of one hundred and boxed with five trays per box. Within forty-five minutes of being cut, the cuttings are placed in a cooler. In the afternoon, refrigerated trucks take the cuttings to the airport. The cuttings are flown overnight to major ports of entry such as Miami and Los Angeles and then delivered to the customer via express mail carrier or refrigerated trucks. Mail shipments arrive approximately forty-eight hours after cutting, while truck shipments arrive between forty-eight and seventy-two hours after cutting.

Figure 2-1. Paul Ecke de Guatemala greenhouses are located in a beautiful valley surrounded by three volcanoes. The climate is ideal for year-round poinsettia stock production.

Figure 2-2. A range of poinsettia stock plants in Guatemala

a

b

c

d

e

f

Figure 2-3. Stock plants are cut (a); cuttings are placed in moistened paper in trays (b); trays are stacked (c); trays are placed in a vacuum cooler to remove the "field heat" (d); then the trays are boxed, with ice packs placed between trays (e) and placed in a cooler prior to shipping to the airport (f).

STOCK PLANT PRODUCTION

A brief overview of stock plant production is provided for those growers still interested in cutting production. The stock plant schedule is based on the number of pinches that are applied to the stock. The more pinches applied, the more potential cuttings per stock plant; however, each pinch adds production time and cost. Two- and three-pinch stock plant programs must be started in April and March, respectively, and will occupy space that could otherwise be used to produce other crops. For this reason, one-pinch (fast-crop) stock plants can be an attractive option since they can be started in May.

Following are the pros of fast-crop stock plant production compared to traditional two- and three-pinch stock plants:

As mentioned above, fast-crop stock plants can be started in May, which will displace fewer spring crops than two- or three-pinch stock plants.

Lighting for photoperiod control in North America is required from mid-September through early May (see the Photoperiodic Lighting section in this chapter). Growers using stock programs starting in March or April must use lights to prevent flower bud induction. Fast-crop stock plants are grown only during natural long-day conditions and do not require light-ing. Any negative impacts that light might have on adjacent crops will be reduced, along with electrical costs. The exceptions are Eckespoint 'Autumn Red', Eckespoint 'Freedom', Eckespoint 'Jester', Peter Jacobsen's 'Pepride', Eckespoint 'Red Velveteen', and Eckespoint 'Winter Rose Early Red', which have a different photoperiodic response and require lighting until mid to late May to prevent flower initiation.

Greenhouse heating costs are higher during spring than during May or June. Traditional stock production begins during cooler months, when more energy is required to provide 68–70°F (20–21°C) night tempera-tures. Fast-crop production begins during May, when the heat requirements and the associated cost of heating are considerably lower.

Reduced production time for fast-crop stock also reduces the labor input per unit required. Traditional programs require more spraying for insect or disease pests, watering, spacing, pinching and other operations needing the attention of production staff. Additional savings result from the reduced quantity of fertilizers, pesticides, and other material costs associated with a longer production cycle.

Fast-crop stock plants can be finished as blooming plants (see the Guidelines for Blooming section in this chapter).

Following are some of the negative aspects of fast crop stock production:

- Fast-crop plants produce about half the total number of cuttings per plant when compared to traditional programs, resulting in double the number of stock plants required and a higher cost per cutting.
- The short production cycle for fast-crop stock does not allow recovery from serious production difficulties, minimizing the margin of error.

SCHEDULING

Table 2-1 provides general schedules for one-, two-, three-pinch stock plants. The peak cutting demand usually occurs in July (weeks 27–31). The first cuttings go toward large plant production (8" [20 cm] pots or larger), while the last cuttings are used for small plants (4" [10 cm] pots or smaller). Cuttings for less-vigorous cultivars are produced before the cuttings for those that are more vigorous. The key is that the final pinch, termed the "critical pinch," occurs approximately six weeks prior to the demand for cuttings. This allows for the shoots to reach the proper maturity when the cuttings are harvested.

Growers should not limit poinsettia stock programs to only one system. An all-or-nothing approach may be easier to manage, but the extra effort of combining traditional and fast-crop programs can be beneficial. For example, cutting production requirements peak during a few short weeks in the summer. To produce enough cuttings during this peak without sacrificing size and quality places an excessive burden on traditional stock plants. Supplying cuttings for this peak also goes beyond the economic viability for fast-crop stock alone. However, when the programs are combined, production is accomplished at a lower total cost. For example, to produce the cuttings during a few weeks of the cycle, traditional stock would require an excessive number of stock plants, resulting in a higher cost to the grower for more greenhouse space, heat, labor, etc. By combining the programs, a smaller base of traditional stock plants can produce the majority of cuttings needed, while a group of fast-crop stock provides the remaining balance. Also, novelty colors or cultivars may not warrant the production cost associated with traditional stock plants or the cost of purchasing summer cuttings. Fast-crop stock may be an ideal program to supply the quantity of cuttings needed without committing long-term space and care.

TABLE 2-1. PINCH SCHEDULE

Months:	March	April	May	June	July	August
3-Pinch Program						
Suggested Container Size: 12"	Plant Rooted Cutting	Initial Pinch	2nd Pinch	Critical Pinch	Begin Harvest	Late Harvest
Spacing: 18" x 18"	Establish Cutting ≅ 2 Weeks	≅ 4–5 Weeks	≅ 4–5 Weeks	Cultivar Dependent ≅ 5–7 Weeks	25 Cuttings	30 Cuttings
		Leave 6 Nodes	Leave 2–3 Nodes	Leave 1–2 Nodes	Developmental time between 1st and 2nd cutting flushes ≅ 5 Weeks	
2-Pinch Program						
Suggested Container Size: 10"	Plant Rooted Cutting	Initial Pinch	Critical Pinch	Begin Harvest	Late Harvest	
Spacing: 15" x 15"	Establish Cutting ≅ 2 Weeks	≅ 4–5 Weeks	Cultivar Dependent ≅ 5–7 Weeks	15 Cuttings	25 Cuttings	
		Leave 6 Nodes	Leave 2–3 Nodes	Developmental time between 1st and 2nd cutting flushes ≅ 5 Weeks		
1-Pinch Fast Crop						
Suggested Container Size: 6½"	Plant Rooted Cutting	Initial Critical Pinch	Begin Harvest	Late Harvest		
Spacing: 12" x 12"	Establish Cutting ≅ 2–5 Weeks	Cultivar Dependent ≅ 5–7 Weeks	10 Cuttings	20 Cuttings		
		Leave 10 Nodes	Developmental time between 1st and 2nd cutting flushes ≅ 5 Weeks			

PHOTOPERIODIC LIGHTING

If stock plants are planted prior to May 5, night-interruption lighting must be provided to keep the stock plants vegetative. During the night interruption, the lamps should provide 10 f.c. (108 lux) at canopy level from 10 P.M. to 2 A.M. Traditionally, night-interruption lighting was provided with strings of incandescent lamps; however, growers have started to use high-pressure sodium lamps for photoperiodic lighting. Cyclic lighting can be used to save energy. Ideally, the plants should receive twenty minutes of lighting every hour from 10 P.M. to 2 A.M. Cyclic lighting can be achieved by mounting high-pressure sodium lamps on irrigation booms and running the booms back and forth across the crop or by adding an oscillating reflector to distribute the light to a wider production area (figure 2-4b). Day-length extension lighting programs are not as effective as night-interruption lighting at keeping the poinsettia vegetative. Appendix C provides guidelines for designing a layout for lamps to provide night-interruption lighting.

a   b

Figure 2-4. Night-interruption lighting can be provided with incandescent lamps (a) or high-pressure sodium lamps with an oscillating reflector (b).

CUTTING MATURITY

The maturity of the cutting affects rooting in propagation. Cuttings that are either immature or overly mature are more difficult to root. A good-quality cutting roots rapidly and uniformly. Cutting maturity is determined by the timely pinching of the stock plants. For most cultivars,

Figure 2-5. 'Lilo' cuttings harvested four, five, or six weeks after pinching of the stock plants. Optimum rooting occurred in the six-week-old cuttings.

cuttings are best taken five to six weeks after the last pinch of the stock plants. Therefore, it is important to schedule the planting and pinching of stock plants to insure optimum maturity when the cuttings are removed.

CUTTING SIZE

The stem length of poinsettia cuttings is usually 2–2.5 inches (5–6 cm). Cutting length is measured from the base of the cutting to the growing tip. This cutting will have approximately two mature leaves. The leaves should not be too large, since large leaves are more likely to wilt and become infected with botrytis in propagation. Large cuttings also require more propagation bench space.

Figure 2-6. The ideal cutting size has a 2" (5 cm) stem and a 6–7" (15–18 cm) leaf span.

The stem diameter (caliper) of cuttings varies among cultivars, but stem caliper of 0.16–0.24" (4 to 6 mm) is desirable. Stems can be cut at a leaf node or between nodes, since roots develop from the base of a poinsettia cutting with or without a leaf node.

GUIDELINES FOR BLOOMING STOCK PLANTS

A benefit of fast-crop programs is the opportunity to finish blooming plants out of the stock plants. Fast-crop stock can be made into compact two-pinch forms or grouped to create larger specimen plants. Stock plants scheduled in the traditional two- to three-pinch program are more likely to have an excessive number of shoots and damaged foliage, resulting in blooming plants of lesser quality. Following are some guidelines for using fast-crop stock for blooming plants:

- Select the best stock plants for blooming, discarding any weak or damaged plants.
- Stock may have to be thinned to reduce the total number of shoots. As these plants are generally grown to ten or more nodes, the total height and shoot count may be excessive for double-pinch forms. Trim the plant using care to shape the plant and to allow uniform side shoots, from which new growth will emerge. The final cutback date should be similar to the pinch date used for a 6.5" (17 cm) pinched plant of the same cultivar in your location.
- Specimen plants can be created by selecting multiple stock plants for uniformity in height, shoot size, and root system and then combining them in a large container (10" [25 cm] or larger).
- Keep only as many stock plants as you have finishing space to accommodate. Double-pinch forms require approximately 2 ft.^{2}/plant, while three plants combined in 10" (25 cm) or larger containers require a minimum of 3 ft.^{2}/plant.

PROPAGATION

A high-quality finished crop begins on the stock plant and continues throughout propagation. Problems that start in propagation can continue to cause trouble throughout the season, so proper attention to detail is critical.

SCHEDULING

Deciding the date to propagate poinsettia cuttings ultimately depends on when blooming plants are scheduled for market. For most cultivars, propagation occurs in July and August to meet the scheduling demands for a poinsettia blooming during the Christmas season. In general, four weeks are needed to produce a well-rooted cutting. There may be some differences in the total amount of time the cuttings remain in propagation depending on the age and condition of the cuttings, environmental conditions, and the cultivars. Cultivars vary in the time required for rooting. Fast-rooting cultivars may require one less week in propagation compared with slow-to-root cultivars.

STAGES OF PROPAGATION

The time that cuttings are in propagation may be divided into three distinct development stages: callus formation, root initiation, and toning.

1. CALLUS FORMATION

Almost immediately after a cutting is placed in propagation, the cut surface at its base begins to heal. New cells, called callus tissue, form in and

JIM FAUST

7   14   21   28

DAYS

Figure 3-1. The progression of root formation during four weeks in propagation.

around the wounded area. In seven to ten days, callus tissue will encompass the base of the cutting. During this time, the cuttings need protection from drying since very little water can be absorbed through the callus tissue. Misting is used to maintain a film of water on the leaves and to slow the loss of moisture from the cuttings until roots are formed. Roots are not formed directly from the callus tissue, but rather from other cells inside the stem that grow through the callus. Because cuttings are closely spaced and in a warm, humid environment, they soon begin to elongate. When callus formation is evident, PGRs can be applied to control stem elongation of the more vigorous cultivars.

Growers can purchase callused cuttings, reducing propagation time by seven to ten days. Callused cuttings are most often directly stuck into the finished container.

2. ROOT INITIATION

Root tips should be evident within ten to fourteen days after sticking cuttings. If roots are not forming by this time, the rooting conditions may be less than optimal. The temperature of the rooting medium may be cooler than optimum for good rooting, the cuttings may be too dry from lack of good mist coverage, or the rooting medium may be too wet, thus excluding oxygen from the rooting zone. Often, if the medium is too wet an unusually large mass of callus tissue forms but roots are not present. Finally, there may be pests or diseases that are inhibiting root formation. As roots begin to form, the cuttings are able to take up more water and nutrients through the roots. Inspect cuttings in propagation daily to help identify problems early in the production cycle, and take timely actions to correct any problems before the damage is too severe.

3. TONING

Although cuttings begin to develop roots after ten to fourteen days, they are not ready to withstand the warmer, drier, and brighter conditions of the greenhouse. It usually takes another week to develop a root system that can fully meet the water and nutrient needs of the cutting. As the mist is gradually reduced, increase the light intensity by removing some of the shade, and increase the air movement. Concurrently, apply low levels of fertilizer and apply fungicides to prevent stem and root rot. During the toning period, apply a PGR to the more vigorous cultivars to prevent excessive stem elongation (see chapter 14, Cultivar Guide, to compare the height potential of different cultivars). The cuttings are ready for transplanting three to four weeks after propagation begins.

HANDLING UNROOTED CUTTINGS

Most U.S. and Canadian growers receive unrooted cuttings (URC) from offshore production facilities located in Mexico, Guatemala, or Costa Rica. The cuttings are typically delivered to the greenhouse in the United States between forty-eight and seventy-two hours after being cut. The cuttings are wrapped in moistened paper and packaged in boxes that have been cooled to 55°F (13°C) prior to shipping. Ice packs are frequently placed in the boxes to maintain cool temperatures throughout the shipping process during the warmer months of the year.

The standard cutting has a 2" (5 cm) stem with two to three mature leaves. The bottom leaf should be removed only if it is within $^1/_2$" (1.3 cm)

Figure 3-2. A standard 2" cutting

of the base of the stem. European-style cuttings are shorter and have smaller leaves and stem caliper.

The cuttings should be immediately stuck upon arrival or placed in a cooler (50–60°F [10–15°C]) and stuck within twenty-four hours of delivery. Some growers purposely plan their sticking schedule so that the cuttings can be placed in a cooler prior to sticking, since pre-cooling can reduce wilting on the propagation bench. It is critical that boxes of cuttings do not sit in direct sunlight or in a warm environment prior to planting.

Once cuttings are removed from boxes, they must be immediately transplanted and placed under mist. It only takes ten to fifteen minutes in a hot summer greenhouse for a cutting to permanently wilt. Avoid re-cutting the stems, as this will open fresh wounds and increase the risk of disease.

ROOTING MEDIA

Poinsettia cuttings are usually rooted in a preformed material, such as foam, Rockwool, or peat moss. These materials, in the form of cubes, wedges, pellets or plugs, are molded into strips or trays to provide easier handling and more efficient space use. Such products are formulated to provide good porosity (approx. 20%) and water holding capacity (approx. 50%) during mist propagation.

Figure 3-3. Cutting rooting in Oasis wedge

Excessively wet media will decrease the oxygen available to the stem tissue. Under low oxygen conditions, callus tissue can become very large, while root initiation and growth is slowed. Excessively wet media also increase the incidence of disease and fungus gnat problems.

Figure 3-4. Root formation of poinsettia cuttings. Left: Normal, Right: Heavy callus formations caused by inadequate air content of the rooting medium.

While designed for efficiency in propagation, rooting media do not provide optimum conditions for growing the plants after the cuttings have rooted. Transplanting well-rooted cuttings into the final growing containers helps to avoid stress on the young plants.

DIRECT STICKING

Cuttings can be directly stuck into the final container to avoid the additional labor of transplanting rooted cuttings. The advantages and disadvantages of direct sticking are listed in table 3-1. Before direct-sticking cuttings, thoroughly wet the medium and then wait until the cuttings develop callus before watering again. It is helpful to dibble a hole to allow air space around the base of the cutting to assist in callus formation and to minimize stem rot. The hole should be larger and deeper than the cutting being placed into the medium. Cuttings should not be "watered in" until roots start to form, about seven to ten days after the cuttings are stuck. This provides air space around the base of the cuttings and supplies oxygen for root generation.

Figure 3-5. Direct-stick propagation of poinsettia cuttings

High concentrations of fertilizer (300–400 ppm nitrogen) may need to be applied to directly stuck cuttings because the preplant fertilizer incorporated into the growing medium can be rapidly leached out under mist propagation. Almost all the nutrients may be leached out of the medium after two to three weeks in propagation, so the fertilizer may be gone just as the roots are starting to grow rapidly. One or two applications of 300–400 ppm nitrogen may be required to get the medium's EC into the target range (1.5–2.5 mmhos/cm for a saturated media extract [SME] test or 0.7–1.3 mmhos/cm for the 1:2 method).

A control plan for fungus gnats should be in place *before* sticking the cuttings. Otherwise, by the time the fungus gnat infestation is evident, the damage could be severe. A pesticide may need to be applied when watering in the cuttings. Keep the floors under benches free of algae, plant debris, and weeds. Hydrated lime and/or copper sulfate have been used successfully to control algae and fungus gnats on walkways and under benches.

TABLE 3-1.
ADVANTAGES AND DISADVANTAGES OF DIRECT
STICKING UNROOTED CUTTINGS

Advantages	Disadvantages
Labor savings, since the transplanting step is eliminated.	More propagation space is required.
Reduced materials cost, since the rooting materials are eliminated.	The growing medium may have a higher water-holding capacity than most rooting media do. This could lead to excessively wet medium that increases disease and pest problems and increases rooting time.
Less production time, since one less week is needed prior to pinching.	
Callused cuttings can be purchased, which can reduce propagation time by one week.	Slow-release fertilizers incorporated into the growing medium may release nutrients too quickly due to the moist, warm propagation environment.
Convenient for pre-finish sales for licensed propagators/distributors, since the cuttings can be propagated pot-to-pot, pinched, and the excess production can be sold when the crop needs to be spaced.	Excess leaching through the mist system may cause low nutrient concentrations in the growing medium.
Fewer foliar diseases and plant growth regulators, since the extra space surrounding the cuttings increases air movement and decreases competition for light.	Fungus gnat control can be more difficult on cuttings directly stuck in a peat-based medium compared to cuttings stuck in an inert rooting medium such as Oasis.

SPACING

Cuttings require approximately 12 in.^{2} (77.4 cm^2)/cutting or twelve cuttings/ft.^{2} (129 cuttings/m^2). Oasis strips often have $1^1/_2$–$1^7/_8$" (3.8–4.5 cm) between cuttings. The strips are then placed 6–8" (15–20 cm) apart so that the leaves of neighboring plants barely touch. The space needs to be adjusted for cuttings from large-leaf cultivars (Eckespoint 'Prestige') or small-leaf cultivars ('Winter Rose' family). After sticking cuttings, leaves should be parted to the sides of the rooting strips to expose all shoot tips to the mist and sunlight.

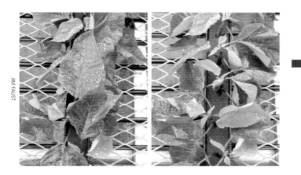

Figure 3-6. Leaves should be parted immediately following sticking in order to expose all shoot tips. Left: Before parting. Right: After parting.

ROOTING HORMONE

Poinsettias root well without the use of a rooting hormone, especially under optimal environmental conditions. However, the use of a rooting hormone can encourage more uniform rooting under less-than-ideal conditions or with difficult-to-root cultivars. Growers commonly use 2,500 ppm indole-3-butyric acid (IBA) or 1,500 ppm IBA plus 500 ppm

Figure 3-7. IBA damage occurring in propagation due to the IBA coming in contact with the shoot.

naphthaleneacetic acid (NAA) as a quick liquid or powder dip to the base of the stem prior to sticking. Powders may be more difficult to uniformly coat the base of the stems compared to liquid dips. It is important that the highly concentrated hormone dip come in contact only with the stem, since hormone on the petioles and foliage can cause twisted and distorted leaves.

MISTING

The mist system must be operating as the cuttings are being stuck in order to limit wilting. The mist frequency will vary with each greenhouse, depending on the light intensity, humidity, and air movement. Table 3-2 provides an example of a misting schedule. The ideal misting frequency should continually provide a film of water on the leaves, maintain the humidity near 100%, and supply little or no water to the rooting medium. Misting during the night is often necessary during the first two or three nights, thereafter misting should only be required during the day.

TABLE 3-2.
EXAMPLE OF A MISTING SCHEDULE DURING POINSETTIA PROPAGATION

Night Misting Schedule

1	2	3	4	5	6	7	8	9	10	11	12	13	14	15	16	17	18	19	20	21	22	23	24	25	26	27	28
3x	3x	3x	3x	3x	3x	3x								1x	1x	1x	1x	1x	1x	1x							
							2x	2x	2x	2x	2x	2x	2x														

Day Misting Schedule (10 sec. per time period)

1	2	3	4	5	6	7	8	9	10	11	12	13	14	15	16	17	18	19	20	21	22	23	24	25	26	27	28
10 Minutes							20 Minutes											45 Minutes									
			15 Minutes											30 Minutes													

Fine mist nozzles are preferred since smaller droplets of water are less likely to drip off the foliage. Surfactants, or wetting agents, can be sprayed on the foliage to improve contact of water to the leaves. These products can allow the mist frequency to be reduced.

ROYAL HEINS

Figure 3-8. Misting provided in propagation with a boom. Note that the mist nozzles are tilted so that the mist does not dislodge or damage the cuttings.

JIM FAUST

Figure 3-9. The hydrophobic surface on poinsettia leaves causes water to form beads and roll off (left). Wetting agents reduce the surface tension of water, which allows the water to form a thin layer across the leaves (right).

CapSil is an organosilicone spray adjuvant for foliar applications. Use CapSil at the rate of 300 ppm, or 4 fl. oz./100 gal. of water (about 0.25 tsp./gal. [0.32 ml/L]. Briefly dip cuttings before sticking or spray onto cuttings immediately after sticking, then begin misting as usual. If dipping cuttings, do not apply to the end of the stem. Treated cuttings will regain turgidity faster following sticking and may root a couple of days faster. Be careful not to apply so much CapSil that the material runs down the stem into the rooting medium, as it could delay rooting. If you have not had experience using wetting agents during poinsettia propagation, trial this treatment on all cultivars before adapting a new procedure.

The mist frequency should be adjusted daily based on the sunlight conditions, since higher light will increase the rate of water evaporation. Leaf rolling is an indication that excessive water loss is occurring, and the environment must be changed immediately. Some wilting will occur midday even under high mist rates. The mist frequency decreases as callus formation occurs and the cutting can absorb more water through the rooting medium. As roots begin to penetrate the growing medium (weeks 3 to 4), misting will not supply adequate water for plant growth, so overhead watering will replace misting.

Figure 3-10. High alkalinity water contains salts that leave a residue on poinsettia leaves during propagation.

Poor water quality can negatively impact cutting performance in propagation by changing the rooting medium pH, increasing the soluble salts, or leaving mineral deposits on the foliage. Water with high levels of calcium, magnesium, or iron can leave an undesirable residue on poinsettia leaves. These salt residues can cause immature leaves to become hard and to expand poorly after transplant. Water with an electrical conductivity (EC) greater than 1 mmho/cm is not recommended for propagation. Filtration systems such as reverse osmosis (RO) can remove salts, or the irrigation water can be diluted with an alternative water source. For high alkalinity water, acid injection can help maintain the rooting medium pH between 5.5 and 6.5; however, it will not reduce the amount of residue that forms on the leaves. Do not use phosphoric acid if the treated water will be used for misting—the damage it can cause to the growing tip and expanding leaves of poinsettia cuttings can be significant.

In recent years, growers have begun to use ZeroTol during poinsettia propagation to reduce disease incidence and algae growth. ZeroTol is a hydrogen peroxide–based product that can be continuously injected into the mist water at a dilution rate of 1:1,000 (check the regulations in your state/country to be sure such use is considered legal). It can kill fungi, bacteria, and algae on contact, so it can provide sanitation and disease control during propagation.

FERTILIZATION

Once a cutting is removed from the stock plant, it loses its main source of nutrient supply. The cutting can sustain itself in a healthy nutritional status for only a short time in propagation without additional fertilization. In addition, most cuttings are rooted under intermittent mist, which leaches nutrients from the cuttings. Cuttings harvested from well-fed stock plants should not require fertilization until roots start to form. Approximately ten days after the cuttings are placed in propagation, a fertilizer solution with 100 to 150 ppm nitrogen and potassium may be applied at weekly intervals to the rooting medium until the rooted cuttings are transplanted. The common fertilizer 15-0-15 is a good choice, since 20-10-20 can cause the immature leaves to become reddened, hard, and distorted. This phenomenon is likely caused by excess phosphorus on the leaves. Phosphorus also promotes stem elongation, which is not desirable in propagation.

Figure 3-11. The plant on the left received a daily overhead irrigation of water, while the plant on the right received a daily overhead fertigation with 20-10-20 for the two weeks prior to transplant. The leaves that emerged during and after treatment were small, thickened, and often exhibited interveinal chlorosis. The leaves can also turn reddish. In some cases, the symptoms persisted on newly developing leaves for many weeks after treatments ceased.

Nutrients need not enter the cutting solely through the roots. Leaves and stems can also absorb them. Both foliar and root feeding methods can be effective in propagation, so soluble fertilizers are sometimes added to the intermittent mist. A supply of nitrogen and potassium at rates of 50–100 ppm is recommended since these are the elements that are leached most heavily by the mist. However, there are inherent risks associated with adding fertilizer to the mist water. The foliage can absorb only a limited amount of fertilizer and excessive salts may accumulate, and the nutrient-rich mist on the plants, greenhouse benches, and floors encourages algae growth. High-quality water (EC less than 1.0) is necessary if fertilizer is added to the mist; otherwise, high salts can cause foliar damage.

TEMPERATURE

The temperature of the growing medium near the base of the cutting has a large impact on the speed of rooting. Rooting medium temperatures in propagation are frequently cooler than the surrounding greenhouse air temperature since the medium is cooled by the continual evaporation of water from the rooting medium, bench, and leaves. So it is important to use a soil thermometer and not rely entirely on air temperature measurements.

The optimal average daily media temperature for callus formation and rooting is 72–78°F (22–26°C). Day temperatures can be 76–82°F (24–28°C), while night temperatures can be 70–74°F (21–23°C). Temperatures below 80°F (27°C) for the first five days will help to alleviate moisture stress and minimize the potential for *Erwinia* soft rot. Cooler night temperatures, between 68–70°F (20–21°C), during the first three nights will also reduce moisture stress. Non-optimal temperatures will significantly slow rooting and reduce the uniformity of rooting. Bottom heat is very effective at heating the growing medium and decreasing the rooting time. The bottom heat can be turned off and the temperatures can be reduced 5°F (2.8°C) after all the cuttings are rooting (week 3).

LIGHT

Shade cloth is initially used in propagation so that the cuttings receive 1,000–2,000 f.c. (11–22 klux) during the brightest part of the day. By the end of propagation (week 4), the cuttings should be acclimated to light levels that will be experienced in the greenhouse after transplant (approx. 4,000 f.c. [43 klux]). Excessive shade will reduce rooting during propagation and vigor following transplant.

AIR MOVEMENT AND HUMIDITY

Excessive ventilation should be avoided during the first two weeks in propagation since this can dehydrate cuttings. High humidity is essential during the first week in propagation to reduce wilting. During the final two weeks in propagation, increased air circulation and lower humidity will help to tone the cuttings and to acclimate them to the harsher environment following transplant.

PLANT GROWTH REGULATORS

The use of plant growth regulator (PGR) spray applications will help to prevent excessive stem elongation in propagation. Use of PGRs in propagation not only reduces stem elongation, but also enhances the green color of the foliage. PGRs should be applied early in the morning or late in the evening when the mist system can be turned off without stressing the cuttings.

Cycocel or a B-Nine/Cycocel tank mix are both commonly used. Growers must experiment to identify the optimal rates for their facility and location. A good starting point is 1,500 ppm Cycocel or 1,000–1,500 ppm B-Nine and 1,000 ppm Cycocel. The application of PGRs can begin during the second or third week of propagation. One PGR application is often sufficient for medium height potential cultivars, while medium-tall and tall cultivars may require two to three applications (See chapter 14, Cultivar Guide, for the height potentials of various cultivars). Proper applications do not delay rooting.

Paclobutrazol (Bonzi and Piccolo) and Sumagic are potent growth regulators that require caution in poinsettia propagation. To be effective as a retardant, these growth regulators must be applied uniformly to the cutting stems. Foliage covering the stem portion of cuttings in propagation makes applying Bonzi and Sumagic difficult. Also, if these products run off the foliage and down the stem, cuttings may receive an excessive dose that results in stunting.

PESTS

FUNGUS GNATS

Fungus gnats can be a severe problem in the warm and wet propagation environment. Adult fungus gnats do not cause damage to poinsettia cuttings, but the larvae injure poinsettia cuttings by feeding on callus tissue and young roots. The extent of the damage is often not noticed until the cuttings are transplanted, at which time irreparable damage may have occurred. Fungus gnats are particularly difficult to control when cuttings are propagated in an organic growing medium, e.g., peat moss, while fewer problems occur in inert rooting media. Fungus gnat populations tend to increase as the poinsettia propagation season progresses, so minor infestations early in the season can result in major problems on the last crops to be rooted. In addition to good sanitation, preventive pesticide applications are frequently required.

ROYAL HEINS

Figure 3-12. Fungus gnats feed on callus tissue and new roots (a), which can cause uneven rooting in propagation (b).

WHITEFLIES

Whiteflies are always a concern on poinsettias, so monitoring must begin in propagation. Pesticides for whitefly control can be difficult to apply in propagation, so it is particularly important to start propagation with pest-free cuttings. If whiteflies are found on cuttings prior to sticking, cuttings can be dipped in a pesticide before they are stuck. Systemic pesticides also work well during propagation. Take precautions against phytotoxicity by testing several cuttings before treating the entire crop.

Cuttings in propagation are more easily damaged by insecticide applications during the first two weeks. After rooting, pesticide applications are safer, although it is difficult to achieve adequate coverage on the undersides of the leaves. Smoke and aerosol formulations can be used late in propagation to control adult whiteflies, although the foliage must be dry before making the applications.

DISEASES

The most commonly encountered diseases in propagation include botrytis, bacterial soft rot (*Erwinia*), and rhizopus.

BOTRYTIS

Figure 3-13. Botrytis is the most common pathogen found on poinsettias during propagation. Damaged tissue should be removed to reduce the spread of this disease.

Botrytis is always a major concern in propagation. It is very important to remove any plant debris from the greenhouse prior to starting propagation. The constant leaf wetness that occurs during the first seven to ten days in propagation is conducive to disease development. Excessive misting should be avoided. Clean and remove damaged leaves daily. Preventive fungicide applications are often used, since airborne botrytis spores are always present in greenhouses. Fungicides are most effective as protectants rather than as curatives. Fungicides should be applied early in the morning or late in the evening, when the mist system can be turned off. The use of a wetting agent may help reduce botrytis blight since the wetting agent disperses the moisture evenly over the cuttings, which allows for a reduction in misting.

ERWINIA

Bacterial plant pathogens survive in water sources as well as plant and soil debris and may not become evident until conditions (heat and humidity) are conducive to development of the disease. *Erwinia carotovora,* the pathogen causing bacterial soft rot, cannot penetrate tissues directly, so it must have a wound to enter the plant. The bacteria multiply rapidly, spreading through the vascular tissue and causing a soft mushy rot that begins at the base of the cutting or at the point of entry. Significant losses of propagation material usually occur during the first few days in propagation. Precooling cuttings at temperatures of 55°F (13°C) for a minimum of four hours prior to sticking reduces the risk of *Erwinia* infection.

Figure 3-14. *Erwinia* causes a soft, mushy rot at the base of the cutting. This disease usually appears during the first week in propagation.

As with all diseases, good sanitation and healthy plants are the best defense. Quickly remove any infected plant material to reduce the spreading of the pathogen. Keep the foliage hydrated without saturating the rooting medium. Waterlogging can seriously aggravate a problem that a healthy cutting can suppress. Copper-based products are often applied to reduce the occurrence of bacterial soft rot.

RHIZOPUS

Rhizopus is a fungal pathogen that resembles botrytis, but is much less common. It can be very destructive under high temperatures and high humidity in propagation. Rhizopus requires wounded or weakened plant tissue to attack poinsettia cuttings, and when wounds callus or heal rapidly, the fungus is unable to become established. Suppression is best attained by sanitation and by careful handling of cuttings to avoid injury. There are no fungicides currently registered to control rhizopus on poinsettias.

CUTTING DISORDERS

BROWN CALLUS

Cuttings that are slow to root often develop callus tissue that turns from white to brown. This may indicate that the cuttings were too mature or that the conditions in propagation are not ideal. Brown callus can also result from drying or wilting of the cuttings. This often occurs if the cuttings are at the end or side of a bench where there is insufficient mist or if the air movement in the greenhouse is blowing the mist away from the cuttings. A dry rooting medium, excessive fertilizers, fungicides, disease, or insect activity in the root zone can also cause brown callus and slow rooting.

HARD GROWTH

Figure 3-15. Hard growth can be caused by cuttings remaining in propagation for too long, acid injection in mist water, excessive growth regulator application, or poor nutrition.

When cutting growth becomes stunted and the tissue hardens in propagation, the quality of the cuttings diminishes. Good-quality cuttings should emerge from propagation vigorous and actively growing, while overly mature cuttings placed in propagation become hardened. These cuttings are slow to root and slow to resume active growth. Often, cuttings are stunted if they are left on the propagation bench too long after they are sufficiently rooted.

Hard cuttings may also result from a low nutritional status or deficiency of one or more nutrient elements. Conversely, excessive amounts of fertilizers on the foliage can cause distorted, hardened tissue. Take care when adding acid to mist water as a method to improve water quality; the acid may cause damage to sensitive cuttings. High rates of PGRs applied during propagation may also result in stunted, hard cuttings that are slow to resume active growth. It is advisable to use no more than 2,000 ppm of B-Nine or no more than 1,500 ppm of Cycocel during any one application.

LEAF SCARRING

Blemishes such as yellow splotches, brown leaf edges, and rough foliage may develop in propagation, especially on dark-leafed cultivars. One cause of leaf scarring is rough handling of cuttings before they are placed in propagation. When cuttings are bundled or harvested by hand, leaves are often creased or broken. These damaged areas turn brown and result in scar tissue when the plants are on the propagation bench.

If cuttings are permitted to get too dry, particularly at night, or if the leaf temperature becomes too high during the day, leaf scarring may occur. This can be reduced by increasing day misting and by timing the night mist to prevent drying when the heat comes on.

Excessive air movement directly over the cuttings prior to root formation increases evapotranspiration and leads to leaf damage. Although ventilation is necessary to control temperatures and avoid excess humidity, the flow of air should be directed away from the cuttings. If leaf movement can be seen, air movement is excessive and scarring will occur.

The accumulation of salts on or in the leaf tissue results from poor quality mist water or water with relatively high levels of salts or nutrients. Generally, it is difficult to propagate quality poinsettia cuttings with poor-quality mist water. Test for alkalinity and the presence of elements so that you can adjust the water accordingly.

YELLOW LEAVES

Leaf yellowing may result from factors within the cutting itself or from the environment that surrounds the cutting. Shipments of unrooted cuttings that are placed in a warm location for several hours prior to unboxing and sticking can exhibit yellow leaves. In severe instances, the leaves will appear yellow during sticking. In most cases, leaf yellowing will appear one to four days after sticking.

Figure 3-16. Leaf yellowing resulting from placing boxes of unrooted cuttings at warm temperatures prior to unboxing and sticking.

Cultivars with medium-green foliage have a tendency to yellow in propagation. Misting leaches nutrients from leaves, so the nutritional status can be very low when rooting starts. Thus, it is important to start applying fertilizers once rooting begins to reduce leaf yellowing.

High light intensity and high leaf temperatures can also cause leaf yellowing. Reducing light intensity in propagation helps to control some of these conditions. Begin with intensities that do not exceed 1,500–2,000 f.c. (16–22 klux) until roots have formed. For the more sensitive cultivars, 1,000–1,200 f.c. (11–13 klux) is recommended. Maintain leaf temperatures at 75–80°F (24–26°C) to minimize leaf yellowing.

DEMAND INCREASES FOR OFFSHORE CUTTINGS

Traditionally, the vast majority of finished poinsettias were grown by greenhouse potted crop growers. Since 1990, a dramatic shift has occurred with poinsettia production. First, the rapid increase in demand for bedding plants in the 1980s and 1990s resulted in additional greenhouse production capacity. To cover fixed costs, bedding plant growers filled this space with poinsettias as a counter-cycle to the spring bedding plant demand. This "new" bedding plant grower did not have the spring space to devote to poinsettia stock plants, nor the desire to invest in a long-term crop. The market forces of this additional supply of poinsettias into the mass market pressured the cutting suppliers to reduce costs. As a result, most cuttings sold to growers in North America today are unrooted and come from offshore production.

VEGETATIVE GROWTH

The primary goal during the time from transplant to flower initiation is to build the foundation, or chassis, of the blooming plant. This entails thorough root penetration into the growing medium, applying the proper pinch timing and technique to achieve excellent branching, controlling stem elongation, and achieving the target plant height so that extreme measures do not need to be undertaken to promote or reduce stem elongation. Insufficient growth during this time will limit the ability to achieve adequate plant height and substance, while excessive growth prior to flower initiation will make height control very challenging.

SCHEDULING

The number of vegetative days (time from transplant to flower initiation) required for a crop is affected by the geographic location of the greenhouse, the height potential of the cultivar, and the plant form. It is particularly important to appreciate the scheduling differences between cultivars due to the differences in vigor. Fast-growing, tall cultivars will not need as much time to achieve the desired height as slower, more compact cultivars, so scheduling of the two types will be different. The benefit to the grower for taking the time to plan and schedule each cultivar will be recognized at the end of the crop when height and fullness is uniform throughout the mix of cultivars, better meeting the desired product specifications of the intended market. Detailed guidelines for developing specific crop schedules during the vegetative stage are presented in chapter 12, Scheduling Flowering Potted Poinsettias.

HANDLING ROOTED CUTTINGS

Purchased rooted cuttings should be unpacked immediately upon arrival. If this is not possible, then the boxes should be placed in a cool environment (50–60°F [10–15°C]) out of direct sunlight and, if possible, opened to allow warm air and humidity to be released from the box. The cuttings must be unpacked within twenty-four hours. If the cuttings cannot be immediately transplanted, then they should be placed in the greenhouse with 7–8" (18–20 cm) between strips. The medium should be well watered to avoid excessive drying, which leads to leaf burn and damage of the root system. Cuttings should be transplanted within two days of the delivery; however, if this is not possible, fertilization should begin at a rate of 200 ppm N applied every other day. It is not advisable to apply phosphorus on the foliage at this time, but if it is necessary, then the foliage should be rinsed following the application. It is common to observe phosphorus damage on the foliage of plants that receive regular overhead applications of 20-10-20 or similar fertilizer blends (figure 3-11 in chapter 3, Propagation).

TRANSPLANTING

Rooted cuttings should be planted so that the top of the rooting medium is at or just slightly below the top of the growing medium. Risk of stem disease and attack on the stems by fungus gnat larvae is greatly increased when cuttings are transplanted so that the stems are in contact with the soil. Exposed rooting medium may lose water more quickly than the surrounding growing medium, so daily application of water to the base of the cutting is recommended until roots establish into the new growing medium.

Figure 4-1. The proper planting depth for rooted cuttings

CROP ESTABLISHMENT

DISEASE AND PEST CONTROL

Many growers will apply a fungicide drench while initially watering in the newly transplanted rooted cuttings. A tank-mix fungicide that has one active ingredient for *Pythium* and one active ingredient for rhizoctonia is highly recommended.

Rooted cuttings should be inspected for fungus gnats. An initial sign of fungus gnats is the presence of unrooted cuttings amongst a strip of rooted cuttings. Unrooted or poorly rooted cuttings may show signs of fungus gnat larvae feeding on the callus tissue. If fungus gnats are present at the time of transplant, then a pesticide should be applied immediately following transplant, and the fungicide treatment should be reserved until the fungus gnats are under control.

WATERING

Water management is the key to establishing a good root system in the weeks following transplant and prior to pinching. During the first few days following transplant, it is critical that the water content of the rooting medium is checked daily since the surrounding growing medium may be well watered while the rooting medium in immediate contact with the roots is dry. This is especially true when cuttings are rooted in Oasis foam or Rockwool Cubes. Roots will begin to grow into the surrounding medium two to four days following transplant.

If cuttings are propagated in a rooting medium at your facility, then it usually requires ten to fourteen days for the roots of the young transplants to reach the sides of a 6" (15 cm) pot. Purchased cuttings that have been shipped often require an additional week to establish a well-developed root system as a result of the shipping stress.

Once the roots are well established, a regular cycle of irrigation followed by drying down the mix is recommended; however, water stress should never be evident on young plants. Using this wet-dry cycle, it is possible to suppress activity of root pests such as fungus gnat larvae. Growers using subirrigation systems can maintain a dry zone at the medium surface to help prevent fungus gnat activity.

FERTILIZATION

Most cuttings come out of a propagation environment with relatively low tissue nutrient levels due to two factors. First, considerable nutrient leaching occurs from leaves under a mist system. Second, most growers limit the amount of fertilizer applied during propagation because they do not want the excessive stem elongation that can easily occur under high temperatures, high humidity, and high nutritional levels.

Fertilization should begin at the time of transplanting to provide immediate access to fertilizer as new roots form. During the first seven to ten days, small amounts of water should be applied to the base of the cutting to help keep this root cube moist and allow easy root penetration to the surrounding medium, so the opportunity to apply fertilizer is somewhat limited initially. Rates of application should be in the 200–250 ppm nitrogen range. Most growers will also apply a fungicide drench during the first week after transplanting to help prevent major disease organisms from attacking the crop. Therefore, whenever a thorough irrigation of the soil can be done, incorporate a balanced fertilizer to get the crop off to a good start.

As was described above, it is still important to avoid contacting the foliage with phosphorous fertilizers. Damage to young growing tips and expanding leaves will result when overhead irrigation of mixes containing phosphorous are applied without being rinsed from the foliage. As it is difficult to apply fertilizer only to the growing medium while pots are spaced closely together, growers can use fertilizer formulations that have little or no phosphorous for best results (e.g., 15-5-15, 14-0-14).

LIGHT

Balancing light intensities at this stage of the crop is challenging. In most greenhouses the temperatures are still very warm at the end of the summer, and shade is used to help reduce stress to the young transplants. However, good light intensities are the key to strong growth, and growers should target to use as much light as is possible to build a good foundation on the plants. If cuttings have been properly toned coming out of propagation, they should be able to withstand light intensities of 4,500 f.c. (48 klux) at time of transplant. Until roots are established, it is likely that growers will need to provide some relief from heat stress by misting the foliage with clear water during the hottest part of the day. Additional airflow in the greenhouse will also help to cool the young plants and avoid stress. Of course, in more severe climates additional shade may still be required until the plants are actively growing and can handle higher light conditions.

Figure 4-2. 'Freedom' leaves are particularly susceptible to leaf burn when shadecloth is removed from the greenhouse and plants experience drought stress.

High light intensities (above 5,000 f.c. [54 klux]) help build good stem strength and prevent stretch as new shoots emerge. Leaf removal at time of pinch is used to prevent apical dominance of branches, but this also results in a clear pathway for light to reach the stems. Crops are typically started pot tight, and this spacing creates significant canopy cover that reduces the light delivered to individual shoots. By removing excess leaves and increasing light penetration to the stems, new shoots are encouraged to grow at a more upright angle and form thicker stem calipers with shorter internodes. When the leaf canopy shades plants, branches may develop in a horizontal pattern as new shoots grow outward to capture light. Horizontal branching is one of the key factors influencing stem breakage at the end of the crop.

Figure 4-3. Horizontal branching caused by shade from the canopy.

PINCHING

The purpose of pinching is to promote lateral shoot development. You can pinch by hand or with a sharp knife. Fresh, turgid cuttings are easy to pinch by hand using a simple back-and-forth movement of the fingers to "snap" the growing tip from the main plant. However, if cuttings are not very turgid because of high temperatures, knives provide a better method for pinching, as the "cut" will be cleaner and less likely to damage the stems. Knives should be disinfected as needed to remove latex buildup or if they come in contact with infected plant tissue. Use sharp knives to avoid damaging the stems.

The timing of pinching depends on several factors, including the desired number of nodes on the cutting stem, the scheduled start of short days (flower initiation), and root establishment. (See chapter 12, Scheduling Flowering Potted Poinsettias, for more details.)

NODE NUMBER

The number of desired flowers on the finished plant and the final plant spacing will influence the number of nodes left below the pinch, although the ideal specifications may vary by cultivar. In general, 4" (10 cm) crops are usually pinched leaving four to five nodes, while 6" (15 cm) and larger crops are usually pinched leaving five to eight nodes below the pinch. High-density plantings (12 x 12" [30 x 30 cm] spacing or closer) should not leave more than five nodes below the pinch unless using a cultivar such as 'Pepride', where the node count should be higher (seven to eight) for optimum results. There is no advantage to leaving more than eight nodes below the pinch on traditional spacings for 6" (15 cm) crops (14 x 14" [36 x 36 cm]), since there is not sufficient space for the plant to have more than five flowering stems in the top canopy. The additional nodes will only produce shoots that stall or break off. Multiple plant forms such as 7" (18 cm), 8" (20 cm), or larger should have individual plants pinched in a similar manner (no more than eight nodes per plant).

PINCHING TECHNIQUE

The pinching technique can have an important impact on plant architecture. A *hard* pinch involves removing all immature (not fully expanded)

JIM FAUST

a   b

Figure 4-4. A soft pinch (a) followed by the removal of one or two immature leaves (b) allows for a higher lateral shoot number than a hard pinch and more even branching than a soft pinch does.

leaves. This technique is acceptable with most poinsettias, but where temperatures and establishing conditions are stressful, stems can become somewhat hardened and compromise the potential branching. Also, it is not unusual for plants that are left for a hard pinch to have lower branches developing prior to pinching, thus an early application of a plant growth regulator may be needed to prevent stretch.

ROB BERGHAGE AND ROYAL HEINS

Figure 4-5. Pinch technique affects plant architecture and the number of shoots in the flowering canopy. Left to right: soft pinch, hard pinch, and soft pinch plus leaf removal.

A *soft* pinch involves removing the shoot tip and the small immature leaves (less than 1" [3 cm] long). It is most common to schedule a poinsettia crop with the intent to perform a hard pinch. However, if the crop is off to a slow start, the plant may lack sufficient nodes to perform a hard pinch on the scheduled pinch date. Pinch dates can not be altered to later dates by more than one week without compromising growth and quality, so a soft pinch can be performed to allow a higher node count than could be achieved with a hard pinch.

ROB BERGHAGE AND KEVIN HEINZ

Figure 4-6. Examples of soft, medium, and hard pinches (left to right)

When a soft pinch is performed, one or two immature leaves are also removed at the time of the pinch. This technique is termed *soft pinch with leaf removal.* The purpose of the leaf removal is to allow for more uniform branching, since the immature leaves will exert some apical dominance over the axillary buds and the immature leaves will continue to expand after the pinch. These leaves often become excessively large and can cause the lateral shoots to grow unevenly. Any immature leaves that have grown excessively large can be easily removed one to two weeks following pinch.

JIM FAUST

Figure 4-7. Immature leaves left below the pinch will continue to expand to form excessively large leaves. These leaves should be removed to allow for better light penetration and to improve branching.

Growers should be careful not to excessively remove leaves. Sometimes work crews are instructed to remove one or two additional leaves per cutting below the pinch. If the cuttings have previously lost a couple of bottom leaves in propagation, then the leaf removal process may result in only one or two leaves remaining on the cutting (three to four leaves are usually adequate). This may provide insufficient leaf area to intercept light, resulting in very slow growth following the pinch.

PLANT GROWTH REGULATORS (PGRs)

Plant growth regulators are used during the vegetative phase to control stem elongation and to improve branching.

HEIGHT CONTROL

Several plant growth regulator options exist for height control during the vegetative phase. During the warm temperatures and high light conditions of August to mid-September, the more active plant growth regulators are often selected. B-Nine/Cycocel tank mixes and Bonzi or Piccolo sprays can be used at this time to control potentially vigorous growth. These products also have the potential to provide excessive height control, so trials should be conducted, and caution is recommended. Cycocel is used alone at this time for a more moderate height control option desired in cooler climates or on moderately vigorous cultivars. (Plant growth regulators are covered in detail in chapter 5, Height Control.)

   The timing of growth regulator applications following pinch should be based on lateral shoot development, not a calendar, because the timing of lateral shoot development is variable. As the time from transplant to pinch increases, the rate at which the lateral shoots emerge following the pinch also increases. In fact, if the pinch date is significantly delayed, lateral branching may occur prior to the pinch.

FLOREL

Florel (ethephon), or Ethrel in Canada, can be used in conjunction with a manual pinch to control stem elongation following pinching and to potentially improve branching. Florel is commonly applied three to seven days before pinch, then repeated three to seven days following pinch. This is referred to as a "sandwich" application. The application rate ranges from 150 to 500 ppm Florel.

   It is critical that growers appreciate that Florel works like traditional growth regulators to reduce stem elongation; therefore, Florel applications usually replace other early-season growth regulator applications. Do not add Florel applications to the production schedule without reducing early season plant growth applications of other products, since Florel applied in addition to other growth regulators at this time may result in excessive height reduction. Also, Florel should not be applied within one week of the start of short days, since flowering may be negatively affected.

Growers have reported that Florel-treated poinsettias will produce more shoots that finish in the top of the canopy and at more even heights. It is not clear whether Florel actually promotes lateral branching or that leaf-size reduction caused by Florel allows for better light penetration into the canopy, which leads to more uniform branching. Regardless, in recent years many growers have begun to use Florel as a relatively inexpensive early-season growth regulator, and any potential improved branching is considered an added benefit.

The response of poinsettias to Florel is more variable from grower to grower, compared to other plant growth regulators. Part of this variability is because Florel is not quickly absorbed into the leaves and is not translocated inside the plant. Therefore, application timing and technique are critical to achieving repeatable results. A few key considerations:

- A surfactant (spreader sticker) is recommended to improve the contact of Florel with the leaves. CapSil, or a similar product, can be used according to the manufacturer's recommendations.
- Apply Florel when the solution will stay wet on the foliage for as long as possible. Early morning or late evenings work well. Applications made during high temperatures will be less effective since the solution will evaporate too quickly from the leaves.
- Complete, uniform coverage is essential. One gallon (3.8 L) of spray solution should be applied to 200 ft.^{2} (18.6 m^2) of crop area, i.e., spray to runoff. If one half of the plant does not receive the spray, that side of the plant will grow differently than the side receiving the spray.

HEIGHT CONTROL

Height control is one of the most challenging areas of poinsettia production. Stem elongation is a complex process that is influenced by many factors, including the greenhouse environment and cultural practices. Temperature, light, humidity, irrigation practices, fertilization, crop spacing, crop scheduling, and cultivar vigor all impact plant height. Understanding how to balance all of these factors to achieve the desired plant height is a challenge for poinsettia growers every year. Several techniques are available to assist growers in controlling stem elongation, including plant growth regulators, DIF, crop spacing, and crop scheduling, while graphical tracking provides growers with a tool to help take some of the guesswork of height management decisions.

PLANT GROWTH REGULATORS

Plant growth regulators (PGRs) are commonly used to reduce stem elongation and, to a lesser extent, to promote stem elongation. Currently, the plant growth regulators used to reduce poinsettia stem elongation are A-Rest (ancymidol), B-Nine (daminozide), Bonzi and Piccolo (paclobutrazol), Cycocel (chlormequat), Florel (ethephon), and Sumagic (uniconazole). Extensive knowledge and experience has been developed for the use of these products on poinsettias. Topflor (flurprimidol) is a new plant growth regulator for the greenhouse industry that has been tested in university trials and is scheduled to be available in the U.S in 2004/05. The use of height-promoting growth regulators is a relatively new phenomenon on poinsettias, and considerable work must be done before these techniques can be recommended. The plant growth regulators used to promote stem elongation are Fascination and ProGibb.

Plant growth regulators vary in their level of activity and their application timing and technique. In order to determine which PGR is the best to apply, growers should evaluate the stage of growth at which the application will be made and the amount of growth control or level of activity desired. Conditions that require higher levels of height control include: vigorous cultivars, warm day temperatures, positive DIF, tight spacing, humid environments, constantly moist soils, high levels of phosphorus applied, and a lack of residual activity from previous PGR applications.

REDUCING STEM ELONGATION

A-REST (ANCYMIDOL)

A-Rest can be applied as a drench early in the season (prior to flower initiation when the shoots are 1–2" [3–5 cm]) or in the late season (after November 1) to control late stretch. Applications should not be made between flower initiation and the end of October. Late-season applications are typically made when the plants are within 1–2" (3–5 cm) of the desired finished height. Rates used should be in the 1–2 ppm range with 4 fl. oz. (118 ml) of solution applied per 6 or 6.5" (15–17 cm) pot. Growing media with pine bark require approximately 25% higher drench application rates than other media since pine bark reduces drench effectiveness.

B-NINE (DAMINOZIDE)

B-Nine is an 85% daminozide water-soluble granular formulation that is applied as a foliar spray. B-Nine is not commonly used alone, although it is effective. The concentrations are typically 1,000–5,000 ppm. B-Nine is very effective at creating dark green leaves. Use of B-Nine is restricted to early-season applications (prior to September 10), since B-Nine can severely reduce bract expansion and delay flowering if applied too near the time of flower initiation.

B-Nine is frequently combined with Cycocel in a tank mix to achieve excellent height control. B-Nine concentrations usually range from 1,000 to 2,500 ppm, while Cycocel concentrations range from 500 to 1,500 ppm. One gallon (3.8 L) of water covers 200 ft.^{2} (18.6 m^2) of bench area. Do

ROYAL HEINS

Figure 5-1. B-Nine/Cycocel tank mixes can delay flowering if applied after flower initiation.

JIM FAUST

Figure 5-2. A B-Nine/Cycocel tank mix is very effective at controlling early-season stem elongation.

Figure 5-3. Cycocel can be used alone or in a tank mix with B-Nine.

not add any spreader-stickers to this mix. For best results, apply in the morning before temperatures reach 80°F (27°C).

BONZI AND PICCOLO (PACLOBUTRAZOL)

Bonzi and Piccolo are 0.4% liquid products that can be used as either a soil drench or as a spray. Spray rates range from 10 to 50 ppm and are most often used by warm-climate growers. Sprays are typically applied prior to flower initiation. Sprays are targeted to the stems and petioles, as uptake through the foliage is poor. Less solution is applied to the foliage compared to B-Nine and Cycocel. Many growers will "spray to glisten" rather than "spray to runoff". Avoid runoff solution since some chemical will run down the stems or drip off the leaves and act as a soil drench, possibly resulting in excessive growth regulation.

Figure 5-4. Bonzi (1 ppm) drenches were applied on Oct. 1, 10, 20, Nov. 1, and 10. The control was untreated. The earlier the application date, the greater the impact on final plant height.

Bonzi and Piccolo are extremely effective when applied as a drench. Drench rates range from 0.25 to 2 ppm. Growing media with pine bark require approximately 25% higher rates than other media do since pine bark reduces paclobutrazol effectiveness. Paclobutrazol drenches are commonly applied during the late season (one to three weeks prior to the market date) to control late stretch. Applications are typically made when the plants are within one inch of the final desired height. Drenches applied too early in the season (September and early to mid-October) have the potential to produce excessively short plants and to reduce bract size. If 6 and 6.5" (15–16.5 cm) pots require 4 fl. oz. (118 ml) of finished solution, then the other pot sizes should be adjusted accordingly. For example, if an 8" (20 cm) pot has twice the media volume of a 6" (15 cm) pot, the application rate would also be doubled to 8 fl. oz. (237 ml) per pot. For smaller pot sizes requiring less than 2 fl. oz. (59 ml) of solution, the volume should be doubled and the rate should be cut in half, e.g., increase the volume to 4 fl. oz. (118 ml) and reduce the rate from 1.0 to 0.5 ppm. Lower rates are also used when paclobutrazol is applied from the bottom of the pot (subirrigation) compared to applications made to the top of the growing medium.

CYCOCEL (CHLORMEQUAT)

Cycocel is a liquid formulation containing 11.8% chlormequat. This is the most commonly used growth regulator on poinsettia crops and is effective

Figure 5-5. Cycocel damage frequently appears on poinsettias. The level of damage increases at higher Cycocel rates and at higher temperatures. The damage usually appears early enough in the season that no marketing problems are created.

as a foliar spray or a soil drench. Foliar applications of Cycocel are made early in the day when temperatures are cooler. Provide coverage of 1 gal./200 ft.^{2} (0.2 L/m^2) of bench area. Cycocel sprays should cease by October 15 in cooler climates or at the appearance of first bract color in warmer, high-light climates. The suggested spray rates of Cycocel are 1,000–1,500 ppm. Higher rates may cause foliar damage. To minimize potential foliar damage, apply Cycocel as a fine mist spray to cover the foliage, but avoid runoff. If leaf yellowing occurs, the foliage often recovers from the initial damage after several weeks.

Figure 5-6. Effect of Cycocel on plant height. Left: Control. Right: One application of Cycocel (1,000 ppm) on October 1.

Drench applications are made at stronger rates (3,000–4,000 ppm) and are relatively expensive in the U.S. Cycocel drenches are more commonly used in Canada, where the cost is less prohibitive.

FLOREL BRAND PISTILL (ETHEPHON)

The use of Florel on poinsettias has become popular in recent years. It is applied as a foliar spray at rates of 150–500 ppm. One application is often made three to seven days before pinch, followed by a second application

Figure 5-7. Florel affects plant height. Left: Control. Right: 8 weekly applications of 500 ppm Florel.

made three to seven days following pinch. This technique is a cost-effective method for controlling early-season stem elongation. Florel has been used to improve branching of difficult branching cultivars such as 'Winter Rose'. Lateral shoots appear to develop more uniformly with more shoots filling in the top of the finished plant canopy. Florel applications must cease prior to flower initiation since there is the potential for causing delayed flowering.

Figure 5-8. An example of delayed flowering as a result of a 500-ppm Florel application made after flower initiation.

SUMAGIC (UNICONAZOLE)

Sumagic is a 0.05% uniconazole liquid that can be used as a foliar spray (2.5–10 ppm) prior to flower initiation. Very precise measurement of the chemical and application technique is essential to success with Sumagic.

TOPFLOR (FLURPRIMIDOL)

Topflor is a 0.38% flurprimidol product that has been used in Europe and is scheduled to be released for use in the U.S. in 2004/05. University trials have been conducted in the U.S., and the results suggest that 8–30 ppm spray applications provide height control for a medium-vigor cultivar such as Eckespoint 'Freedom'. Spray applications should not be made after flower initiation.

INCREASING STEM ELONGATION

The following products promote stem elongation, although there is limited experience with their use on poinsettias. So no recommendations are currently available, nor should any be implied.

FASCINATION (BENZYLADENINE/GIBBERELLIC ACID_{4+7})

Figure 5-9. Early-season applications of Fascination (3 ppm) can increase stem elongation. Left: 'Freedom White' received 3 ppm Fascination on October 4. Right: Control plant.

BRIAN WEESIES

Fascination contains 1.8% of each of two plant hormones, benzyladenine (BA) and gibberellic acid (GA). A similar product has previously been available under the name Promalin. Growers have recently been experimenting with Fascination for promoting stem elongation on plants that are elongating slowly or have been excessively growth regulated and will not make their target heights. Initial trials suggest that 2–3 ppm Fascination can work effectively; however, much research must be conducted before any recommendations can be made concerning the use of this product on poinsettias. One key appears to be that the application(s) should occur early in the season (September and early October) since late applications (late October and November) can cause stretching of the internodes between the transitional bracts, which creates an undesirable appearance. Applications of Fascination made immediately prior to marketing can promote bract expansion. These are experimental results, so extreme caution is urged. Fascination is not currently labeled for use on poinsettias.

JIM BARRETT

■ Figure 5-10. Late-season applications of Fascination can cause stretch between the transitional bracts.

JOE MOORE

■ Figure 5-11. Late-season applications of Fascination can accelerate bract expansion. Left: 'Prestige' Control. Right: 'Prestige' bracts ten days after a 3-ppm Fascination application

PROGIBB (GIBBERELLIC ACID₃)

ProGibb is a 4% gibberellic acid product. Spray applications of 2–5 ppm have been used to promote stem elongation in September or early October. Insufficient data and experience exist for any recommendations to be made. Extreme caution is urged since excessive stem elongation can result in unsightly plants.

■ Figure 5-12. Gibberellic acid can produce excessive stem elongation.

PLANT GROWTH REGULATOR STRATEGIES

PROPAGATION

The use of plant growth regulator spray applications will help to prevent excessive stem elongation in propagation. Growth regulators should be applied early in the morning or late in the evening, when the mist system can be turned off without stressing the cuttings. Cycocel (1,500 ppm) or a B-Nine/Cycocel tank mix (1,000–1,500 ppm B-Nine and 1000 ppm Cycocel) are commonly used. The application of growth regulators can begin during the second or third week of propagation. One PGR application is often sufficient for moderately vigorous cultivars, while more vigorous cultivars may require two or three applications. Proper applications do not delay rooting.

Paclobutrazol (Bonzi and Piccolo) and Sumagic are potent growth regulators that require caution in poinsettia propagation. To be effective, these growth regulators must be applied uniformly to the cutting stems. Foliage covering the stem portion of cuttings in propagation makes applying paclobutrazol or Sumagic difficult. Also, if these products run off the foliage and down the stem, cuttings may receive an excessive dose, resulting in stunting. Growers should definitely experiment with these products prior to making an application to a large number of cuttings. It is suggested to trial rates that are less than 5 ppm for paclobutrazol and less than 1 ppm for Sumagic.

TRANSPLANT TO PINCH

The need for PGRs is generally limited during this stage unless no PGRs were used in propagation. Newly transplanted cuttings typically have plenty of surrounding space, so less stretch is likely to occur at this time. If the cuttings already have adequate node count, any new growth is likely to be removed by pinching. Stretch is most likely to occur when the plants must be grown to a greater node count before pinching. It is important that the internodes remain compact (less than 1" [2.5 cm] between nodes) prior to pinch, otherwise the pinch height may be higher than desired, which can result in uneven branching.

PGRs may be needed at this stage when premature lateral shoots develop before the pinch or when the plants are grown as non-pinched forms. Cycocel as a spray (1,000 ppm) is usually adequate to control stem elongation. Florel applications that are used to reduce stem elongation as well as to promote branching are often applied as a "sandwich" treatment, which refers to applications made three to seven days prior to pinch and repeated three to seven days following pinch.

PINCH TO FLOWER INITIATION

The use of PGRs generally begins when lateral shoots are $3/4$–1" (1.9–2.5 cm) long. At this stage, many PGR options exist. For light control, use Cycocel at a rate of 1,000–1,500 ppm or B-Nine at 2,000–3,000 ppm. For moderate control, spray foliage with a tank mix of B-Nine (1,000–2,500 ppm) and Cycocel (1,000–1,500 ppm). If stronger control is required, spray applications of paclobutrazol (10–25 ppm), Sumagic (2.5–10 ppm), or Topflor (8–30 ppm) may be used.

Drench applications of PGRs provide longer lasting and more uniform effects than spray applications. For moderate control, Cycocel may be applied as a drench at a rate of 3,000 ppm. A-Rest, paclobutrazol, and Sumagic drenches are not recommended at this stage due to the potential to excessively reduce stem elongation.

FLOWER INITIATION TO FIRST COLOR

Cycocel is the PGR of choice for most growers during this stage of development. Spray or drench applications are acceptable under a wide range of conditions. Spray applications should be made when greenhouse temperatures are below 80°F (27°C) to reduce the incidence of phytotoxicity (see figure 5-5). Other application options become more limited once flower initiation begins (generally the third week of September for crops grown under natural day lengths). Spray applications of A-Rest, B-Nine, Florel, paclobutrazol, Sumagic, and Topflor are not recommended except in regions of extreme heat, such as southern Florida, the Gulf States, and the tropics, due to the potential for delaying flowering and significantly reducing bract size.

FIRST COLOR TO FLOWER

Ideally, all PGR applications should be completed prior to first color; however, in the event of late stretch due to weather conditions or an unusual growth pattern, it is possible to apply a drench of A-Rest (1–3 ppm) or paclobutrazol (0.5–2.0 ppm) without significant bract size reduction or flower delay. The rates used should be maintained at the low end unless you are located in the extreme heat regions of the southern U.S. A single drench application usually provides sufficient height control; however, two applications are occasionally needed in warm climates when high temperatures prevail in October and November.

Apply drenches using the volume of solution that is proportional to the container volume. For 6–6.5" (15–17 cm) pots, apply 4 fl. oz. (118 ml) of the PGR solution to a uniformly moist medium. It is not advisable (or legal by some product labels) to apply the PGRs through irrigation systems since it is difficult to accurately control the volume applied. The most common application method is "dipping" the chemical out of solution tanks or using equipment designed to provide accurate doses to each container. Drench applications are extremely effective with hanging baskets, where spray applications are difficult to apply without drift onto adjacent plants and growing conditions often encourage rapid stem elongation. For 10" (25 cm) hanging baskets, apply 15 fl. oz. (443 ml) of the PGR solution per container.

H. MARC CATHEY

A leader in horticulture science, Dr. Marc Cathey is both a friend and an ally to the Ecke Ranch. Through his research, poinsettia growers have been given tools that make their work better and easier.

Dr. Cathey has helped us understand the application of lighting to crop production for photoperiod control. In poinsettia production this is used to manipulate plants to either maintain the vegetative growth needed for mother plants or to schedule and time flowering plants for market. The work he did in the development of plant growth regulators helps control stretch of poinsettias and has brought an end to the technique of stem folding, once a required step for poinsettia producers when plants grew too tall for commercial sale.

His contribution to the science of crop production is matched only by his contributions to the entire green industry as a promoter and advocate for the use of plants and flowers in every aspect of our lives.

PGR CALCULATIONS

PGRCALC is a Microsoft Excel spreadsheet developed at North Carolina State University that allows growers to calculate the amounts of A-Rest, Atrimmec, Bonzi, B-Nine, Cycocel, Fascination, Florel, GibGro, Piccolo, ProGibb, and Sumagic needed to create any spray or drench solution desired. If you enter your costs for each PGR, it will also calculate your materials cost per application as well as per plant treated. By entering plant dimensions and application rate per unit area, the spreadsheet will calculate the amount of active ingredient each plant received during the application. The software is available at www.floricultureinfo.com.

DIF

DIF refers to the difference between day and night temperatures (Day Temperature – Night Temperature = DIF). As the DIF becomes more positive, stem elongation increases. In contrast, as DIF becomes more negative, stem elongation decreases. The DIF effect is a combination of two separate responses. First, stem elongation increases as day temperatures increase. Second, stem elongation increases as night temperatures decrease. Thus, the combination of warm days and cool nights (positive DIF) results in the most rapid stem elongation, while cool days and warm nights (negative DIF) result in the slowest stem elongation rates.

Figure 5-13. The effect of DIF on poinsettia height. Left: Poinsettia grown with warm day temperatures (74°F [23°C]) and cooler night temperatures (64°F [17°C]). Right: Poinsettia grown with cool days (64°F [17°C]) and warm nights (74°F or [23°C]). Leaves have been removed to better see the habit.

A "zero DIF" occurs when the day temperature equals the night temperature. Zero or negative DIF conditions are much easier to achieve during poinsettia season in northern greenhouses. In warmer climates, the morning temperatures can be dropped at or before sunrise and the greenhouse kept cool for two to four hours until temperature control is lost. This technique will provide a moderate negative DIF response.

Once flower initiation begins, high night temperatures (72°F [22°C]) can delay flowering. So, growers must be careful to not attempt to provide a negative DIF environment that results in the night temperature exceeding 72°F (22°C).

Hanging baskets grown in the top of the greenhouse tend to have warmer day temperatures and cooler night temperatures than do bench crops. This large positive DIF encourages stem elongation; therefore, higher PGR rates are often required to control the height of hanging basket crops.

CROP SPACING

Spacing plays a crucial role in stem elongation, crop quality, and crop profitability. The number of 6" (15 cm) pots that can be grown at different spacings (table 5-1) demonstrates the effect of spacing on crop profitability. Nearly twice as many plants can be grown at 10 x 10" (25 x 25 cm) spacing compared to 14 x 14" (36 x 36 cm) spacing, so greenhouse space use efficiency is much improved at tighter spacing. Economics push growers to produce poinsettias at high densities; however, the downside to tighter spacing is the increased potential stem elongation and the loss of plant quality.

TABLE 5-1.
THE EFFECT OF CONTAINER SPACING ON THE NUMBER OF POTS

Spacing	Grown per Unit Area Area per pot	Pots per unit area
10 x 10" (25 x 25 cm)	100 in.² (645 cm²)	1.4 pots/ft.² (15.5 pots/m²)
12 x 12" (30 x 30 cm)	144 in.² (929 cm²)	1.0 pots/ft.² (10.8 pots/m²)
14 x 14" (36 x 36 cm)	196 in.² (1,265 cm²)	0.7 pots/ft.² (7.9 pots/m²)

LIGHT QUALITY

In nature, neighboring plants compete for light, so the plant that elongates the fastest can position its leaves to intercept the most sunlight. Therefore, stem elongation is promoted by competition for space from neighboring plants and has nothing to do with low light conditions such as cloudy weather. The neighboring plant response is due to the interception of light that has been filtered through or reflected from neighboring plants. Leaves absorb red light, while they reflect or transmit far-red light. Therefore, the light environment near a neighboring plant is relatively low in red light and high in far-red light. Plants respond to this altered light environment by partitioning their energy into stem elongation. When plants respond to specific wavelengths (or colors) of light, this is termed a *light quality* response.

Poinsettias are particularly responsive to neighboring plants. For example, many cultivars elongate relatively slowly when the plants are grown in isolation, i.e., no neighbors. However, those same cultivars will elongate very rapidly if placed closely to a neighboring plant.

Figure 5-14. Two poinsettias that have been grown in the same greenhouse and are the same age. Left: Poinsettia grown with additional space. Right: Poinsettia grown pot-to-pot.

CANOPY CLOSURE

Poinsettias begin to elongate in response to competition for light with neighboring plants when the tips of the leaves of neighboring plants begin

Figure 5-15. An example of the leaves of neighboring plants beginning to overlap. Stem elongation increases at this point when neighboring plants compete for light.

to overlap. This point in time is referred to as *canopy closure* and is a key factor for making height-control decisions. When a grower evaluates a crop to determine PGR applications, the degree of canopy closure should be part of the decision-making process. The greater the leaf overlap, the greater the increase in stem elongation rate.

HEIGHT POTENTIAL

The number of nodes per stem and the length of the individual internodes determine the height potential for a particular poinsettia crop. Internode length is very sensitive to crop spacing and the degree of canopy closure,

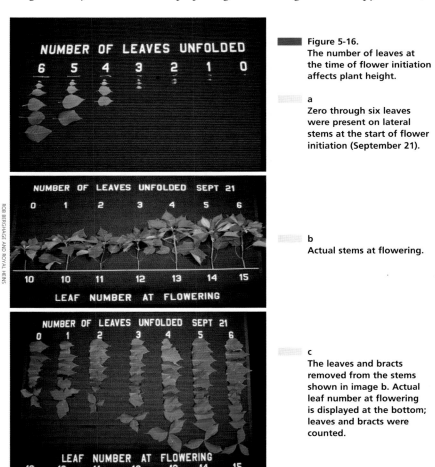

Figure 5-16.
The number of leaves at the time of flower initiation affects plant height.

a
Zero through six leaves were present on lateral stems at the start of flower initiation (September 21).

b
Actual stems at flowering.

c
The leaves and bracts removed from the stems shown in image b. Actual leaf number at flowering is displayed at the bottom; leaves and bracts were counted.

ROB BERGHAGE AND ROYAL HEINS

while node number is determined by the length of the time from pinch to flower initiation. Once flower initiation occurs, the number of leaves left to unfold is fixed to approximately seven leaves. Prior to flower initiation, poinsettias will typically develop a new leaf every four to five days. Thus, if a grower is having problems growing crops of sufficient height, the schedule can be altered to allow additional days from pinch to flower initiation. Adding four or five days will add one leaf and one internode per stem, thus the potential height is typically increased by 0.5" (1.3 cm) to 1.5" (3.8 cm). In contrast, growers can reduce the height potential by decreasing the number of days between pinch and flower initiation.

Figure 5-16 provides an example of how the leaf number at the start of short days (September 21) affects the height potential. Plants were grown and pinched so that zero to six leaves were unfolded on the lateral stems on September 21. The plants were then grown to flower and stems and leaves were removed. The greater the number of leaves at the start of short days, the greater the height potential. In each example, the plants produced six to seven additional leaves on the stems and a whorl of three true bracts at the top of the shoot that subtend the cyathia.

The height potential varies among cultivars. Cultivars that tend to be short (see chapter 14, Cultivar Guide, for the height potential ratings for each cultivar) require a longer vegetative phase (time from pinch to flower initiation) to achieve adequate height, while tall cultivars require shorter vegetative phases so that plants will not be excessively tall.

STEM ELONGATION PATTERNS

Poinsettias follow a distinct **S**-shaped growth pattern from the time of pinch to flower. The **S**-shape has three distinct growth phases. First, there is a *lag phase* associated with initial slow growth that occurs immediately after pinching. The lag phase can last for one to two weeks. Occasionally, lateral shoots will begin to grow prior to pinching. This most often occurs when the pinch date is delayed. The result is that the lag phase may only be a few days. The second growth phase is the *linear phase*. At this time, poinsettias will elongate at their most rapid rate. The stem elongation rate may actually increase throughout the linear phase due to the canopy closure that usually occurs during this time. The linear phase presents the greatest possibility to affect plant height since the most height is achieved during this time. Thus, growth regulator applications should be timed to be effective during the linear phase. The third growth phase is the *plateau phase*. This phase occurs as the plant ceases to add new leaves and the flowers start to develop. Most crops experience this plateau during the two weeks prior to market; however, some cultivars have a tendency to exhibit late stretch. This phenomenon can catch growers by surprise and cause a loss of height control at the very end of the crop. Paclobutrazol drenches are very effective at controlling late stretch.

GRAPHICAL TRACKING

Graphical tracking is a tool that assists growers in making decisions about height control. A graphical tracking chart consists of two **S**-shaped growth curves that describe the minimum and maximum desired height throughout the duration of the crop. The curves start at the pinch date and end at flowering. The space between the two curves is termed the *window*. This provides the target height throughout the duration of crop. A spreadsheet (UNH FloraTrack) has been developed to assist growers in creating their own graphical tracking charts and as a means of recording and managing crop height records. The software is available at www.ecke.com.

A normal **S**-shaped curves works well for most growers; however, some growers have found that curves that have a slower initial elongation rate (longer lag time) and a smaller plateau at the end of the crop work well for some cultivars. This curve has been coined the "late-season curve" and is most often used for small pots, high-density production, and cultivars such as Eckespoint 'Freedom' that have a tendency to elongate up until the market date. In addition, an unpinched curve is available for non-pinched forms (straight-ups).

Graphical tracking requires the grower to record plant height once or twice per week and plot the measurement on the height chart. If the crop is growing below the window, steps can be taken to increase stem elongation. Options include increasing the DIF, delaying crop spacing, and/or avoiding water stress. If the crop is growing above the window, steps can be taken to decrease stem elongation. Options include decreasing the DIF, providing a cool morning temperature pulse, applying a growth regulator, and/or spacing the crop. The process of making regular measurements forces the grower to regularly evaluate crop height. The value of this process should not be underestimated. It is much easier to make small adjustments throughout a crop rather than to allow a couple of weeks of unchecked growth to occur and then have to make more drastic adjustments to overcome excessively slow or fast stem elongation.

ROYAL HEINS

Figure 5-17. Plant height is measured to the top of the poinsettia canopy. The measurements are recorded on the graphical tracking charts.

Figure 5-18. A graphical tracking chart hanging in front of the poinsettia crop.

Figure 5-17 demonstrates how to make a poinsettia crop height measurement. Many growers find it valuable to hang a chart in front of each bench or greenhouse bay so measurements can be easily recorded and the records can be easily accessed. It can be difficult to create a graphical tracking curve for each variety and each crop, so the following tips are suggested:

- Create curves for the most important cultivars and separate by location and/or flowering schedules
- Group cultivars with similar growth patterns and height potential, e.g., Peter Jacobsen's 'Peterstar', RAI Beckmann's 'Maren', and RAI Bevelander's 'Marblestar'.

TRACKING HEIGHT WITH DIGITAL PHOTOGRAPHY

The advent of digital photography has created an opportunity for growers to create a visual diary of poinsettia crops for the purpose of record-keeping and production staff training. Table 5-2 displays an example of weekly pictures taken of Eckespoint 'Enduring Pink' and the corresponding text. A graphical tracking chart is also shown for this particular crop. The combination of text, graph, and images creates a powerful record that can be referenced in future years. This process is not particularly expensive nor does it require excessive time to compile. It does require a strong commitment so that the appropriate data can be gathered weekly throughout the production season.

TABLE 5-2.
WEEKLY NOTES FOR 'ENDURING PINK'

'Enduring Pink' grown in Gainesville, Florida. Note that height control decisions reflect a warm climate production scenario and do not reflect the choices that would be made for locations across most of the U.S. Photos and text provided by Dr. Jim Barrett and Carolyn Bartuska, University of Florida.

9/9 'Enduring Pink' is a very promising new variety that will likely become the main pink in warm climates. It is less vigorous than 'Freedom Red' and finishes with 'Freedom'. This is a late plant-and-pinch schedule for this variety, so we will guard against using too much growth regulator.

9/16

For this 'Enduring Pink' crop we anticipate spraying it once before October 1, and that will probably be on September 30.

9/23

'Enduring Pink' seems to be more sensitive to PGRs than 'Freedom' and most other varieties are, yet it can elongate and stretch as much as 'Freedom' can. Thus, we must control this crop's growth but avoid putting on too much chemical. We decided to spray this week rather than wait for next week as planned. The reason is the plants grew more than the curve this week and the shoot tips show they are continuing to elongate at a good pace. If we do not spray now, they could be well above the curve next week. The low rate of B-Nine/Cycocel (1,000 ppm each) is being used.

9/30

Considering the change in the weather, we are pleased with the growth of this crop. Last week's spray does not appear to have been too strong.

10/7

'Enduring Pink' has now grown out of the spray applied two weeks ago and has resumed rapid elongation. We need more experience with this crop to make a better decision this week. If it continues at the current rate, it will finish at the desired height; spraying could make it finish too short. If the rate of elongation increases, it will become too tall. Last year we had great success with a late drench on 'Enduring Pink', so this week we are not spraying the crop since we feel that we can stop it if needed and want to guard against making it too short.

10/14

This 'Enduring Pink' crop is in almost the same situation as the 'Freedom' crop; however, we are not spraying this crop. This decision may be a mistake, but we want to see how it grows without any PGR. We anticipate that it will probably need a late drench about November 4.

10/21

The 'Enduring Pink' crop is showing color now and is on schedule. The plants look good. They project to be between 14 and 15" (36 and 38 cm) in two weeks and will likely need a drench.

10/28

This is another crop that slowed down, and now we hope it can make two more inches. After looking at the shoot tips, we think this crop might have a better chance than the 'Freedom' crops.

11/4

With 1.5" (4 cm) of growth, this was another surprise after looking like it was slowing down. The plants look like they could add another 2" (5 cm) by the time they finish in ten to fourteen days. The appearance will be a little better if we can hold that down to about 1" (3 cm), so we are applying a 1-ppm Bonzi drench today.

11/11

This 'Enduring Pink' crop responded nicely to the 1-ppm Bonzi drench applied last week, and final height will not be a problem. The drench seems to have had minimal effect on bract development.

11/18

We wish all poinsettias were this easy. 'Enduring Pink' finished on time and the crop is very uniform. The late drench is very effective on 'Enduring Pink' and has little effect on bract size.

Height (inches)

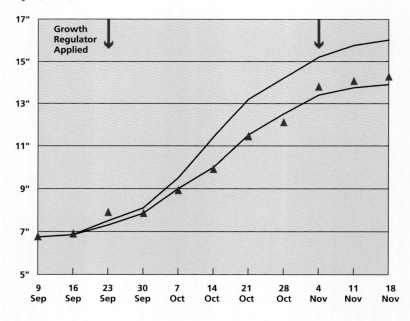

6

❧⟨⟨⟨❀⟩⟩⟩❧

WATER QUALITY

Water quality refers to the chemical composition of the irrigation water. When formulating a nutritional program for poinsettias, water quality should be given top priority. Irrigation water sources vary considerably with location, so a water analysis is required to determine the water quality. Consideration of water quality helps determine what adjustments should be made to the water, what amendments need to be added to growing media, and which fertilizers should be used to supply optimum nutrition for poinsettias.

Several facets of water quality should be explored before deciding on your irrigation practices, fertilizers, or growing media. Alkalinity, pH, EC, nutrient content, and toxic elements should be analyzed and evaluated before a nutritional program is developed.

ALKALINITY

Alkalinity is perhaps the most important consideration in determining water quality. The degree of alkalinity in irrigation water affects the pH of growing media, which in turn affects the availability of plant nutrients in the media. Alkalinity is defined as the water's capacity to neutralize acids and is a measure of bicarbonates (HCO_3^-), carbonates (CO_3^{2-}), and carbonic acid (H_2CO_3). Alkalinity is measured by the quantity of acid required to neutralize the bicarbonates and carbonate ions and is expressed as parts per million (ppm) calcium carbonate ($CaCO_3$) equivalent in a water supply (ppm $CaCO_3$/L). For poinsettia nutrition, 100–200 ppm alkalinity is considered the borderline level for irrigation water, and an acid treatment may be necessary if the alkalinity exceeds this level.

Alkalinity is important to poinsettia production because it can alter the

73

pH of the growing medium. High alkalinity water increases the pH of the medium, restricting the uptake of essential plant nutrients, especially the minor elements (iron, manganese, zinc, copper, and boron). Recommended methods for controlling alkalinity in the water supply involve treatment with fertilizers and/or acid injection. For many years, growers have alternated 20-10-20 and 15-0-15 to help manage media pH and counteract the alkalinity of the water source. For example, with high alkalinity water, an acid-residue fertilizer such as 20-10-20 can be used to counteract the alkalinity. In contrast, with low alkalinity water, an alkaline-residue fertilizer like 15-0-15 can be used to assist in keeping the pH from dropping too low.

Historically, alternating different fertilizers had the additional benefit of supplying all the plant nutrients that could not be supplied in a single fertilizer source. However, in more recent years, many growers have started to use fertilizers that contain all of the essential macro- and micronutrients, such as Peters Excel 15-5-15 Cal Mag fertilizers. These fertilizers are neither strongly alkaline or acidic, so alternating multiple fertilizers is not necessary.

pH

pH is a measure of acidity or basicity. The pH of the water supply is not necessarily an indication of its alkalinity because it is possible to have high pH water with relatively low alkalinity. Ideally, the water pH should be between 5.0 and 6.0. Higher pH water (greater than 6.0) can cause solubility issues for iron sulfate, and some pesticides, fungicides, and plant growth regulators. With high-alkalinity water, more acid is required to neutralize the bicarbonates and lower the pH of the water. With low alkalinity water, a relatively small amount of acid is required to lower the pH. Acid-injection is covered in more detail later in this chapter. For poinsettia growing considerations, the pH of the growing medium is more often a concern than the pH of the water (see Growing Media, chapter 8, for a discussion on media pH).

ELECTRICAL CONDUCTIVITY

Electrical conductivity (EC), or soluble salts, refers to the total amount of dissolved salts in a water supply. Water EC is important in that it contributes to the EC of the growing medium and it restricts the amount of fertilizers that can be added to the irrigation water. A water source with an EC reading of 0.5 mmhos/cm or less is considered desirable. By adding fertilizer to irrigation waters, the EC of the fertilizer solution is automatically increased. In most cases, it is not advisable to have the fertigation solution exceed an EC of 3.0 mmhos/cm. If irrigation water has a high EC, it is very easy to exceed an EC of 3.0 mmhos/cm by adding fertilizer. When the irrigation water EC is low, there is more flexibility in terms of the amount and kind of fertilizers to be used.

PLANT NUTRIENTS

Most irrigation water supplies a few plant nutrients that are essential to poinsettias. However, irrigation water is usually not considered a prime source for nutrients other than calcium or magnesium, whose presence should be considered when formulating a nutritional program. For example, an irrigation source may contain 50 ppm magnesium. This is more magnesium than many plant fertilizers supply; therefore, a grower using this water source should never have to add further magnesium in a fertilization program.

TOXIC ELEMENTS

Sodium and boron are two elements that are often found in irrigation water and may reduce poinsettia growth. Although boron is essential for adequate nutrition, levels above 0.8 ppm in irrigation water may lead to plant injury and decreased growth. Sodium, on the other hand, is not an essential element, and levels above 50 ppm may cause marginal leaf or bract burn. High sodium levels can sometimes be counteracted to some degree with the addition of other cations, such as calcium, potassium, or magnesium.

WATER TESTING

EC, pH, and alkalinity can be easily tested in-house with water test kits. A commercial lab is needed to measure the remaining items in the water.

TABLE 6-1. WATER ANALYSIS INTERPRETATION.

Item	Desirable Range	Comments
Alkalinity (bicarbonates)	40–100 ppm*	The major factor affecting media pH. Low alkalinity can cause media pH to decrease, while high alkalinity can cause media pH to rise. Additional lime can be incorporated into the growing medium prior to potting to compensate for low-alkalinity water (less than 40 ppm). If the alkalinity is greater than 200 ppm, acid injection is used to reduce water alkalinity.
pH	5.5–7.0	Alkaline ground water is due to contact with limestone. Acidic waters may evolve from areas of decomposing organic matter or unusual mineral deposits. Very high values may indicate high sodium.
EC (electrical conductivity)	0.1–0.5 mmhos/cm	The conductivity indicates dissolved mineral content, or soluble salts. High EC water can cause the medium's EC to become excessively high, which can reduce growth and cause marginal leaf and bract burn. The higher the EC, the greater the leaching requirement.
Hardness	less than 100 ppm	A measure of the calcium and magnesium concentrations in the water. Can cause a white residue on foliage, particularly when in mist propagation water.
Calcium	less than 100 ppm	Levels equal to or higher than sodium are desirable. A plant nutrient, it is relatively harmless at fairly high concentrations.
Magnesium	less than 24 ppm	A plant nutrient normally present in lower concentration than calcium. Higher values are not apt to be harmful. It can cause a white residue on foliage, particularly when in mist propagation water.
Sodium absorption ratio (SAR)	less than 4	Sodium absorption ratio (SAR) is a calculated value indicating the sodium hazard. Values above 8 indicate potential for impairing the growing medium structure.
Iron	less than 2 ppm	Can cause a rust-colored residue on foliage if present at high levels in mist propagation water.
Boron	less than 0.8 ppm	An important element for plant nutrition, but it is toxic in high concentration.
Sodium	less than 100 ppm	Small amounts are not harmful and can beneficially substitute for potassium when deficient. Excess causes leaf necrosis and burn.
Chloride	less than 70 ppm	Although required in minute amounts for plant nutrition, high levels can be toxic.
Sulfate	less than 50 ppm	An important plant nutrient.

*Divide ppm by 50 to calculate the milliequivalents per liter (meq/L).

WATER QUALITY AND MIST PROPAGATION

Water quality affects rooting performance of poinsettia cuttings in the following ways:

1. it may change the pH of the rooting medium,
2. it may change the soluble salts (EC) of the rooting medium, and
3. it may leave mineral deposits on the foliage or cause leaf distortion.

The same guidelines for irrigation water (table 6-1) are applicable for mist propagation water. However, good water quality is more critical for successful propagation than for irrigation of rooted plants.

The optimum pH range for rooting media is 5.8–6.3. An alkalinity level in the irrigation water greater than 200 ppm may raise the pH of the medium and slow the rooting process. EC has a direct effect on rooting, e.g., high EC water will delay rooting. Water with an EC of 1.0 mmho/cm or greater is not recommended, and water with high levels of dissolved minerals such as calcium and magnesium often leaves unsightly residues on foliage of cuttings under mist (see figure 3-10). It is best to avoid these water sources. Acid treatment of mist propagation water does not reduce the residue problem.

Treating mist propagation water with phosphoric acid is *not* recommended for two important reasons. First, phosphorus reacts with calcium to form an insoluble calcium phosphate precipitate and increases the foliar residue problem. Second, soluble phosphorus is absorbed by poinsettia leaves, forms insoluble complexes with minor nutrients, and causes deficiencies, distorted leaves, and hardened plant tissues (see figure 3-11). If there is a choice, use the best quality water available for mist propagation. Collection of rainwater or treatment of water by reverse osmosis may greatly improve the success of mist propagation.

WATER TREATMENT

Water can be treated for toxic elements and for pathogens. Filtration systems can be used to reduce the concentration of elements such as bicarbonate, calcium, iron, sodium, and many others. Reverse osmosis (RO) is one of the most common filtration systems used in commercial greenhouses. RO water purification systems work on the principle that pressure can be applied to water that has a high solute concentration and the water will be pushed through a membrane while the solutes are left behind. The energy required to pressurize the system, the membranes, and membrane maintenance are significant costs for this system. Brine waste water (high solute) resulting from the RO process must be properly disposed of.

Pathogens in the irrigation water are a particular concern for surface water sources and in re-circulation irrigation systems. Root rot organisms, such as *Pythium* and *Phytophthora*, are of particular concern. Ultraviolet light, ozonation, and chlorination are frequently used to disinfect irrigation water if pathogens are present. Ozone is an effective ozidizer and leaves no residual in the water. However, the ozonation process can produce a residual ozone gas, which is considered an air contaminant and thus some air pollution agencies might require it to be collected. Water that is exposed to ultraviolet light treatments must have a high clarity so that suspended particles do not scatter the light; therefore, ultraviolet light treatments are performed after the water has passed through a filtration system. Ultraviolet light and ozonation provide no residual disinfection beyond the initial treatment. In contrast, chlorine does provide residual disinfection. The amount of chlorine added to the water depends on the amount of contaminants in the water that will break down the chlorine. The residual chlorine should be approximately 0.5 ppm in order to achieve adequate disinfection. Residual chlorine of 2.5–10.0 ppm can cause damage to plants. The dose will be higher than the residual chlorine levels since some chlorine will break down when it comes into contact with organic matter and contaminants in the irrigation water prior coming into contact with the plants.

ACID INJECTION

Injecting acid into irrigation water containing high levels of alkalinity or pH (table 6-1) can reduce those levels. Acids are commonly injected into irrigation water simultaneously with fertilizer solutions. For the best results, use a separate injector for acid or an injector with multiple heads to avoid stock solutions of acid being mixed with fertilizer stock solutions.

Three different factors need to be considered to determine the amount of acid to treat irrigation water. They are:
 1. the pH of the water,

2. the alkalinity of the water, and

3. the type of acid being used.

Therefore, the amount of acid injected will vary with each water supply.

The target alkalinity is 40–100 ppm. The most common acids used in commercial greenhouses include phosphoric acid (H_2PO_4, 75 and 85%), sulfuric acid (H_2SO_4, 35 and 93%), and nitric acid (HNO_3, 61 and 67%). A North Carolina State University Web site (www.floricultureinfo.com) contains a spreadsheet (Alkalinity Calculator) that assists users in calculating the acid required for different water sources.

Acids also supply plant nutrients such as phosphorus, sulfur, and nitrate-nitrogen. The concentrations of these nutrients should be considered when developing the fertilization program. The Alkalinity Calculator mentioned above allows you to calculate the concentration of nutrients supplied by the acid. The pH of acid-injected water should be tested regularly to determine that the injector is functioning properly.

Before using liquid mineral acids, adhere to the following precautions:

• Handle with care! Mineral acids are extremely corrosive.

• When diluting acids, always pour acid into water and not the reverse. Pouring water into concentrated acid may cause a violent reaction.

• Injection equipment should be designed to handle acids; otherwise equipment may be damaged.

• Acid-treated water may corrode iron or galvanized pipe and release toxic levels of zinc or other metals. Plastic pipes are recommended.

• Acids should not be added to concentrated stock solutions containing calcium fertilizers; insoluble precipitates may form.

• Water treated with phosphoric acid should not be used for mist propagation or overhead watering of poinsettias. Foliar absorption of phosphorus causes deformed leaves and hardened growth.

7

✧❀✧

IRRIGATION AND IRRIGATION SYSTEMS

In recent years the largest change in poinsettia irrigation has been the increased use of mechanical irrigation systems. Mechanical systems can be divided into three types: overhead watering (boom or sprinkler watering), surface watering (microtube and drip irrigation), and subirrigation (flood floor, ebb-and-flow, trough, and capillary mat irrigation). Although installation expenses are high, long-term savings will be realized due to reducing the labor costs associated with hand watering. The following table lists some of the advantages and disadvantages of different irrigation systems.

TABLE 7-1. ADVANTAGES AND DISADVANTAGES OF DIFFERENT IRRIGATION SYSTEMS.

Irrigation Systems	Advantages	Disadvantages
Overhead Booms Sprinklers	Overhead systems are versatile since they can also be used to irrigate other crops following poinsettias, such as bedding plants. Overhead irrigation is the least expensive system to install and allows for a large area to be irrigated at one time.	Overhead irrigation results in frequent wetting of the leaves and bracts, which will increase poinsettia susceptibility to foliar fungal pathogens such as botrytis. Also, the increased splashing of water can quickly spread bacterial pathogens. Overhead watering can compact the growing media, resulting in lower porosity. Overhead watering may also flush media out of the pots resulting in lower media water retention. Due to the relatively high leaching fraction, higher fertilizer rates generally are needed to get the same quality plants compared to subirrigation. Overhead systems use large amounts of water and can produce excessive runoff.

81

Irrigation Systems	Advantages	Disadvantages
Surface Microtubes	There is little media compaction and washing out of media from the pots. Microtubes work well with standard, pulse, or no-leach irrigation methods by adjusting the amount of water applied to each pot. Adapt well to hanging baskets and large pot sizes. Installation costs for microtube systems are relatively low. No wetting of the foliage reduces the potential for the spread of pathogens.	Lack versatility. The number of pots to be irrigated prescribes the dimensions of the microtubes and the header pipe. If spacing is changed, the irrigation system must be adapted. Best suited for large containers or spaced crops. Cost becomes prohibitive for pot sizes less than 4" (10 cm) in diameter. Poor water quality can result in the microtubes becoming plugged. Regularly monitoring is required to catch dry plants and clean or replace the tubes.
Subirrigation	No runoff. Lower water and fertilizer required. Little media compaction and media loss during irrigation, which allows the media to retain its initially high water holding capacity. No water on foliage.	Requires well-designed (level) benches or floors. High installation costs. Pathogen pressure and ease of spread in recirculation systems. Non-uniformity of water application (depending on system design).
Ebb-and-flow (Dutch trays)	Reduced labor for moving plants in and out of the greenhouse.	May not supply adequate water to plants grown in large containers (greater than 7" [18 cm]).
Ebb-and-flow (flood floors)	All sections of the greenhouse are easily accessible with forklifts and carts which decreases the labor and time needed for planting and shipping. High greenhouse space use efficiency due to limited aisle space Mechanical pot placement and pot spacing machines are available. Low maintenance.	May not supply adequate water to plants grown in large containers (greater than 7" [18 cm]). Large-scale production is required to have a single, uniform crop in each irrigation zone. Requires highly uniform plants. Plants closest to the inlets/drains receive more water than plants along the edges. Managing disease can be challenging, especially *Pythium*.
Trough	Ideal for small containers (4" [10 cm] and smaller).	Some spacing limitations. Larger containers may not fit in the troughs.

Irrigation Systems	Advantages	Disadvantages
Capillary mats	Ideal for small containers (4" [10 cm] and smaller).	Algae formation on the mats.
		Salts accumulate in the mats.
		Good contact must be made between the medium in the pot and the mat. To insure this, the first irrigation must be a top watering to establish the connection.
		If the plants dry to wilting, or are moved, they will have to be irrigated again from the top. Pots with "legs" or other projections can't be used if they don't allow contact between the media and the mat.
		May dry out too quickly in sunny and dry climates.

WATERING

Watering requires the proper combination of water volume applied and irrigation timing. The goal is to avoid extreme conditions that create stresses that weaken the plants, result in poor growth, and increase disease susceptibility. Watering technique influences many factors, such as salt buildup in the root zone, the porosity (or compaction) of the growing medium, and greenhouse relative humidity. These factors can affect product growth and quality. Proper irrigation decisions require knowledge about how the irrigation water, growing medium, and plants interact.

GRADING FOR MORE UNIFORM CROPS

The challenge that growers face with automated irrigation systems is maintaining uniform moisture content within an irrigation zone. Lack of uniformity results from different sized plants growing in the same irrigation zone or an irrigation system that provides a different volume of water to different pots. Any differences in plant size will result in some plants being too wet or too dry. Often, the best solution is to properly grade plants to maintain a high degree of uniformity within the irrigation zone.

Grading and sorting the crop based on plant size can be performed any-time workers are handling the plants. Grading can be done during sticking unrooted cuttings, transplanting rooted cuttings, pinching, and spacing. Poinsettia growth often displays the most plant-to-plant variation following the pinch, when the lateral shoots are first emerging. Thus, grading at the time of spacing provides an excellent opportunity to even out the crop, and this may be the last time the plants will be individually handled prior to shipping. Grading also improves the ease of plant growth regulator applications, since all the plants in a particular greenhouse or bench are a similar size and can receive the same growth regulation treatments.

GROUPING CULTIVARS

Small-leaf poinsettia cultivars and short cultivars have a lower water requirement than the standard size and vigor cultivars. For example, Eckespoint 'Max Red', Eckespoint 'Jester', Peter Jacobsen's 'Pepride', and 'Winter Rose' have lower water requirement than most cultivars do. If these cultivars are mixed together with standard cultivars, the cultivars needing less water are likely to stay too wet, grow poorly, and become more susceptible to pathogens. Therefore, it is useful to place similar cultivars on the same irrigation lines or sections.

LEACHING

The leaching percentage (or leaching fraction) is the amount of water that drains from the bottom of the pot divided by the total amount of water applied. While only small amounts of leaching are recommended, e.g., approximately 10% of the total water applied, leaching percentages as high as 40–50% are not uncommon with drip irrigation. The effects of leaching on the medium's nutrient concentration must be understood to fully appreciate the differences in nutrient management with top-watering versus subirrigation systems.

   With a constant liquid fertilization program, the greater the leaching fraction applied with top-watering, the lower the root medium nutrient levels. Lower concentrations of fertilizer can be applied with less leaching to achieve the same root medium concentration as when higher concentrations are applied with high leaching.

Irrigation practices that alter the amount of water applied also influence the amount of salts applied from the irrigation water. For example, if the water supply has a high alkalinity, the more water applied, the greater the effect the water will have on driving the pH upward.

Regardless of the irrigation strategy, water quality determines leaching frequency. Water with a high EC (more than 0.5 mmhos/cm) will require more frequent leaching with clear water than will water with low EC. When leaching, plants should be irrigated twice within a few minutes. Poinsettias can be grown with no leaching, but high-quality water, low fertilizer rates, and an experienced grower are required.

IRRIGATION SYSTEMS AND GROWING MEDIA CHARACTERISTICS

Many different growing media can be used to produce poinsettias, but the window of acceptable physical properties is smaller with subirrigation than with top-watering. With top-watering, the grower can dry down media if desired, or heavily water media that will not re-wet quickly. With subirrigation, the media can not dry down too far since re-wetting may be a problem. Also, a moist medium may absorb more water during subirrigation than the same medium when it is drier.

JIM FAUST

Figure 7-1. Flood floor irrigation of a poinsettia crop.

The length of a subirrigation cycle seems to have less effect on the amount of water uptake than does the medium's moisture content at the time of the irrigation. Allowing the plants to sit in water longer does not achieve the same goal as letting microtubes run longer and is not recommended. Wetting agents will increase the amount of water absorbed by either moist or dry media. The importance of media moisture content is dependent on pot size. During subirrigation, water uptake by dry root media is usually not limited with 4" (10 cm) and smaller pots. Water uptake may become limited with the increase in height from a 6" (15 cm) to an 8" (20 cm) pot.

IRRIGATION SYSTEMS AND FERTILIZATION PRACTICES

To insure quality crops, the irrigation system must provide the proper amount of water, maintain adequate nutrient levels, and achieve optimum soluble salt levels. Any irrigation system is capable of providing excess fertilization and high salts. Plants grown with overhead irrigation systems accumulate salts in the bottom of the container. Large amounts of water will leach the excess salts from the container, but excessive leaching may be problematic if the growing medium remains saturated too long, depriving the root system of necessary oxygen levels and predisposing the root system to pathogens.

With subirrigation systems, water is absorbed through the bottom of the container and salts accumulate at the upper surface of the growing medium. The lack of leaching with subirrigation systems allows for a reduction in the amount of fertilizer required. Plants produced with subirrigation systems perform as well as those produced with surface irrigation when the fertilizer is reduced to account for the lack of leaching with subirrigation benches. With subirrigation systems, termination of fertilizer does not result in a rapid decrease of soluble salts or nutrient levels, as is the case with overhead systems.

High quality, long-lasting poinsettias can be produced with both overhead and subirrigation systems provided the fertilizer levels are properly maintained. Poor postproduction longevity is a direct result of excessive fertilizer or overwatering, which is more likely to be the result of human error rather than the type of irrigation system used.

SURFACE EVAPORATION AND SALT LAYERS

Salts accumulate in the top layer of the growing medium as water evaporates from the medium's surface. The extent of salt layer formation with top-watering depends on the amount of leaching and whether the salts are washed back down into the root zone. At times the top layer is high in salt accumulation, while at other times it is almost nonexistent with top watering.

During subirrigation, water and fertilizer flow from the bottom of the pot to the medium's surface, then water is lost by evaporation but salts are left behind, accumulating at the surface. Since no leaching occurs, the salt layer is more concentrated with subirrigated crops. The rapid movement of fertilizer salts to the surface of the root medium with subirrigation makes it difficult to raise the soluble salt level in the root zone. Application of clear water by subirrigation during a rapid growth phase will likely result in very low nutrient levels in the medium and is not recommended. If nutrient levels become very low, it is more difficult to raise the nutrient level with subirrigation than with top-watering.

The salt accumulation in the top layer does not appear to have any detrimental affect on poinsettia growth or postproduction keeping quality. However, growers must be careful about top-watering a crop that has been grown entirely with subirrigation. It is possible to quickly flush a lot of salts into the root zone, which can cause bract and leaf margin burn.

8

GROWING MEDIA

Poinsettias can be successfully grown in a wide variety of growing media, and there is no one "best" growing medium. The selection of a growing medium is dependent on the availability of media components, mixing and handling equipment, the size of the growing operation, and the irrigation system.

A growing medium serves four functions:
- to supply water,
- to supply nutrients,
- to permit gas exchange to and from the roots, and
- to provide support for the plants.

It is interesting to note that the first three functions on this list are grower controlled. So it is important for growers to approach growing media with the awareness that greenhouse practices influence the choice of media. Also, the process of blending the media components and additives, filling the pots, and the irrigation methods will influence the physical and chemical properties of the growing media.

PHYSICAL PROPERTIES

For any growing medium, the most important characteristics are a favorable physical structure and freedom from toxic constituents and pathogens. Today, growing media are comprised primarily of blends of sphagnum peat moss, perlite, vermiculite, sand, pine bark, and coir. These components allow for sterile, inert, reliable, and reproducible mixes for quality propagation and growing.

Growing media have a high porosity (75–85% pore space) that creates spaces for water, oxygen, and other gasses. These media are easily compressed and compacted, causing a reduction in the number of large pores, therefore reducing aeration and drainage. Whether one purchases a pre-mixed growing medium or mixes the components in-house, it is important to not compact the medium while handling and filling pots. Rough handling can reduce the pore space and can increase the susceptibility to root and stem rot pathogens. Maintaining porosity is a key component of successful poinsettia production.

Water should be added to peat prior to mixing and/or pot filling since an overly dry medium will shrink when initially watered in the pot, thus reducing pore space. The proper amount of moisture in the growing medium can be determined by squeezing the medium in your hand. If water can be squeezed out of the medium, it is too wet. If the medium crumbles apart after squeezing, it is too dry. Growers can usually add 1–2 gal. of water per 3 ft.^{3} (45-90 L/m^3) of a peat-based growing medium. Ideally, the water is added the day before filling pots.

The depth of the medium or height of the pot also affects aeration and moisture retention. Shallow pots have greater moisture retention and lower the air space after irrigation. There is always a waterlogged zone at the bottom of the container following a thorough irrigation. The more finely textured the medium, the deeper this zone will be. Therefore, it is easier to overwater plants grown in smaller containers and plants grown in fine-textured media.

PRE-PLANT MEDIA AMENDMENTS

Most commercial growing media will contain a starter charge of fertilizer, lime, and a wetting agent, so that the media properly wets with the initial irrigation and sufficient nutrients are immediately available following planting.

STARTER CHARGE

The media EC usually starts at 1.5–2.0 mmhos/cm (SME test). The starter charge of fertilizer typically provides enough nutrients to sustain growth for the first week or two after transplant; however, little fertilizer remains in the root zone after a couple of weeks of plant growth, leaching during irrigation, and evaporation of water from the medium's surface.

Starter charges often contain:
- Calcium nitrate and potassium nitrate to provide nitrate-nitrogen, calcium, and potassium.
- Triple superphosphate (0-45-0) or soluble phosphate salts to provide phosphorus.
- Gypsum (calcium sulfate) to supply calcium and sulfur.
- Dolomitic limestone to provide calcium and magnesium and to adjust the medium's pH.
- A minor nutrient mix that provides iron, manganese, boron, copper, zinc, and molybdenum.

LIME

Adding lime to the growing medium accomplishes two important things: it helps adjust the media pH to a desirable level, and it supplies a source of calcium and/or magnesium, which are often not included in many commercially blended fertilizers. Many growing media contain a large component of sphagnum peat moss that is acidic (low pH). Adding lime raises the pH to an optimum level. Pulverized dolomitic limestone is the most common form of lime used. It is relatively slow to dissolve, so it usually lasts for the duration of poinsettia crop. However, the growing medium pH may not reach the initial target pH of 6.0 during the first few days after the initial irrigation, so hydrated lime may be used in addition to dolomitic lime. Hydrated lime is more soluble and will cause the medium pH to immediately rise to the target pH with the first irrigation. Hydrated lime is quickly leached from the medium, so dolomitic lime is still required to maintain the pH through the duration of the crop. If the pH is already sufficiently high, gypsum can be added as a source of calcium without further increasing the pH.

WETTING AGENT

Wetting agents can be incorporated into the growing medium prior to potting or applied as a drench to decrease the surface tension of water, making it easier to wet the medium's components. Wetting agents are particularly important for plants grown with subirrigation.

CHEMICAL PROPERTIES

MEDIA pH

Media pH affects the solubility and availability of nutrients for uptake by the roots. Some elements are not greatly affected by changes in pH, but others are highly affected. Those elements that are relatively unaffected by pH include boron, chloride, nitrate, potassium, sodium, and sulfur. Elements that become more soluble as the pH rises include calcium, magnesium, and molybdenum. Aluminum, copper, iron, manganese, and zinc become more soluble as pH decreases. Consequently, growers should target a pH of 6.0 since all nutrients are readily available at this pH.

TABLE 8-1. pH AFFECTS NUTRIENT AVAILABILITY.

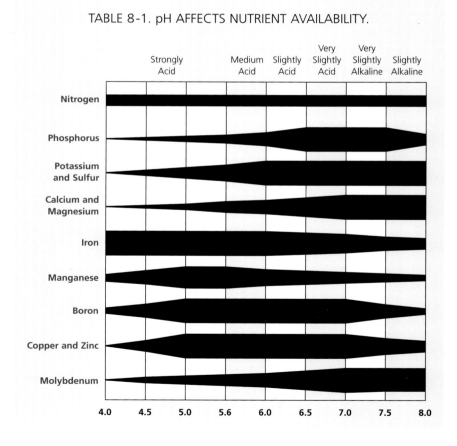

Compared to many other greenhouse crops, poinsettias are relatively tolerant of a wide pH range; therefore, relatively few problems occur when the medium's pH is maintained between 5.5 and 6.5. Media pH measurements provide a valuable clue to potential nutritional problems and suggest an approach to correct existing problems. A high pH may result in chlorotic foliage caused by minor nutrient deficiencies or sodium toxicity. High pH can be caused by high alkalinity water, repeated use of alkaline residue fertilizers (potential basicity greater than 50 ppm $CaCO_3/L$), and excessive lime added to the growing medium. High pH in the medium can be corrected with the injection of acid into the irrigation water and/or repeated applications of acid-residue fertilizers (potential acidity greater than 200 ppm $CaCO_3/L$).

Figure 8-1. At high media pH, minor nutrient deficiencies occur

A low pH frequently signifies a low supply of calcium and/or magnesium and can increase the solubility of certain microelements to a toxic concentration. Low pH in the medium can be caused by low water alkalinity, repeated applications of acid-residue fertilizers, and/or insufficient lime in the growing medium. Low pH can be corrected with a drench application of flowable limestone and/or repeated applications of alkaline-residue fertilizers. If low pH is a frequent problem resulting from low alkalinity irrigation water, additional lime should be incorporated in the growing medium prior to planting.

MEDIA SOLUBLE SALTS

Fertilizers are salts; therefore, one can estimate the amount of fertilizer in the growing medium by measuring how much salt it contains. Salts dissolved in solution affect the solution's ability to conduct an electrical current, thus one can collect a medium sample, add water to dissolve the salts, then measure the electrical conductivity (EC, or soluble salts) of the solution. This is an easy test to perform and provides an accurate assessment of the overall fertility of the growing medium. Weekly testing can be conducted to track crop fertility. Soluble salt tests do not reveal any information about the concentration of individual plant nutrients such as nitrogen, phosphorus, potassium, etc.

IN-HOUSE pH AND EC TESTING

The pH and EC of the growing medium can be easily measured. Many growers perform weekly in-house tests to regularly monitor the fertilization program. There are two different techniques for testing pH and EC. One technique involves removing a sample of growing medium from the container, while the other involves pouring water through the growing medium and collecting the solution that comes out the bottom of the pot.

EXTRACTED MEDIA TESTS

A sample of the growing medium is taken from the bottom two-thirds of the container (the top inch of the medium should not be sampled since this area has a much higher salt content than the root zone). The sample is mixed with distilled or de-ionized water for thirty minutes. During this time, the salts dissolve in the water. The solution is then squeezed from the slurry into the EC meter, and the soluble salt concentration is recorded. This measurement is expressed as millimhos per centimeter (mmhos/cm) or milliSiemens per centimeter (mS/cm) or deciSiemens per meter (dS/m). These units are all equivalent, so they can be used interchangeably. The target medium EC for poinsettias is 1.5–2.5 for an SME test.

   These tests are commonly performed with one of two different methods. The difference is the amount of water added to the medium sample. For a saturated media extract (SME) test, enough water is added to create a "glisteny" surface. This is the procedure used by most commercial media testing labs. For a 1-to-2 test (or sometimes called a 2:1 test), one volume of medium is added to two volumes of water. Because more water is added in the 1-to-2 test, the results have lower numbers (more dilute soluble salts). The target medium EC for poinsettias is 0.7–1.3 for a 1-to-2 test.

POUR-THROUGH TESTS

Pour-through testing provides a potentially time-saving alternative to extract tests. The general procedure for pour-through tests is as follows:
1. Saturate the growing medium with the standard constant liquid fertilizer solution being used on the crop.
2. Wait one hour.
3. Apply enough distilled water (approximately 75 ml) into the pot so that 50 ml can be collected while coming out the bottom of the pot.
4. Measure the pH and EC of the solution that has been flushed out of the pot. The target EC is 2.2–3.8 mmhos/cm, which is higher than extract test results.

Figure 8-2. Insufficient fertilizer application and/or excess leaching can cause a low soluble salt content in the growing medium.

Figure 8-3. Excess fertilization and/or insufficient leaching can result in high levels of soluble salts in the growing medium.

If the test results indicate low fertility, the concentration of fertilizer can be increased and/or the frequency of fertilizer applications can be increased. Low soluble salts can cause leaf chlorosis and can slow plant growth. If the test indicates excessive fertility, clear water can be applied to leach the medium until the EC is in the target range. High soluble salts can increase plant susceptibility to root rot pathogens, can cause leaf and bract edge burn, and can inhibit plant growth.

Keep in mind that EC is a measure of all soluble salts, but not all salts are essential nutrients. Soluble salts come from irrigation water, fertilizers, and chemicals inherent to the growing medium. Irrigation water often contains such elements as calcium or magnesium that are essential for plants, but it may also contain sodium, chlorides, and other salts that are not needed but contribute to the medium's EC. It is essential to know the EC of the irrigation water because many water sources have an EC of 1.0 or greater, yet it is important to maintain the growing medium's EC below 3.0 (SME test). If the EC of the irrigation water is unusually high, it may be necessary to treat the water to remove soluble salts or find another source of water with less salinity.

a   b   c

Figure 8-4. Media testing sequence: A media sample is removed from the root zone, avoiding the salty top layer (a). Water can be rapidly extracted from multiple media samples by placing the media in a Buchner funnel and then pulling a vacuum with a pump (b). Electrical conductivity (EC) and pH tests can be easily and rapidly done in an in-house laboratory (c).

GROWING MEDIA ANALYSIS

In some cases, the EC and pH of the growing medium may be on target, yet the plants exhibit symptoms that suggest a nutritional problem. Often, the cause is that a particular nutrient or two is out of balance with the other nutrients. In this situation, a growing medium analysis from a soil-testing laboratory is needed to identify the specific concentration of the individual nutrients in the growing media. Table 8-2 shows the target ranges of the various nutrients for poinsettias. Note that the balance of nutrients can be as important as the absolute concentration of the nutrients.

TABLE 8-2. GROWING MEDIA NUTRIENT ANALYSIS INTERPRETATION KEY FOR POINSETTIAS.

	Low Level	Acceptable Range	High Level
pH	< 5.2	5.8–6.3	>7.0
Electrical conductivity (EC, mmhos/cm)			
SME test	<1.0	1.5–2.5*	> 3.0
1:2 Test	<0.5	0.7–1.3*	>1.5
Pour-through test	<1.5	2.2–3.8*	>4.5
Nitrate-N (ppm)	<40	100–200	> 300
Ammonium-N (ppm)	–	0–20	> 20
Phosphorus (ppm)	<5	5–40	> 50
Potassium (ppm)	< 35	80–180	> 250
Calcium (ppm)	< 70	100–200	> 200
Magnesium (ppm)	< 30	50–100	>150
Sodium (ppm)	–	0–50	> 50

*Poinsettia cultivars with dark green leaves perform well at the lower end of this range, while medium-green-leafed cultivars perform well at the higher end of this range.

Occasionally, the results of a growing medium analysis are acceptable, yet the plants exhibit symptoms pointing to a nutritional problem. Tissue analyses can reveal if the plants are actually taking up the nutrients in the medium. In situations where root damage has occurred or root growth is poor, the proper nutrients may be present in the growing medium, but they may not be absorbed by the plants in sufficient quantities to support healthy growth. Plant tissue analysis is discussed in further detail in chapter 9, Poinsettia Nutrition.

9

POINSETTIA NUTRITION

Fertility management of poinsettias involves three important considerations. They include:
1. to supply all the essential nutrients,
2. to provide these nutrients in a balanced ratio, and
3. to provide nutrients in quantifies that correspond to the plant's growth requirements.

Thirteen mineral nutrients are required for poinsettia growth. Each of these essential nutrients is supplied through the irrigation water and fertilizer.

THE ESSENTIAL NUTRIENTS

Poinsettias require a balanced ratio of all essential nutrients. Six of the thirteen essential elements (nitrogen, phosphorus, potassium, calcium, magnesium, and sulfur) are called *macronutrients* because they are needed in relatively large quantities, while seven elements (iron, manganese, zinc, boron, copper, molybdenum, and chlorine) are termed *micronutrients* because they are required in relatively small quantities.

Following is a brief description and use guide for each essential element:

NITROGEN

Nitrogen is absorbed primarily as nitrate (NO_3^-) or ammonium (NH_4^+). Reduction of nitrate to ammonium occurs in cells where the nitrogen becomes a constituent of amino acids, proteins, chlorophyll, nucleotides, and enzymes. Nitrate is readily mobile within the plant and can be stored in the vacuoles in the cells.

In fertilizers, nitrogen is available in three different forms: urea, ammonium (or ammoniacal), and nitrate. Urea is not recommended for poinsettias.

Ammonium nitrogen (NH_4^+)

Ammonium is supplied in water-soluble fertilizers in the form of ammonium phosphate or ammonium nitrate. Ammonium nitrogen has an acidic effect on growing media pH. Fertilizers that contain 20–40% of the nitrogen in the ammonium form usually have little or no calcium and magnesium. Growers that have high alkalinity water often use fertilizers with moderate to high rates of ammonium. The ammonium helps to counteract the effect that high-alkalinity water has on media pH.

Growers have often observed that fertilizers that are relatively high in ammonium appear to promote stem elongation; however, recent research has demonstrated that, in fact, phosphorus promotes stem elongation. Interestingly, ammonium is most often incorporated into fertilizers in the form of ammonium phosphate. Thus, when growers thought ammonium was promoting stem elongation, it was actually the phosphorus.

High ammonium in the growing media in the postharvest environment decreases the longevity of poinsettias as well as many other potted flowering plants. Therefore, the rates of ammonium nitrogen applied should be decreased to 20% or less during the last few weeks of the poinsettia season. Also, high ammonium (greater than 40%) applications can cause ammonium toxicity during cloudy and cool growing conditions, so these should always be avoided. Fertilizers that are termed "dark-weather" fertilizers tend to have high nitrate and little or no ammonium.

Nitrate nitrogen (NO_3^-)

Nitrate is supplied in liquid fertilizers in the form of calcium nitrate, potassium nitrate, and ammonium nitrate. Nitric acid used to neutralize high-alkalinity water also supplies nitrate. The percentage of nitrogen in the nitrate form ranges from 60 to 100% in poinsettia fertilizers. Nitrate tends to cause the medium's pH to increase over time; therefore, growers that have low-alkalinity water tend to rely more heavily on high-nitrate fertilizers. Many growers have observed that high-nitrate fertilizers produce smaller, darker green leaves and shorter plants.

Deficiency

A nitrogen deficiency manifests itself through uniform yellowing of foliage occurring on the older leaves first. Growth is also reduced. When insufficient fertilizer is being applied to a poinsettia crop and the medium's EC is low, nitrogen deficiency is often the first symptom visually observed. Decomposing organic matter in the growing medium, such as bark, can tie-up nitrogen resulting in insufficient nitrogen levels. Multiple applications of 300–400 ppm nitrogen can be used to correct a deficiency.

Figure 9-1.
Nitrogen deficiency

Toxicity

Poinsettias react unfavorably to excessive quantities of ammonium or urea, resulting in poor root development, yellowing of foliage, and leaf drop. No more than 40% of the nitrogen supplied to poinsettias should be in the form of ammonium, and urea should be omitted completely. During the last few weeks of a blooming poinsettia crop the ammonium concentrations are often reduced to 20% or less of the total nitrogen applied since high ammonium can reduce the longevity of poinsettias in the postharvest environment.

PHOSPHORUS (P)

Phosphorus is absorbed as phosphate and is essential in every living cell as the key factor in energy transfer. Phosphorus is a component of sugar, phosphates, nucleic acids, nucleotides, co-enzymes, and phospholipids. Stem elongation is promoted as phosphorus levels increase.

Phosphorus is usually provided in water-soluble fertilizers in the form of ammonium phosphate. Phosphoric acid used to neutralize high-alkalinity water also supplies phosphorus. Superphosphate is often incorporated in the growing medium prior to planting.

Deficiency

A phosphorus deficiency results in stunting, older leaf yellowing, and necrosis. Phosphorus deficiency is not common on poinsettias, but it can occur if a fertilizer lacking phosphorus, such as 15-0-15, is used continuously for several weeks.

Figure 9-2. Phosphorus deficiency

Toxicity

Phosphorus applied to the foliage of poinsettias can cause severe leaf distortion. This occurs most frequently when rooted cuttings are held in the rooting medium prior to transplanting. Cuttings at this stage may require daily irrigation. If a fertilizer containing phosphorus is applied overhead daily, the symptoms can appear after one week. It is possible that the symptoms are not phosphorus toxicity, per se, but rather a complex of micronutrient deficiencies resulting from the micronutrients being tied up by the phosphorus.

POTASSIUM (K)

Potassium is absorbed as elemental potassium (K^+). Potassium is highly mobile within the plant and plays an important role in plant water relations, enzyme activation, photosynthesis, stomatal regulation, cell extension, and protein synthesis. Next to nitrogen, potassium is the mineral nutrient required in the largest amount by plants.

Potassium is supplied in liquid fertilizers in the form of potassium nitrate, potassium chloride, and potassium sulfate. Potassium is often applied at a concentration (ppm) similar to nitrogen (1:1, nitrogen-to-potassium ratio [ppm basis]).

Deficiency

Potassium deficiency results in lower leaf margin yellowing followed immediately with necrosis. To correct a deficiency, apply 300–400 ppm potassium one or two times.

Figure 9-3. Potassium deficiency

Toxicity

Although phosphorus toxicity is not commonly observed, excess potassium may accentuate calcium or magnesium deficiency and may cause salts damage.

CALCIUM (Ca)

Calcium is absorbed as elemental calcium (Ca^{2+}); this element functions as a structural component of cell walls and thus plays a fundamental role in membrane stability and cell integrity. Calcium also functions as a secondary messenger in the signal transduction between environmental factors and plant growth and development responses.

Calcium is supplied in liquid fertilizers primarily in the form of calcium nitrate. Dolomitic lime incorporated into the growing medium also supplies calcium and magnesium, while gypsum supplies calcium. Irrigation water can also be a significant source of calcium.

Calcium fertilization can be easily overlooked since many "balanced" fertilizers that contain nitrogen, phosphorus, and potassium, such as 20-10-20, do not provide calcium. The rates of potassium, calcium, and magnesium applied are often linked since these nutrients are the primary cations applied in a fertilization program and they can act antagonistically if not well balanced, i.e., an excess of one nutrient can cause a deficiency in the other. A 3:1 to 5:1 calcium-to-magnesium ratio (ppm basis) in the fertilizer is recommended.

Deficiency

Calcium fertilization is a primary focus for poinsettia growers since calcium deficiencies are relatively common. Leaf cupping is the most common symptom. Calcium transport within the plant occurs passively, i.e., it requires water movement. Thus, greenhouse conditions that limit evapo-transpiration, such as high humidity, low air movement, high salts in the growing medium, and low solar radiation, increase the incidence of calcium deficiency. Bract edge burn increases on susceptible cultivars when calcium levels in the plant are low. In addition, calcium is immobile within the plant, meaning that the older leaves do not mobilize calcium when the actively growing tissues are deficient in calcium. Foliar applications of calcium chloride (anhydrous or dehydrate) or a high-quality calcium nitrate can be applied weekly from first color to flower in order to prevent bract edge burn. The typical application rate ranges from 300–350 ppm calcium. A wetting agent is often added to improve coverage of the leaves and bracts.

Figure 9-4. Calcium deficiency

Toxicity

Excess calcium may accentuate magnesium or boron deficiency.

MAGNESIUM (Mg)

Magnesium is absorbed as elemental magnesium (Mg^{2+}) and is best known as the nucleus of the chlorophyll molecule. Magnesium is also required by enzymes involved in phosphate transfer and plays a role in carbohydrate partitioning.

Magnesium is supplied in liquid fertilizers primarily in the forms of magnesium nitrate or magnesium sulfate (Epsom salts). Dolomitic lime incorporated into the growing medium also supplies calcium and magnesium. Irrigation water can also be a significant source of magnesium.

Magnesium fertilization can be easily overlooked since many common fertilizers such as 20-10-20 and 15-0-15 do not supply magnesium. Ideally, 30–40 ppm magnesium is supplied in a constant liquid fertilization program. The rates of calcium and magnesium applied are often linked since these nutrients can act antagonistically, i.e., an excess of one nutrient can cause a deficiency in the other. A 3:1 to 5:1 calcium-to-magnesium ratio (ppm basis) in the fertilizer is recommended.

Deficiency

Magnesium deficiency usually causes interveinal chlorosis of older leaves. Magnesium is not present in many standard commercial fertilizers; therefore, magnesium nutrition is often overlooked and deficiencies are common. Excess levels of calcium can also cause deficiencies. A one-time 200-ppm magnesium application with Epsom salts (magnesium sulfate)

Figure 9-5.
Magnesium deficiency

is recommended to correct magnesium deficiency.

Toxicity

Excess magnesium may induce potassium or calcium deficiency.

SULFUR (S)

Sulfur is absorbed as sulfate (SO_4^{2-}) and is a constituent of many proteins and enzymes. Sulfur fertilization is not often consciously undertaken since sulfur is available in the sulfate forms of several common fertilizer salts, namely potassium sulfate, magnesium sulfate, and iron sulfate. Sulfur is also provided by gypsum (calcium sulfate) incorporated into the growing medium. However, sulfur deficiencies occasionally do occur on poinsettias.

Deficiency

A sulfur deficiency causes uniform yellowing of upper leaves with the topmost leaves showing the most severe symptoms.

Toxicity

An excess of this nutrient may accentuate potassium, calcium, or magnesium deficiency.

MICRONUTRIENTS

Micronutrients are most often applied as a complex rather than as individual salts, such as iron sulfate. Common sources of micronutrients include: STEM (Soluble Trace Element Mix), Fritted Trace elements, Micromax, and Compound 111. Chelated nutrients (iron EDTA, manganese EDTA, etc.) are more soluble and hence more readily available than sulfate forms (iron sulfate, manganese sulfate, etc.)

The micronutrient rates in pre-blended fertilizers are based on relatively high rates of nitrogen application. Since dark-leaved poinsettia cultivars became prominent, nitrogen fertilization levels have decreased. When macronutrient rates are reduced, the micronutrients are also reduced. As a result, micronutrient deficiencies have increased in occurrence in recent years due to the overall reduction in nitrogen rates applied throughout the crop. Many growers have found that supplemental applications of micronutrients can be beneficial. STEM (2−4 oz./100 gal. [150−300 mg/L]) can be applied as a corrective micronutrient application.

IRON (Fe)

Iron is absorbed as elemental iron (Fe^{2+} or Fe^{3+}) or iron chelate (Fe-EDTA). Iron is a constituent of cytochrome, certain proteins involved in photosynthesis, and other enzyme systems.

Deficiency

Iron deficiency results in the chlorosis of younger foliage, and an extreme deficiency may result in severe bleaching of the newest leaves. Insufficient iron, high media pH, or excess manganese can cause iron deficiencies. If the media pH is greater than 6.5, then lowering the pH may be the best method to increase iron uptake. Otherwise, iron sulfate or iron chelate (4-6 oz./100 gal. [300-450 mg/L]) can be applied as a fertilizer application. Water pH greater than 6.0 may cause iron sulfate to precipitate out of the stock tank solution, resulting in no iron actually being applied to the crop. Avoid getting iron sulfate on the foliage, as it may cause leaf burn. Finally, old supplies of iron sulfate should not be used, since the iron may have oxidized in the bag, making it insoluble when mixed with water.

Figure 9-6. Iron deficiency

Toxicity

Excess iron can reduce manganese uptake.

MANGANESE (Mn)

Manganese is absorbed as elemental manganese (Mn^{2+}) or as a chelate (Mn-EDTA), manganese is required in many enzyme systems including those responsible for photosynthetic evolution of oxygen.

Deficiency

Manganese deficiency usually causes mottled yellowing of young mature leaves, which become highly chlorotic and rough appearing as plants mature. High media pH or excess iron can cause manganese deficiencies. Deficiencies can be corrected by reducing the pH if it is above 6.5 or by applying manganese sulfate (2 oz./100 gal. [150 mg/L]).

Figure 9-7. Manganese deficiency

Toxicity

Excess manganese results in toxicity symptoms with older leaf yellowing and necrosis or edge burn. Manganese can cause iron or molybdenum deficiency.

BORON (B)

Boron is absorbed as borate and is involved in carbohydrate transport. It is associated with cell wall synthesis, cell division, and cell enlargement.

Deficiency

Boron deficiency causes terminal growth to cease and may result in distorted leaf and stem development. In some instances, a boron deficiency causes the plant to resemble a witch's broom.

Toxicity

Boron can be very high in some water sources. Excess boron results in foliar edge yellowing or burn starting with the oldest leaves.

Figure 9-8. Boron toxicity

ZINC (Zn)

Zinc is absorbed as elemental zinc (Zn^{2+}) or as a chelate (Zn-EDTA). Zinc is required for many enzymes and particularly with those responsible for hydrogen transfer.

Deficiency

A zinc deficiency causes chlorosis and stunting of new developing leaves. High levels of phosphorus can induce zinc deficiency.

Figure 9-9. Zinc deficiency

Toxicity

Excess zinc causes death of exposed plant parts. Zinc is a component of some fungicides, which may increase tissue concentrations.

COPPER (Cu)

Copper is absorbed as elemental copper (Cu^{2+}) or as a chelate (Cu-EDTA); it is essential in many oxidase respiration reactions.

Deficiency

A copper deficiency causes interveinal chlorosis of young leaves and can eventually lead to leaf necrosis. Middle-aged leaves are affected first.

Toxicity

Excess copper may cause death of roots and plant decline. Copper is a component of some pesticides and fungicides, so foliar applications may increase tissue concentrations.

MOLYBDENUM (Mo)

Molybdenum is absorbed as molybdate (MoO_4^{2-}). It is required by poinsettias as a catalyst in nitrate reduction and is also a component of certain other enzyme systems.

Deficiency

Figure 9-10.
Molybdenum deficiency

A molybdenum deficiency causes leaf yellowing of newly mature leaves, upward rolling, and edge burn. In some crops, a molybdenum deficiency causes distorted foliar growth from the failure of interveinal areas to expand normally. Continuously apply 0.1 ppm molybdenum using sodium molybdate or 1 ppm as a corrective measure. Maintaining the media pH above 5.5 will also improve molybdenum uptake.

Toxicity

High levels of this element are reported to cause little or no plant damage.

CHLORINE (Cl)

Chlorine is absorbed as elemental chloride (Cl⁻) and is required in photosynthetic reactions involved in oxygen evolution.

Deficiency

Although seldom observed because poinsettias require extremely minute quantities of chloride, a deficiency may cause stunting and dieback.

Toxicity

Excess chlorine causes typical salinity effects with older leaf and edge burn.

DIAGNOSING NUTRITIONAL PROBLEMS

The Ecke Ranch Web site (www.ecke.com) contains a complete diagnostic key for assisting growers in diagnosing nutritional problems. The first clue at diagnosing nutritional problems is the location of the symptoms on the plant. This provides an indication of the mobility of the nutrient causing the problem. In-house pH and EC tests provide additional information about the general nutritional status of the crop. Growing media and foliar tissue analyses performed at a commercial laboratory can provide the specific details that are often required for problem-solving.

NUTRIENT MOBILITY

When deficiencies occur, certain nutrients can be mobilized from the older leaves to the younger leaves to support new plant growth. Nitrogen, phosphorus, potassium, and magnesium are mobile nutrients; therefore, deficiency symptoms of these elements will first appear in the older leaves. In contrast, calcium, iron, manganese, boron, zinc, and copper are immobile nutrients that can not be moved from older to younger leaves. When the roots do not take up immobile nutrients, the new growth will display deficiency symptoms since the nutrients cannot be mobilized from the older leaves.

TABLE 9-1.
MOBILE AND IMMOBILE NUTRIENTS

Mobile Nutrients	Immobile Nutrients
Nitrogen	Calcium
Phosphorus	Iron
Potassium	Manganese
Magnesium	Boron
Sulfur	Zinc
	Copper

FOLIAR TISSUE ANALYSIS

Leaf analysis is a valuable tool for assessing the fertility of many horticultural crops. The use of tissue analysis in combination with growing medium analysis usually provides a very clear picture of the nutritional status of the poinsettia crop. A monthly growing medium and tissue sample is recommended even if nutritional problems are not observed. Growing medium analysis is covered in chapter 8, Growing Media.

Nutrient concentration will vary with the plant tissue sampled. Thus, it is critical that tissue samples are consistently the same tissue in order for the results to be meaningful. For example, when leaves down the entire stem have been sampled, the upper leaves had a nitrogen concentration of

5–6%, while the lower leaves were 3–4% nitrogen. Other mobile nutrients exhibit a similar pattern, where the tissue concentration increases as the leaves are closer to the shoot tip. In contrast, the concentration of the immobile nutrients decreases as the leaves are closer to the shoot tip. For example, the upper leaves may have less than 0.5% calcium while the lower leaves may be as high as 2% calcium.

The proper tissue to send for analysis is the youngest fully mature (fully expanded) leaves, including petiole. Approximately twenty leaves are required per sample. Table 9-2 displays the target ranges for poinsettia tissue analysis. For the most accurate and informative monitoring, both growing media and leaf tissue analyses should be used.

TABLE 9-2. LEAF TISSUE NUTRIENT MINERAL ANALYSIS INTERPRETATION KEY FOR POINSETTIAS

	Low Level	Acceptable Range	High Level
Nitrogen (%)	3.5	4.0–6.0	7.0
Phosphorus (%)	0.2	0.3–0.6	0.8
Potassium (%)	1.0	1.5–3.5	4.0
Calcium (%)	0.5	0.7–1.8	
Magnesium (%)	0.2	0.3–1.0	
Sulfur (%)	0.05	0.1–0.3	
Iron (ppm)	50	100–300	
Manganese (ppm)	40	60–300	650
Zinc (ppm)	20	25–60	
Boron (ppm)	15	25–75	100
Copper (ppm)	1	2–0	
Molybdenum (ppm)	0.5	1–5	

Concentrations based on oven-dry tissue.

IN-HOUSE pH AND ELECTRICAL CONDUCTIVITY (EC) TESTING

Relatively easy and inexpensive media testing procedures can be quickly performed in any greenhouse. A media pH and EC test can solve many nutritional problems. Regular testing procedures can help identify trends and potential problems prior to the crop displaying visual symptoms. (Specific testing procedures and interpretation are covered in chapter 8, Growing Media.) Keep in mind that pH and EC tests cannot reveal information about specific nutrients. If the pH and EC are both within the target ranges, then growing media and tissue analyses from a commercial laboratory may be required to identify the specific nutrients that may be lacking, excessive, or out of balance.

FERTILIZATION

Historically, poinsettias have been considered to be heavy feeders; however, in recent years growers have used more moderate fertilization rates. This has occurred as a result of several factors. First, several popular cultivars in the 1990s were susceptible to bract edge burn. These large-bracted cultivars, such as Gross 'Supjibi', were more prone to bract edge burn when the plants were fertilized with high rates. Second, the advent of subirrigation systems resulted in poinsettia crops grown with no leaching. In these systems, the amount of fertilizer applied is often cut in half. This process made growers more aware that less fertilizer could be used if less leaching occurred during irrigation. Finally, as the choice of cultivars changed primarily to dark-leaf types, less fertilizer was required to maintain healthy-appearing foliage.

Growers can use commercially blended fertilizers or purchase individual fertilizer salts and mix their own. For most small to mid-sized growers, commercial formulations are economical and reduce the risk associated with mixing your own fertilizer. Also, some blended fertilizers contain all of the essential nutrients required for plant growth, thus reducing the need to alternate different fertilizers. There is not a perfect fertilizer for poinsettias since the fertilization program depends on the irrigation water source and the growing medium used. The best fertilizer choice for one water source may not work well with another water source.

DEVELOPING A FERTILIZATION PROGRAM

In greenhouses that have a single fertilizer injector, growers can continuously use commercial fertilizer blends that provide all the essential nutrients, such as Peters Excel 15-5-15 Cal-Mag. In greenhouses that have multiple-headed injectors, a balanced nutrient solution can be achieved by simultaneously injecting two or three different fertilizers into the water line. Fertilizers such as 20-10-20 or 15-5-25 contain adequate amounts of nitrogen, phosphorus, potassium, and micronutrients but do not contain calcium or magnesium. These formulations can be balanced with a simultaneous injection of 15-0-15 or calcium nitrate (15.5-0-0). Also, magnesium sulfate may be added to the 20-10-20 or 15-5-25 as a source of magnesium. *Caution:* Do not mix magnesium sulfate (Epsom salts) with a calcium fertilizer in a concentrated stock solution. The two chemicals react to form an insoluble precipitate.

A fertilizer calculator (FertCalc) is available online at www.floricultureinfo.com. This Microsoft Excel spreadsheet allows users to input the injector ratio, the number of injectors, the stock tank size, the desired concentration of nitrogen, phosphorus or potassium, and the elemental analysis of the fertilizer. The software calculates the proper amounts of fertilizer to mix in the stock tank(s). Fertilizer costs, the percentage ammonium- and nitrate-nitrogen, nutrients supplied with cid injection, and nutrient ratios are also calculated.

FERTILIZER CONCENTRATION

The proper fertilizer concentration depends on several factors: namely water quality, growing medium amendments, watering practices, frequency of fertilizer application, and stage of plant development. Most growers start with 250 ppm nitrogen and modify the program based on plant growth, appearance, and the growing medium's EC. If the growing medium does not possess a starter charge of fertilizer, then 300–400 ppm nitrogen may be applied during the first week after transplant.

The amount of leaching that occurs with each irrigation has a large impact on the fertilization program. If more than 10% of the solution applied to the top of the pot pours out the bottom of the pot, then higher fertilizer concentrations may be necessary to supply adequate nutrients. Recirculating irrigation systems do not create any leaching of excess nutrients from the growing medium. For this reason, fertilizer solutions are used at a lower concentration than would be used when overhead watering poinsettias.

Poor-quality water may have a high EC (1.0 mmhos/cm) prior to the addition of fertilizer salts. In these cases, high concentrations of fertilizer cannot be applied without subjecting the plants to excess salts, and leaching is required to keep the media EC from increasing excessively. Finally, the concentration of fertilizer is often reduced during the last weeks of production since the plants are past the rapid growth phase and poinsettia longevity in the postharvest environment improves if the growing medium does not contain excess salts.

FERTILIZATION METHODS

Several methods exist for supplying fertilizer to poinsettias. Each method has advantages and disadvantages. The choice depends on grower preference, facilities available, and economics.

Constant liquid fertilization (CLF)

This method is the very popular and is probably the most foolproof as well as the most economical approach. It automatically limits the quantity of fertilizer applied in case of under-watering and prevents excessive buildup of salts, even plants are overwatered. If all irrigation water contains fertilizer of a desired concentration, there are no problems in administration of the feeding program. Plants receive more fertilizer when water demand is high due to high light, warm temperatures, and rapid growth. Plants receive less fertilizer during cloudy and cool weather, when plant growth is relatively slow. The entire crop can often be produced with one or two different fertilizer formulas. Clear water is used while spot watering between fertilizer applications to the entire crop.

Liquid fertilizer applied at fixed intervals

A popular approach that varies from the above is to inject fertilizer at weekly or fixed periods using higher concentrations than for the constant liquid program in order that levels will not be depleted when clear water is being applied. This type of program may require adjustment of fertilizer concentrations at different stages of growth due to increasing frequency of interim irrigation as plants become larger and use more water. Otherwise, more frequent irrigation may lower the fertility level of the growing medium.

Incorporation of controlled-release fertilizer in the medium

Controlled-release fertilizers provide a similar effect to the constant liquid feed program, except that the grower has less control over fertilizer availability since the fertilizer release rate is affected by growing medium temperature and water content. Since commercial greenhouses nearly always have the ability to apply water-soluble fertilizers through the irrigation system, controlled-release fertilizers are usually reserved for a supplemental program. When controlled-release fertilizers are used to supplement a liquid fertilizer product, the low rate on the product label is recommended. Do not use more than half the high rate listed on the label.

Dark- and medium-green-leaf cultivars have different nutritional requirements, yet it can be difficult to apply different rates of fertilizer to different cultivars growing in the same greenhouse. Controlled-release fertilizers can be incorporated into the medium or top-dressed on the medium of medium-green leaf cultivars. Then, all cultivars receive the same liquid feed program.

Controlled-release fertilizers can also be beneficial in direct-stick propagation programs. There is very little opportunity to apply liquid fertilizer while poinsettia cuttings are rooting under a mist system. Regular misting can leach all the nutrients that initially existed in the starter charge incorporated into the growing medium. Thus, controlled-release fertilizer can meet the nutritional requirements of rooting cuttings.

10

THE GREENHOUSE ENVIRONMENT

The greenhouse environment controls the growth and development of roots, leaves, and flowers. Growers can manipulate greenhouse temperature, light, and humidity to "build" the poinsettia to meet the market's requirements in terms of the proper height, leaf number, bract size, and timing of flowering.

TEMPERATURE

Temperature influences the growth and development of roots, shoots, and bracts. There are three aspects to be considered when defining the effects of temperature on poinsettias:

1. the average daily temperature,
2. the difference between the day and night temperatures, and
3. the specific effect of night temperature on poinsettia flower development.

Each of these different measures of temperature has a unique effect on poinsettia growth and flowering. The average daily temperature affects the rate of leaf and flower development, the difference between the day and night temperature influences stem elongation, and high night temperatures can delay poinsettia flowering.

AVERAGE DAILY TEMPERATURE

The average daily temperature represents the twenty-four-hour average temperature and controls how fast new leaves develop on stems, the time to flower, and how fast roots initiate in propagation. The rates of root growth, leaf development, flower development, and bract expansion

119

increase as the average daily temperature increases from 50 to 73°F (10 to 23°C). Between 73 and 78°F (23 and 26°C), poinsettias develop at their optimal rates. Above 78°F (26°C), the rate of development slows. Development does not occur on poinsettias at average daily temperatures below 50°F (10°C) or above 86°F (30°C).

Figure 10-1. Effect of temperature on shoot development.

For example, at 77°F (25°C), a new leaf unfolds from the shoot tip every 3.5 days, while at 68°F (20°C) a new leaf unfolds every 5 days. Also, the flowering response time for poinsettia cultivars represents the time from flower initiation to anthesis at typical commercial greenhouse temperatures, such as 68°F (20°C). However, flowering can occur faster or slower if the average daily temperature is higher or lower than 68°F (20°C). For example, a cultivar that is listed with a nine-week response time may require ten weeks at 65°F (18°C) or twelve weeks at 62°F (16°C).

It is important to note that the "optimal" temperature may not be the "best" temperature. The optimal temperature refers to the temperature at which plants develop at their fastest rate; however, the growth achieved may not necessarily be the highest quality. Temperatures from 68 to 72°F (20 to 22°C) can create a desirable "toned" appearance, while warmer temperatures can produce larger leaves and a "softer" appearance. Plant quality is often determined by the interaction of temperature and light, which is covered later in this chapter.

DIF

The relationship between day and night temperatures, called DIF, is an important tool for controlling stem elongation. DIF is the DIFference between the day and the night temperatures (DIF = DT − NT). DIF influences cell elongation in stems and thus the length of the internodes and the height of the plant. A positive DIF means the plant is growing under a warmer day than night temperature. Stem elongation is promoted under warm days and cool nights. In contrast, a negative DIF is created when the night temperatures exceed the day temperatures. Stem elongation is inhibited under cool days and warm nights.

The response of a poinsettia to DIF depends on a number of factors. First, the magnitude of the response to a change in DIF is not the same across all values of DIF. Plant height is affected more when the DIF is shifted from a positive to a zero DIF than from a zero to a negative DIF. Second, the use of DIF to influence the final height of the poinsettia crop is most effective during the time of rapid stem elongation. Unfortunately, this is also a time of warm day temperatures in most regions of North America, so a zero or negative DIF environment can be difficult to achieve.

During warm outdoor weather, it may not be physically possible to provide a negative DIF environment. In these situations, a cool temperature can be provided during the morning to reduce stem elongation. Vents can be opened at sunrise to rapidly drop the greenhouse temperatures. The greenhouse is kept cool for several hours until the sunlight eventually warms the greenhouse. Growers commonly allow greenhouse temperatures to drop between 60 and 62°F (15 and 17°C) at sunrise. Dropping the temperatures below 55°F (13°C) may cause chilling injury or latex eruption. Maintaining the low temperatures for longer periods of time will lower the average daily temperature and slow down crop development. It is best to start to drop the temperature about forty-five minutes prior to sunrise in order to achieve the low temperatures by sunrise.

NIGHT TEMPERATURE

High night temperatures (above 72°F [22°C]) cannot be used after the start of short days or flower initiation due the potential to delay flowering. Poinsettias are unique among most plant species in that high night temperatures can delay flowering, regardless of the day temperature. Night temperatures should remain below 72°F (22°C) once flower initiation begins, near September 15 to 25, depending on the cultivar. Therefore, growers must be careful not to attempt to provide a negative DIF environment that would require the night temperature to exceed 72°F (22°C).

Zero DIF and cool morning temperature drops can be used to achieve moderate height control.

ROB BERGHAGE AND ROYAL HEINS

Figure 10-2. Each plant was grown at a different day and night temperature combination. Poinsettias grown at night temperatures above 74°F (23°C) experienced delayed flowering regardless of the day temperature.

TABLE 10-1.
SUGGESTED TEMPERATURES FOR POINSETTIAS

Production Phase	Day Temperature	Night Temperature	Average Daily Temperature
Stock plants	70–80°F (21–26°C)	70–75°F (21–24°C)	70–78°F (21–26°C)
Propagation*	74–80°F (23–26°C)	70–75°F (21–24°C)	72–80°F (22–27°C)
Establishment (from transplant to flower initiation)	70–80°F (21–26°C)	70–75°F (21–24°C)	70–78°F (21–26°C)
Flowering (from initiation to bract expansion)	70–80°F (21–26°C)	65–68°F (18–20°C)	68–72°F (20–22°C)
Finishing (last 2 weeks before market)	70–75°F (21–24°C)	65–68°F (18–20°C)	65–70°F (18–21°C)
Shipping	55–60°F (13–15°C)	55–60°F (13–15°C)	55–60°F (13–15°C)
Retail	65–70°F (18–21°C)	65–70°F (18–21°C)	65–70°F (18–21°C)

*Refers to media temperatures; all other temperatures listed are air temperatures

LIGHT

The light requirements for poinsettias can be expressed with two different types of measurements. Foot-candles (f.c.) is a light intensity measurement that is the traditional method for identifying the proper light levels. (Lux is the metric equivalent that equals lumens/m². Lux and klux equivalents will be in parentheses after foot-candle measurements.) A foot-candle measurement is typically recorded during the brightest part of a sunny day. A newer measurement concept for the greenhouse industry accounts for the total light quantity delivered throughout the day. This concept is termed the daily light integral (DLI), and the unit is "moles/day" or mol·m⁻²·d⁻¹. This measurement requires a light sensor attached to a data-logging device. DLI is currently not a common measurement, but it will continue to become more widely used in the coming years; therefore, the light requirements for poinsettias will be reported in this chapter with both units. One cannot directly convert foot-candles to moles/day, so approximate numbers are provided. Appendix B provides a table that estimates the relationship between foot-candles and DLI.

Figure 10-3. An example of a meter that records the daily light integral, DIF, average daily temperature, minimum daily temperature, and maximum daily temperature.

The light requirements for poinsettias vary with the stage of production. Stock plants have the highest light requirement. Traditionally, stock plants were grown outdoors in full sunlight (10,000 f.c. [108 klux, 40–55 moles/day]). Today, poinsettia stock plants are grown in greenhouses in order to provide exclusion (screening) from whiteflies. Stock plants should only be covered with enough shade cloth in order to prevent excessively high greenhouse temperatures, otherwise, high light levels result in the better cutting production. Poinsettia stock plants will produce a high yield of well-toned cuttings when grown at 4,000–5,000 f.c. (43–54 klux, 15–25 moles/day).

The lowest light requirement occurs during propagation; however, excessively low light can slow rooting. During the first week of propagation, cuttings are grown at 1,000 f.c. (11 klux, 2.5-5 moles/day) in order to minimize water stress. As callus and rooting occur, the light levels are increased to 2,000 f.c. (22 klux, 5-7.5 moles/day). By the end of propagation, cuttings should be acclimated to light levels that will be delivered in the greenhouse following transplant (3,000 f.c. [32 klux, or 7.5–15 moles/day).

Following transplant, 3,000–4,000 f.c. (32–43 klux, 10–20 moles/day) are usually provided. Light levels at this stage impact lateral branching and stem strength. Low light (below 3,000 f.c. [32 klux, 10 moles/day]) in September can cause weak lateral stems that are more prone to break during shipping in November and December. As light levels decline during the fall, it is important to remove shade cloth or whitewash from the greenhouse. In northern climates, all shade can usually be removed by mid-September, while in warmer climates the shade cloth can usually be removed by early October.

Figure 10-4. Two plants grown with the same amount of light (or daily light integral). Left: Poinsettia shaded with a 50% shade cloth. Right: Poinsettia receiving 50% of the ambient light due to shading of leaves placed above the poinsettias.

It is important to understand that the low light conditions caused by clouds or shade cloth *do not* cause poinsettias to stretch, while low light conditions caused by the shading of neighboring plants *do* cause poinsettias to stretch. The shading by neighboring plants alters the spectral light quality received by plants; when the red-to-far-red light ratio is reduced, stem elongation is promoted. This light quality response is covered in more detail in chapter 5.

TABLE 10-2.
SUGGESTED LIGHT LEVELS FOR POINSETTIAS

Production Phase	Light Intensity Foot-candles*	Daily Light Integral Moles/Day
Stock plants	4,000–5,000	15–25
Propagation* Week 1	1,000	2.5–5
Week 2	2,000	5–7.5
Weeks 3–4	3,000–4,000	7.5–15
Transplant to Flower	3,000–4,000	10–20

*1 foot-candle = 10.8 lux.

Figure 10-5. Temperature and light interact to affect plant quality. Left: Poinsettia (leaves removed) grown under high temperatures and low light. Right: Poinsettia (leaves removed) grown under cool temperatures and bright light.

INTERACTION OF TEMPERATURE AND LIGHT

Light impacts plant growth (stem caliper, branching, fresh and dry weights), while temperature influences development (time to develop new leaves and flowers). Temperature and light interact to affect overall plant quality. For example, excellent quality occurs when poinsettias are grown under moderate temperatures (68–74°F [20–23°C]) and moderate to high light levels (3,000–5,000 f.c. [43 klux, 10-25 moles/day]). Under these conditions, there is plenty of energy to pack into the developing leaves and flowers. In contrast, the poorest quality occurs under high temperatures (75–85°F [24–30°C]) and low light (less than 2,000 f.c. [22 klux, 5.0 moles/day]). Under these conditions, the leaves and flowers develop very rapidly, but there is little energy to pack into those leaves and flowers. As a result, the stems are thin and the plants lack substance. Excess shade from July through September can inadvertently create low light conditions while temperatures remain relatively high.

PHOTOPERIOD

The effect of photoperiod on poinsettia flowering is covered in chapter 11, Flowering.

HUMIDITY

Humidity does not have a large direct impact on poinsettia growth, but humidity does indirectly affect several important factors. High humidity conditions reduce evapotranspiration, which results in the growing medium drying out more slowly. Slower water loss can result in less water stress, which can result in larger leaves and softer growth. High humidity can also cause plant temperatures and greenhouse temperatures to be higher, since the evaporative cooling effect of water evaporating from leaves or from cooling pads is reduced. In contrast, low humidity allows for very effective evaporative cooling, so plant and greenhouse temperatures can remain relatively cool even under high light.

Perhaps the more critical issue concerning humidity involves pathogens. Poinsettias are more susceptible to many fungal pathogens under high humidity conditions than under lower humidity levels. Botrytis, powdery mildew, and other foliar fungal pathogens are more likely to infect plant tissues during periods of high humidity.

During winter, disease pressure can be especially high for the following reasons:

- A large number of plants and relatively low ventilation rates create high humidity conditions.
- Condensation forming on the inside surface of the glazing material can cause the drops of water to continually wet the crop leaves and flowers.
- Cool leaf temperatures during the night can cause condensation to form on the plants.

Reducing greenhouse humidity or keeping the plants warmer at night can decrease the disease pressure. The best method for reducing greenhouse humidity involves exhausting the humid greenhouse air and bringing in cooler, drier air and heating that air. This cycle is repeated once the greenhouse air becomes humid again. Keeping plant temperatures from dropping below the dew point can reduce condensation. Exhausting very humid air will reduce the dew point, while increasing foliage temperatures will keep condensation from forming. Plant temperatures can be made warmer at night by increasing the air temperature or by using thermal blankets. Horizontal airflow fans are also useful at reducing the humidity immediately surrounding the plant canopy (microclimate) by stirring the saturated air in the canopy with the drier overhead greenhouse air. Finally, compounds can be applied to the inside of the greenhouse glazing material to reduce the formation of condensation. Some plastic films contain anti-condensation properties.

11

FLOWERING

Poinsettias have an unusual flower, termed the cyathium (*pl.* cyathia). The cyathia produce stamens and pollen followed by pistils. The ovary emerges from the center of the flower and then nods toward the side as the seeds develop. The ovaries are not often seen on commercial cultivars prior to marketing and the low-light postharvest environment does not often allow for further flower development. However, if poinsettias are kept in the greenhouse in December and January, ovaries are often seen developing. Colorful bracts below the cyathia and nectaries located on the cyathia attract pollinators.

Figure 11-1.
Cyathia with pistil (right) and stamens (left).

Figure 11-2.
Pollinators are attracted by the bracts and the nectaries.

JIM FAUST

129

The bracts can be subdivided into true bracts and transitional bracts. True bracts directly subtend the cyathium in a whorl of three, and they are already red when they emerge from the shoot tip. Transitional bracts are initially green, then change to red as they expand and mature. Transitional bracts appear on the stem below the true bracts and have internodes between each bract. The bracts that provide the most color and the timing of color development vary with cultivar. For example, Eckespoint 'Freedom' has large transitional bracts that allow the plants to be marketed relatively early in the season. 'Freedom' is often shipped to customers prior to pollen shed and prior to the true bracts fully expanding. In contrast, Eckespoint 'Success' has a few small transitional bracts, and the true bracts provide the primary color. As a result, the true bracts need sufficient time to fully expand before 'Success' can be marketed.

**Figure 11-3.
True bracts and
transitional bracts.**

FLOWER INITIATION

Flower initiation refers to the first stage of flowering. The first sign of a physical change of the meristem inside the shoot tip begins five to seven days after the critical day length is reached, or approximately September 20–October 1 under natural day lengths. Figure 11-4 displays a series of scanning electron microscope pictures of a poinsettia meristem as it transitions from a vegetative to a reproductive state. These eight stages of flower development require approximately twenty consecutive short days.

Figure 11-4. Flower development in the poinsettia shoot tip occurring during the first twenty days in an inductive photoperiod (short days). Note: Visible bud appears after approximately thirty consecutive short days.

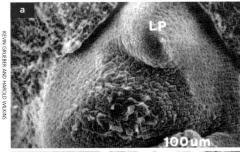

(a) Dome-shaped vegetative meristem.

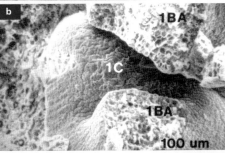

(b) Flat, triangular meristem. The three primordia that abut the sides of the meristem become the first bracts. Occurs after approximately six to eight consecutive short days.

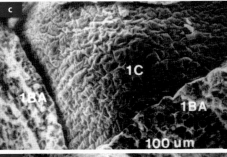

(c) Triangular, prism-shaped meristem. This structure becomes the first cyathium. Occurs after approximately nine to ten consecutive short days.

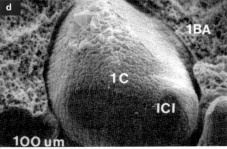

(d) Notching at corners of meristem are the involucral cup initials. Occurs after approximately eleven to twelve consecutive short days. Secondary cyathium meristems evident in axils of primary bracts. Occurs after approximately thirteen to fourteen consecutive short days.

(continued on page 132)

■■■ **Figure 11-4. (continued)**

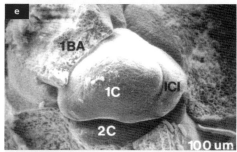

(e) Involucral cup initials expand upward to cover the staminate (male) primordial and, eventually, the pistillate (female) primordium. Occurs after approximately fifteen to sixteen consecutive short days.

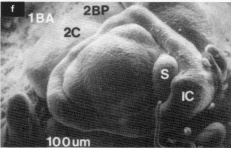

(f) Staminate flower primordial raised and involucral cup initials fused in primary cyathium. Secondary bracts elongate and cover the secondary cyathia. Occurs after approximately seventeen to eighteen consecutive short days.

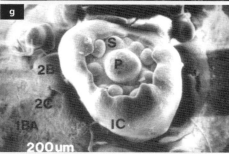

(g,h) Pistillate flower primordium raised in primary cyathium. Secondary bract primordia cover secondary meristem. Occurs after approximately nineteen to twenty consecutive short days.

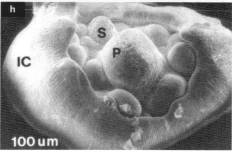

Abbreviations

LP	leaf primordium
1C	first order cyathium primordium
1BA	first-order bract attachment (bract removed)
ICI	involucral cup initial
2C	second-order cyathium primordium
S	stamenate flower primordium
IC	involucral cup
2BP	second-order bract primordium
P	pistillate flower primordium

FLOWER DEVELOPMENT

After flower initiation, flower development occurs as a continuous process from microscopic changes in the growing point to macroscopic development of the flower parts and bracts. The time from flower initiation to pollen shed is referred to as the *response time*. This time varies from eight to ten weeks, dependent upon cultivar.

Figure 11-5. Visible bud

Different markers indicate progress in flower development. *Visible bud* describes when the first cyathium is visible to the eye without the aid of a hand lens. *First color* represents when the bracts show the first transition from green to their final color. *Anthesis* refers to the first visible pollen shed from the stamens. Historically, anthesis has been the marker for the time when poinsettias are ready for market; however, certain varieties, such as 'Freedom', have considerable bract size prior to anthesis and thus can be marketed before anthesis.

Figure 11-6.
First color appearing
on the bracts

FLOWERING SEQUENCE

The following photographs illustrate the flowering sequence of six cultivars over a five-week period. These should be a benchmark for where you want your crops to be at these given dates. These poinsettias were grown under natural day lengths.

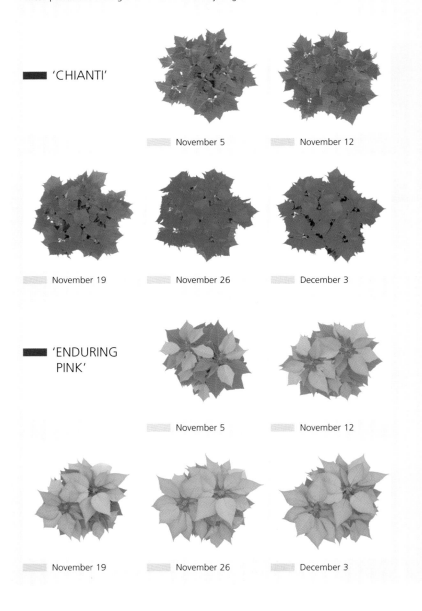

'CHIANTI'

November 5   November 12

November 19   November 26   December 3

'ENDURING PINK'

November 5   November 12

November 19   November 26   December 3

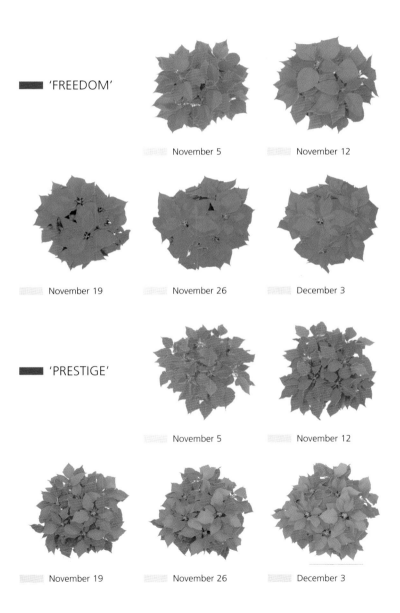

'FREEDOM'

November 5   November 12

November 19   November 26   December 3

'PRESTIGE'

November 5   November 12

November 19   November 26   December 3

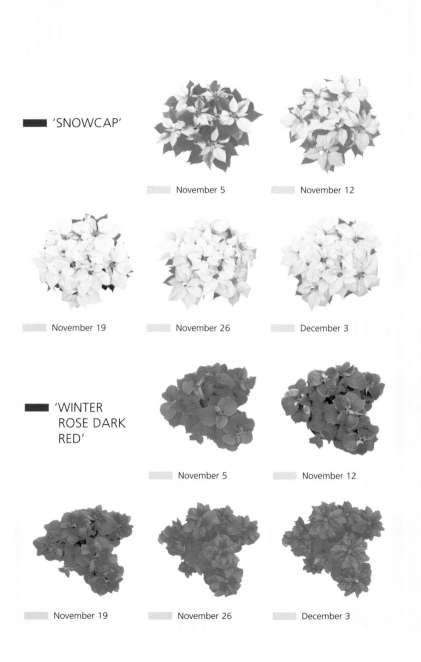

'SNOWCAP'

November 5

November 12

November 19

November 26

December 3

'WINTER ROSE DARK RED'

November 5

November 12

November 19

November 26

December 3

CONTROLLING FLOWERING

Precise control of flower initiation and development is required to produce poinsettias for specific market dates. Photoperiod and temperature are the main tools that growers use to control flowering.

PHOTOPERIOD

Poinsettias are short-day plants or, more correctly, long-night plants whose flowering is initiated when the length of the night exceeds a critical duration. The critical night length has been estimated to be approximately 11 hours and 40 minutes, i.e., the day length must be shorter than 12 hours and 20 minutes for the flowering process to be triggered.

NATURAL DAY LENGTH

In the Northern Hemisphere, the day length is sufficiently long from May to August to keep poinsettias growing in a vegetative, non-flowering state. The day length is sufficiently short around September 20–25 to allow flower initiation to proceed. Early-season cultivars initiate flowers at slightly earlier dates than mid- and late-season cultivars. The day length on September 21, the autumn equinox, is considered to be exactly 12 hours; however, this refers to the time from sunrise on the eastern horizon to sunset on the western horizon. Plants actually "see" sunlight during twilight hours, i.e., the 10 minutes before sunrise and the 10 minutes after sunset. Therefore, poinsettias grown under natural day lengths will begin flower initiation around the third week in September when the day length "seen" by the plants is approximately 12 hours and 20 minutes.

Once the critical day length for flower initiation is reached, the day length must continue to shorten for development to proceed. If a poinsettia is returned to longer day lengths, the terminal flower will abort and three vegetative branches will develop immediately below the terminal flower. This is termed splitting (see chapter 17).

LONG DAYS

Poinsettias can be kept in a continuous vegetative state by manipulating the night length with artificial lamps. Lighting can be provided in the middle of the night (night-interruption lighting) or at the end of the day (day length extension lighting). The lamps must provide a minimum of 10 f.c. (108 lux) for the plants to perceive "daylight". Night interruption lighting is provided to the plant canopy between 10 P.M. and 2 A.M. It is not necessary for the lamps to be on continuously. To conserve energy, cyclic lighting may be used in which the lamps are on for only a portion of each hour. For example, lamps may be turned on for twenty minutes every hour during the four-hour night interruption. No specific lamp type is required; however, incandescent lamps are the most common. In recent years, high-pressure sodium lamps have become more popular for providing night interruption lighting. These lamps can be mounted on irrigation booms that move back and forth above the crop or an oscillating reflector can be used to light a larger area. In either case the individual plants effectively receive cyclic lighting.

Photoperiod is frequently manipulated to sequence the flowering of a particular cultivar. For example, Eckespoint 'Freedom' is an early-season cultivar that will flower about November 15–25 under natural photoperiods. A mid-season crop (late November) of 'Freedom' can be forced by providing long days from September 5–25. The night-interruption treatment is started two weeks before the natural start of short days as an insurance policy that no premature flower initiation occurs. A late-season (first week of December) 'Freedom' crop can be forced by providing night interruption lighting from September 5–October 5.

SHORT DAYS

Short days can be provided with blackcloth to restrict sunlight from being intercepted by the poinsettias. Most growers will provide a ten-hour day length to stimulate flowering. Blackcloth is pulled over the crop in the early evening (6 P.M.) and then opened the following morning (8 A.M.). Heat buildup under the blackcloth can cause heat delay, so it is important not to pull the cloth too early in afternoon when the solar radiation levels are relatively high. Greenhouses outfitted with computer-controlled retractable blackout curtains often program the curtains to re-open following sunset, then close again prior to sunrise in order to reduce the possibility of heat delay while the crop receives fourteen continuous hours of darkness.

Poinsettia flowers develop faster at a ten-hour photoperiod than at an eleven- or twelve-hour photoperiod. Consequently, a crop that is grown under a blackcloth (ten-hour day length) starting September 21 will flower a few days earlier than a crop that begins flower initiation on September 21 and is grown entirely under naturally decreasing photoperiods from September through November.

Short days provided with blackcloth are often used to force mid- or late-season cultivars for earlier market dates. For example, Eckespoint 'Prestige' grown under natural day lengths will flower during the last week of November. Short days can be started on September 15 to provide 'Prestige' for marketing during the third week of November. Further scheduling guidelines are provided in the scheduling section (chapter 12).

LIGHT POLLUTION

Extraneous light that shines onto a poinsettia crop during the night can delay or prevent flowering. A light intensity of merely 2 f.c. (22 lux) is sufficient to inhibit normal flower initiation. So, it is critical that external light sources do not shine into the greenhouses. Street lighting, cars traveling on nearby roads, and parking lots can be sources of light pollution. Lights inside the greenhouse must also be checked to make sure that they are off throughout the night.

Figure 11-7. Light pollution can delay or prevent poinsettia flowering.

TEMPERATURE

Photoperiod is the trigger that is used to start the flowering process (flower initiation), while temperature influences the time from flower initiation

POINSETTIA TRIALS

JIM BARRETT

Established to bring the most current poinsettia research information to growers across the country, the U.S. National Poinsettia Cultivar Trials are conducted each year by Dr. Allen Hammer at Purdue University, Drs. Jim Barrett and Terril Nell at the University of Florida at Gainesville, John Dole at North Carolina State University, and by commercial growers, Homewood Nursery and Heartland Growers.

For growers in northern areas, there is a Canadian trial site that provides significant information on performance and finishing in low-light conditions. Westcan Greenhouses, Langley, British Columbia, Canada, sponsors this annual event.

Following the October and November production period, an open house is held annually at each site to give the public an opportunity to observe the trial cultivars firsthand.

For a real-time look into the Purdue University poinsettia trial greenhouse during the growing season, go to www.poinsettiatrial.org and click on "Live Poinsettia Cam". The site also posts open house dates, cultivar recommendations, and grower guidelines.

to anthesis. The rate of flower development increases as the average daily temperature (twenty-four-hour average) increases from 60 to 72°F (16 to 22°C). The optimal temperature for flower development occurs between 73–78°F (23–26°C). The optimal temperature only means that the plants progress toward flowering at the fastest possible rate at these temperatures. Optimal does not necessarily imply that the best quality occurs at this temperature range, only the fastest flowering.

The one caveat for poinsettias is that night temperatures exceeding 72°F (22°C) will delay flowering (see figure 10-2). Greenhouse night temperatures are often quite warm in the southern U.S. during the third week in September, when flower initiation begins. As a result, flower initiation can be delayed by several days in warm climates; however, these locations tend to also have warmer temperatures throughout October and November, so flower development occurs at a faster rate than cooler northern climates. The result is that poinsettias flower in a remarkably uniform pattern across the U.S. and Canada.

Average daily temperature also impacts bract expansion. The largest bracts occur at temperatures of 73–78°F (23–26°C). Growing different cultivars in the same greenhouse can create challenges for managing the temperature to provide the proper bract expansion. This is especially the case in November. Early-season cultivars such as 'Freedom' may have fully expanded bracts, while late-season cultivars such as Eckespoint 'Chianti' may still have unexpanded bracts. If the greenhouse temperatures are reduced in order to slow 'Freedom', then the bracts of 'Chianti' may not expand to an adequate size, delaying the market date.

When energy costs are high, growers consider growing poinsettias at reduced temperatures. Lower temperatures (65–68°F [19–20°C]) can work well with cultivars such as 'Freedom', 'Pepride', 'Jester', 'Punch', and 'Prestige'. Cooler temperatures do not work well for some small-bracted cultivars and/or mid- to late-season cultivars such as 'Chianti', 'Jingle Bells 3', 'Monet Twilight', 'Red Velvet', 'Success', and 'Winter Rose'.

12

SCHEDULING FLOWERING
POTTED POINSETTIAS

Well-planned crop schedules increase the ease of growing and marketing poinsettias. This chapter will demonstrate how schedules should be adjusted for different climates, cultivars, and container sizes and will provide general plans for growing several unique forms, such as miniatures, mini trees, trees, and wreaths.

SCHEDULING PINCHED POINSETTIAS IN 3–10" (8–25 CM) CONTAINERS

PRODUCT SPECIFICATIONS

Before developing a production schedule, define the product specifications.
- How tall do these poinsettias need to be?
- How many branches and bracts are required?
- What pot size(s) will the crop be grown and sold in?
- How many plants per container are required?
- What is the target market date?

CULTIVAR

Factor in the height potential and flowering response time for each cultivar. These characteristics influence the amount of vegetative growth needed to achieve the desired finished height. The flowering response time also defines how early or late plants will be ready to sell. Chapter 14, Cultivar Guide, identifies these characteristics for poinsettia cultivars offered by the Ecke Ranch.

FLOWER INITIATION DATE

For crops grown under natural day lengths, determine the flower initiation date by using the market date and count backward by the flowering response time of each cultivar used. For example, if Eckespoint 'Freedom' is targeted to flower on November 20, then subtract the response time (8–8.5 weeks) from November 20, which indicates a flower initiation date of September 21–25.

In most regions of the U.S, poinsettias initiate flowers in late September (20–30). The cultivars 'Freedom', 'Jester', 'Autumn Red', 'Red Velveteen', 'Winter Rose Early Red', and Peter Jacobsen's 'Pepride' initiate earlier, generally around September 15–25. Later initiation may occur in warmer regions where night temperatures are higher than 72°F (22°C). However, in these same regions, the warm temperatures and higher light intensities cause a faster rate of flower development, allowing the crop to flower for normal sales.

PHOTOPERIOD MANIPULATION REQUIREMENTS

If the flower initiation date does not fall within the dates outlined above, use of photoperiodic lighting or blackcloth may be required. If the initiation date is prior to September 20 (September 15 for 'Freedom', etc.) blackcloth is required to create fourteen-hour nights. If the initiation date is after September 30 (September 25 for 'Freedom', etc.), night-interruption lighting is required, e.g., lights on between 10:00 P.M. and 2:00 A.M. to prevent plants from initiating flowers until these lights are discontinued.

VEGETATIVE GROWTH REQUIREMENTS & PINCH DATE

The time from pinch to flower initiation is adjusted to determine the final plant height. This phase must be sufficiently long to allow the plants time to form enough leaves to achieve the desired finished height. The ideal time is based on the two key factors: geographic location and cultivar height potential. Table 12-1 suggests the production time for various forms based on geographic location. Table 12-2 provides the adjustment for the vegetative growth time based on height potential of the cultivar, which is listed in the Cultivar Guide (chapter 14).

For example, a 6" (15 cm) 'Freedom' crop grown in the "central" location will require twelve additional vegetative days based on the location (from table 12-1) and five additional days based on its "medium" height potential (from table 12-2). Thus, seventeen days are suggested between pinch and flower initiation. If the flower initiation date is scheduled for September 20, then the pinch date for this crop should be near September 3.

TRANSPLANT DATE

Before pinching poinsettias, it is advisable to have adequate root systems established. The size of growing container and volume of medium influence the time required for rooted cuttings to develop adequate roots prior to pinching. Small pots with less growing mix volume take the least amount of time for root establishment, while large pots with more mix (and greater moisture holding capacity) will take longer. Table 12-3 suggests the number of days typically needed to develop adequate root systems prior to pinching. As a general guideline, plants are established when they no longer wilt or droop from the shock of transplanting, even during the warmest part of the day. Roots should be visible to the side and bottom of the pot. Using the values in table 12-3, subtract the number of days from the pinch date to determine the optimum transplant date. Less time may cause sporadic branching and less uniform development.

For example, a 6" (15 cm) 'Freedom' crop requires ten to fourteen days for establishment prior to pinching (from table 12-3). Therefore, a crop that is scheduled to be pinched on September 3 needs to be transplanted between August 20-24.

PROPAGATION DATE

Cuttings that are stuck into plugs or cells require a four-week propagation period for most cultivars. Therefore, an August 20 transplant date would require a July 23 propagation date. If direct sticking, the amount of time required for cuttings to sufficiently root and be ready to pinch is usually five weeks. Therefore, a September 3 pinch date would require a July 30 propagation date.

TABLE 12-1.
VEGETATIVE GROWTH REQUIREMENTS FOR PINCHED POINSETTIAS

Number of days of vegetative growth between pinching and flower initiation as determined by product form and geographic location.

Product Form	South	Geographic Location Central	North
2–3" (5–8 cm), 1 plant	0	3	5
4–4.5" (10–11 cm), 1 plant	5	7	9
6" (15 cm), 1 plant	9	12	15
6.5" (17 cm), 1 plant	12	16	22
7" (18 cm), 2 plants	18	22	27
8" (20 cm), 2–3 plants	21	26	31
10" (25 cm), 3–4 plants	25	30	35

TABLE 12-2.
VEGETATIVE GROWTH ADJUSTMENTS FOR PINCHED POINSETTIAS

Number of additional days vegetative growth suggested between pinching and flower initiation as determined by product form and cultivar height potential. Height potential is listed for all cultivars in chapter 14.

Product Form	Short	Height Potential Medium	Tall
2–3" (5–8 cm), 1 plant	5	0	0
4–4.5" (10–11 cm), 1 plant	5	5	0
6" (15 cm), 1 plant	10	5	0
6.5" (17 cm), 1 plant	10	5	0
7" (18 cm), 2 plants	10	5	0
8" (20 cm), 2–3 plants	15	10	0
10" (25 cm), 3–4 plants	15	10	5

TABLE 12-3.
ESTABLISHING REQUIREMENTS FOR PINCHED POINSETTIAS

Number of days required to establish rooted cuttings into container prior to pinch.

Container Size	Number of cuttings per container	Number of days to establish rooted cuttings prior to pinch
2–3" (5–8 cm), 1 plant	1	5
4–4.5" (10–11 cm), 1 plant	1	8
6" (15 cm), 1 plant	1–2	10–14
6.5" (17 cm), 1 plant	1–3	14
7" (18 cm), 2 plants	1–5	14–17
8" (20 cm), 2–3 plants	1–7	17–20
10" (25 cm), 3–4 plants	1–10	20–25

TABLE 12-4.
GROWING FLOWERING POINSETTIAS

Cultivar	Colors	Response Weeks	Height	E.C.	Durability	Shelf Life
Early Season						
'Autumn Red'	R	7.5	Medium–tall	2	Excellent	Excellent
'Freedom' family	Red bright red, white, bright pink, rose, marble, jingle bells, coral, salmon	8	Medium	1.5–2.0	Best	Excellent
'Freedom Fireworks'	Red	8.5	Medium	1.5–2.0	Best	Excellent
'Enduring Pink'	Pink	8	Medium	1.5–2.0	Very good	Very good
'Jester'	Red, jingle bells	8	Short	1.5–2.0	Excellent	Excellent
'Pepride' family	Red, white, pink, marble	7.5–8	Short	1.5–2.0	Best	Best
'Punch' family	Red, white, light pink, rose, cranberry	8	Medium	1.5–2.0	Best	Excellent

Cultivar	Colors	Response Weeks	Height	E.C.	Durability	Shelf Life
Early Season (continued)						
'Red Velveteen'	Red	8	Medium–tall	2	Excellent	Excellent
'Winter Rose Early Red'	Red	8	Short–medium	1.5–2.0	Excellent	Excellent
Early Season Novelty						
'Jingle Bells 4.0'	Two-tone red/pink	8	Medium	1.5–2.0	Very good	Very good
'Strawberries 'N Cream'	Two-tone pink/white	8.5–9	Short	1.5–2.0	Best	Best
'Shimmer Pink'	Pink	8.5	Medium	2	Very good	Very good
Mid Season						
'Bright Red Sails'	Red	9	Medium	1.5–2.0	Excellent	Excellent
'Maren'	Pink	8.5	Medium	2	Excellent	Very good
'Max Red'	Red	8.5–9	Short–medium	1.5–2.0	Best	Best
'Peterstar' family	Red, white, pink, marble	8.5	Medium	2	Very good	Very good
'Petoy'	Red	8.5–9	Medium	2.0–2.5	Very good	Very good
'Prestige'	Red	8.5	Medium	1.5–2.0	Best	Best
'Red Velvet'	Red	9	Medium	2	Excellent	Excellent
'Snowcap'	White	8.5	Medium–tall	2	Excellent	Excellent
'V-17 Angelika' family	Red, white, pink	9	Tall	2	Very good	Very good
Mid Season Novelty						
'Amazone Peppermint'	Two-tone pink/peach	9	Medium	2	Very good	Very good
'Heirloom Peach'	Peach	9	Short	2.0–2.5	Very good	Very good
'Holly Point'	Red	9	Short	1.5–2.0	Very good	Very good
'Marblestar'	Marble	8.5	Medium	2	Excellent	Very good
'Plum Pudding'	Purple	9	Tall	2.0–2.5	Very good	Excellent

Cultivar	Colors	Response Weeks	Height	E.C.	Durability	Shelf Life
Late Season						
'Chianti Red'	Red	9	Short–medium	1.5–2.0	Very good	Very good
'Red Splendor'	Red	10	Medium	1.5–2.0	Best	Very good
'Success' family	Red, Light pink, coral	9.5	Medium	2.0–2.5	Best	Excellent
'Winter Rose' family	Red, white, pink, deep pink, marble, jingle bells	9.5	Short–medium	1.5–2.0	Best	Best
Late Season Novelty						
'Jingle Bells 3'	Two-tone red/pink	9.5	Medium	2.0–2.5	Very good	Very good
'Monet Twilight'	Two-tone red/pink	9	Medium	2.0–2.5	Best	Excellent

SPECIALTY FORMS

MINIATURES IN 2.5–3" (6–8 CM) CONTAINERS

Figure 12-1. Miniature poinsettia grown in a 2.5" (6 cm) pot

Recommended cultivars

Eckespoint 'Chianti', 'Freedom' family, Eckespoint 'Jester' family, Eckespoint 'Punch' family, 'Strawberries and Cream', 'Winter Rose' family, and Peter Jacobsen's 'Pepride' family.

TABLE 12-5. BLOOMING POINSETTIA PRODUCTION SCHEDULE

1. Product form: _____

              Pot size: _____   Finished height: _____

              Plants per pot: _____   Blooms per plant: _____

2. Required market date: _____

3. Cultivar: _____

       (per table 12-4) Flowering response time: _____   Height potential: _____

4. Flower initiation date (market date less response time): _____

5. If the date in step 4 is before 9/20, black cloth will be required. Start black cloth on the flower initiation date and continue until 10/15.

       Black cloth start date: _____

If the date in step 4 is after 9/30, lighting will be required. Start lighting around 9/10 and continue until the flower initiation date.

       Lighting stop date: _____

6. Vegetative growth requirements will be influenced by the height characteristics of the cultivar being grown, by the geographic location, and by the product form being produced (refer to tables 12-1 and 12-2).

     A. Number of days required due to product and location (table 12-1): _____

     B. Number of days required due to height characteristics (table 12-2): _____

                Total vegetative growth required (A+B): _____

7. Pinch date (pinch date: flower initiation date less vegetative growth required): _____

       Additional pinch dates: _____

8. Transplant date will be determined by the product form.

       Branched plants: pinch date less approximate establishing time (see table 12-3): _____

       Non-branched plants: flower initiation date less vegetative growth required: _____

       Specialty product forms (i.e., trees): _____

9. Propagation date will be determined by propagation method. If rooting in small container or root cube, allow a production period of four weeks to produce the cutting.

       Propagation date for transplant: _____

If direct sticking into the finished container, allow a production period of five weeks from stick until the plant is ready to pinch.

       Propagation date for direct stick: _____

Production

The schedule below provides a basic guideline of key activities for growing a successful miniature crop (pinched or non-pinched). An ebb-and-flood irrigation system is recommended, as overhead fertilization will cause unacceptable foliar damage. Capillary mats are not recommended, as they often stay too wet and encourage stretch.

TABLE 12-6.
PINCHED MINIATURE POINSETTIAS

Date	Activity	Comments
August 22–28	Stick unrooted cuttings	Use small cuttings (1.5" [4 cm])
September 3–October 25	Early to mid-season height control	Cycocel sprays (1,000 ppm) weekly or as needed
September 12–20	Pinch	Leave 4–5 nodes only on 'Pepride' or 'Winter Rose', 3–4 nodes on other cultivars
October 3–11	Remove old leaves	Remove only large leaves to allow new, smaller leaves to show
November 1–12	Late-season height control	Paclobutrazol drench (0.25 ppm), if needed
November 15–25	Sell	

TABLE 12-7.
NON-PINCHED MINIATURE POINSETTIAS

Date	Activity	Comments
September 5–13	Stick unrooted cuttings	Use small cuttings (1.5" [4 cm])
September 17–October 25	Early to mid-season height control	Cycocel sprays (1,000 ppm) weekly or as needed
November 1–12	Late-season height control	Paclobutrazol drench (0.25 ppm), if needed
November 15–25	Sell	

Fertilizer levels should be maintained at 200 ppm using a balanced fertilizer appropriate for poinsettias. With frequent watering (two or three times per day depending upon weather), fertilizer should not be applied at every irrigation. Clear water will help avoid any salts buildup and will minimize burn in the event the soil becomes too dry.

Regular application of chemical growth regulators is required to keep plants short; the final height of the plant and pot should be 8" (20 cm). Cycocel sprays at 1,000 ppm should begin approximately one week after sticking the unrooted cutting. For 'Winter Rose', try to apply all growth regulators in the initial six weeks of the crop since a reduction in bract size is not desirable. Later applications on large-bracted cultivars such as 'Freedom' will reduce bracts to a desirable size. Use paclobutrazol (Bonzi or Piccolo) as a light drench (0.25 ppm) late in the crop only if needed. 'Freedom' is more likely to stretch than 'Pepride', but the height of both should be tracked closely.

Grow under lower light intensities of 3,500 f.c. (38 klux) since rapid growth is not required and lower light reduces the irrigation requirements. Temperatures are similar to standard poinsettia production, but high light and limited soil moisture retention make it easy to stress plants and cause leaf damage.

Accurately timing flowering and the market date is important since the small size of these finished plants makes it important to manage crop timing for maximum freshness. The following tables provide timing schedules for both pinched and non-pinched forms.

SINGLE STEM

Before the development of free-branching cultivars, florist-quality poinsettias were grown as multiple, non-pinched plants in a pot. Although the "branched"

Figure 12-2. Single-stemmed poinsettias grown with three plants in a 6" (15 cm) container

plant is the most commonly grown form today, non-branched poinsettias, or "straight-ups," continue to be grown for elite "florist quality" blooming crops. This plant form offers something different from the standard branched plant, creating increased sales opportunities in the market. Some considerations when producing single stem poinsettias include the following:

Shorter production time compared to branched plants

Cuttings may be planted later than required for branched plants. Using rooted cuttings, the plant date for a three-stem non-pinched plant in a 6–6.5" (15–17 cm) pot typically would be two to three weeks later than for branched plants. If larger forms are produced (five bloom, seven bloom, etc.), then earlier start dates are required. The table below is based on an anticipated flower initiation date of September 25. Adjust dates for cultivars that initiate flowers earlier (September 15–25), such as 'Autumn Red', 'Freedom', 'Jester', 'Pepride', 'Red Velveteen', and 'Winter Rose Early Red'.

TABLE 12-8.
APPROXIMATE PLANTING DATES FOR ROOTED CUTTINGS

| | Geographic Location | | |
Product	South	Central	North
3 bloom	September 16	September 13	September 10
4 bloom	September 13	September 10	September 3
5 bloom	September 7	September 3	August 30
7 bloom	September 3	August 30	August 25
10 bloom	August 30	August 25	August 20

When using cultivars with a "short" height potential (see chapter 14), add five to ten days of vegetative growth prior to flower initiation.

Flexibility of poinsettia cultivar choice

Outstanding quality single-stem plants may be grown using most cultivars. Some growers may prefer the extra fullness that results from the side shoot growth of free-branching cultivars. However, if you remove the side shoots, do so when growth is large enough to remove easily but is less than 3" (8 cm) in length. Waiting longer to remove shoots results in injury to the stem and allows entry points for disease.

Opportunity to use late cuttings produced from stock plants

Single-stem production works well for growers that produce their own stock plants for two reasons. First, cuttings can be harvested for additional weeks. This allows cuttings that are too late to produce pinched crops to be used for a non-pinched crop. Second, single-stem crops require more cuttings per pot. So, late cuttings make stock plants more productive, lowering the unit cost of each cutting.

Increased plant symmetry and uniformity

Symmetry and uniformity are achieved by selecting rooted cuttings of similar height, caliper, and root development at the time of planting. This will also help reduce the amount of selective growth regulator sprays required to even out the pots. It is more difficult to get uniform growth and development if cuttings are rooted directly in pots. Generally, an odd number of cuttings (three, five, or seven per pot) create the most attractive finished product. However, four or ten cuttings per pot also works well. Suggested planting patterns are shown in figure 12-3.

Figure 12-3. Suggested planting patterns for single-stem poinsettias. Plant cuttings around the outside edge of the pot with a slight outward tilt.

3-Bloom
(6–6.5" pot)

4-Bloom
(6–6.5" pot)

5-Bloom
(7–7.5" pot)

7-Bloom
(8–8.5" pot)

10-Bloom
(10" pot)

Reduced breakage or damage during shipping

Stems of non-pinched plants are sturdier than those of branched plants, allowing greater durability in shipping. Sleeves with more flare may be needed to accommodate larger bracts of single-stem crops.

Increased return based on higher market prices

Non-pinched poinsettias command a higher price than branched plants. For example, wholesale prices for 6" (15 cm) pinched plants range from $2.25 to $4.00, while prices for three plants non-pinched in a 6" (15 cm) pot range from $6.00 to $9.00. The price differential more than offsets the increased cutting costs. Often, large pots with seven or more stems bring even higher prices.

DOUBLE PINCH

The one-plant, pinched, multi-bloom poinsettia is the most commonly grown form. However, as the market trend continues toward different forms, growers are looking for ways to expand their product line. With the superior branching habit of today's cultivars, it is possible to create larger, fancier double-pinched plants with ten to thirteen flowers. This is also an outstanding form for novelty cultivars such as 'Winter Rose'.

Transplant

Transplant rooted cuttings four weeks earlier than traditional one-pinch programs. For most regions of the U.S., this will be mid-July.

Container size

Because of the larger finished height and size of a double-pinched plant, the suggested container size is 6.5–7" (16–18 cm). This should provide adequate weight and stability to the finished product.

Pinch schedule

The initial pinch should be made once cuttings have established a root system in the pot, generally two weeks after transplant. For most growers, this
will be approximately the first week of August. Use a soft pinch with leaf
removal for best branching results. Leave four to six nodes below this pinch.
Four weeks later (early September), apply the second pinch. Leave three to
four nodes per shoot, shaping the plant for a more symmetrical form.

Space required

Double-pinch poinsettias are shorter in height than large, multi-plant forms
that require more space. Final spacing on the bench should average 16 x 16"
(41 x 41 cm), or 1.8 ft.² (0.16 m²) per pot. 'Winter Rose' will require less,
approximately 14 x 14" (36 x 36 cm), or 1.4 ft.² (0.13 m²) per pot.

Height control

For maximum stem strength and reduction of stem breakage, use plant
growth regulators to control stem elongation. Spray applications of Florel,
Cycocel, or B-Nine/Cycocel should be applied prior to and after pinching
because of the longer production time. A finished height of 17–18"
(43–46 cm) is desirable for this form.

MINIATURE TREES

Miniature poinsettia trees offer growers an opportunity to produce a unique
form for the upscale florist market without the commitment of space and
production time required for standard tree forms. The ideal miniature tree

**Figure 12-4. Miniature tree poinsettias
grown in 5" (13 cm) pots**

has a total height (including the container) of 18" (46 cm) and can be grown at 14 x 14" spacing (36 x 36 cm), or 1.4 ft.^{2} per pot (0.13 m^2).

Cultivars

The best cultivars for miniature trees have smaller leaf and bract size. 'Freedom Bright Red' and 'Freedom Salmon', 'Punch' family, 'Winter Rose' family, 'Pepride' family, or novelty types such as RAI Beckmann's 'Heirloom Peach' or 'Strawberries and Cream' work well.

Transplant

Rooted cuttings should be transplanted the last week of June (week 26). Use pots no smaller than 5" (13 cm) for plant stability. For increased retail value, terra-cotta pots, clay pots, or other nontraditional containers have the greatest appeal.

Pinch dates

The first pinch should be done in mid-August. A soft pinch with leaf removal is recommended to encourage strong branching in the upper five nodes. The second pinch should be completed by September 15, bringing each shoot down to about two nodes. Shape the plant during this final pinch to create a compact, symmetrical form.

Growth regulators

Apply plant growth regulators after the first pinch to prevent stretch on side shoots. Spray treatments of Florel, Cycocel, or B-Nine/Cycocel tank mix are effective with these cultivars. After the final pinch, treat these trees much like you would a 4" (10 cm) poinsettia for height control.

Shoot removal

Prior to the first pinch, remove the lowest shoots on the stem as they reach 2–3" (5–8 cm) in length. Do not remove any of the shoots near the top of the plant that will contribute to the branch structure after pinching.

Leaf removal

Do not remove lower leaves from the miniature tree until October unless leaves become infested with insects, disease, or are otherwise damaged. When removing leaves, pinch near the base of the petiole to minimize risk of disease or damage to the main stem. Before sale, remove any leaves that distract from the tree's shape and form.

Value-added ideas

To further increase the value of miniature trees, growers should consider several enhancements.
- Upgrade containers to increase interest and value of the finished product. Clay pots should include the saucer. Terra-cotta pots with designs or relief details or other decorative features increase interest and value.
- Cover the growing medium surface with moss, clean pea-gravel, etc. to add drama to the look of these trees.
- Use variegated ivy, flowering bacopa, or other trailing plants to create a "conservatory" look to these trees.

TREES

Poinsettia trees can be a challenge to grow, but these unique forms offer expanded sales and marketing opportunities. Producing high-quality trees requires a commitment to an extended growing season, considerable greenhouse space, and diligent pruning and crop maintenance.

The height of the poinsettia tree is directly dependent upon growing time prior to the first pinch. For taller trees (4–5' [1.2–1.5 m]), rooted

Figure 12-5.
Poinsettia tree

cuttings are transplanted in late May to early June. Trees can be double- or triple-pinched to attain the final shape and size desired for the finished plant. Double-pinched trees create an umbrella shape, while the triple-pinched trees have a more rounded lollipop form. The following guidelines can assist growers in producing exceptional poinsettia trees.

Cultivars

Some poinsettia cultivars are better adapted to this form than others, with strong stems and large bracts being desirable characteristics for trees. Cultivars that are susceptible to splitting should not be used for trees.
- For 4–5' (1.2–1.5 m) trees: Use Gross 'Amazone Peppermint', Eckespoint 'Snowcap', Eckespoint 'Success', Gutbier 'V-17 Angelika' family
- For 3–4' (0.9–1.2 m) trees: Use Peter Jacobsen's 'Peterstar' Family, Eckespoint 'Red Velvet', Eckespoint 'Red Velveteen', Eckespoint 'Prestige'
- Novelties: Use Eckespoint 'Monet Twilight', Eckespoint 'Jingle Bells 3', 'Winter Rose'

Planting

Plant rooted cuttings into 6" (15 cm) pots. Establish these plants in a warm, humid environment to help develop an active root system and vigorous growth. Begin night-interruption lighting at the time of transplant to keep plants vegetative and to minimize the potential for premature floral initiation. Stake plants at this time to prevent crooked stems, leaving at least 1" (3 cm) between the stem and the stake. As plants elongate, lightly tie them to the stakes, using floral tape or similar materials that will not girdle or damage the stem. Always maintain a margin of space between the plants, and avoid crowding the crop. Space several times during the growth cycle to provide good light and adequate air movement for the development of symmetrical trees.

Transplanting

Before the roots of the plant begin to wrap themselves around the base of the pot, transplant trees into the final growing container (8–10"

[20–25 cm] for small plant trees, 12" [30 cm] pots for larger trees).
Produce trees under light intensities of 2,500–3,000 f.c. (27–32 klux),
and avoid excessively high light that may cause heat stress or restrict
stem elongation.

Leaf and shoot removal

Remove the lower side shoots when they are approximately 2" (5 cm)
long. Be sure to always leave the top ten shoots on the plants to form the
branches. Do not remove foliage until September, unless it is necessary due
to insects, diseases, or chemical burn (phytotoxicity). To remove damaged
leaves from the tree, cut the petiole about 0.5" (13 mm) from the main
stem. The remaining petiole will dry up and abscise naturally without
causing injury to the stem.

First pinch

The first pinch should be a soft pinch, removing 0.25–0.5" (6–13 mm)
of the terminal growth. At the time of pinch, remove the top two or three
immature leaves remaining on the plant. If the plant has split, pinch
immediately below this split to induce new vegetative growth.

Second pinch

The second pinch should be done approximately four weeks after the
first. If this is a double-pinched tree, the lower shoots should be pinched
to leave three or four nodes per stem, while the upper shoots should be
pinched harder, leaving two or three nodes. If this is a triple-pinched
tree, all shoots (upper and lower) should be pinched to two or three nodes
each. At this time, increase the light intensities to about 5,000 f.c.
(54 klux) and use growth regulators as required to prevent stretch of the
new growth. For triple-pinched trees, the final pinch should take place
about four weeks after the second pinch, and two to three weeks prior
to floral induction. Trim each shoot to two or three leaf nodes. Remove
any older foliage that may be shading the growth and development of
new shoots.

Plant supports

Support the branches by loosely tying them to the support stake next to the main stem. This should be done near the time of the final pinch to avoid breakage of new shoots and stems.

Fertilizer

Fertilizer requirements for trees will vary with the growing season. During the hot summer growing period, use fertilizer with high (20–40%) ammonium nitrate and additional calcium and magnesium. Once into fall, a finisher-type feed (higher in nitrate nitrogen) is more appropriate. Avoid the buildup of soluble salts in the medium, and monitor the nutritional status on a regular basis with media and tissue analysis.

TABLE 12-9.
TREE PRODUCTION SCHEDULE

	Triple-pinch, 4–5' (1.2–1.5 m) tall	Double-pinch, 4–5' (1.2–1.5 m) tall	Double-pinch, 3–4' (0.9–1.2 m) tall
Transplant rooted cutting	April 15	May 1	June 1
First pinch	Late July	Mid-August	Mid-August
Second pinch	Mid-August	September 5–10	September 5–10
Third pinch	September 5–10	NA	NA

Packing and shipping

Packing and shipping trees can be difficult due to their large size and potential for breakage. If trees are going to be trucked any distance, it is advisable to sleeve and box them individually. If trees are going to be delivered within a local market, consider securing the pots in some type of larger container to prevent the tree from falling over, and sleeve the upper canopy with a large flared sleeve or plastic bag. To avoid damage to bracts and stems, do not crowd the plants in transport.

WREATHS

Poinsettia wreaths are specialty forms that create great interest and value at retail outlets. Although large wreaths are the most dramatic looking, the long production time makes this a fairly difficult product to grow. Smaller wreaths may be created using a 6.5–7" (16–18 cm) pot and a wire framework approximately 18" (46 cm) in diameter.

Figure 12-6. Poinsettia wreaths in production

Cultivars

Select cultivars that are fairly aggressive in both their growth and branching characteristics and not prone to splitting. 'Prestige', 'Red Velvet', 'Monet Twilight', 'Amazone Peppermint', 'Snowcap', and the 'Peterstar' family make excellent wreaths.

Transplant

Using two cuttings per pot, transplant rooted cuttings in early August (approximately week 31). Position cuttings with the root cubes toward the center of the pot and stems at an angle to be trained along the wire framework.

Training

Stems should be loosely tied along the wire framework weekly using a twist tie or string.

Leaf removal

As stems elongate and lower shoots begin to develop, remove leaves that create shade on the young shoots. Avoid excessive leaf removal during the life of this crop.

Pinching

As shoots emerge from the nodes of each stem, pinching will be required to limit the elongation of these shoots. Pinch all significant side shoots back to one node by mid-September. Pinch the growing tips out of the cuttings once they have reached the center of the upper wire support or by November 1st at the latest. If stems have not completely covered the wire support, do not pinch.

Growth regulators

Apply Florel, Cycocel, or B-Nine/Cycocel to the pots as side shoots develop. It is important to prevent inside shoots from elongating, as this will distort the look created by this form. A hole should always be clearly visible through the center of the wire framework and plants. Applications of Cycocel may continue through October 20, as bract size reduction is not a problem with wreaths.

13

CUT POINSETTIAS

While poinsettias are remarkably popular potted plants, poinsettias are much less well known as cut flowers. Interestingly, poinsettias were first marketed commercially as a cut flower in the early 1900s. Cut poinsettias were field grown for local fresh flower markets or grown in greenhouses throughout Europe up to the early 1960s.

While cut poinsettia production has been minimal in the last thirty years, it has the potential to become an important component of the specialty cut flower industry. Cut poinsettias can be produced for the Christmas holiday, a time period when relatively few other cut flowers are available to grow and market. In addition, the bright red, pink, and white bracted cultivars make cut poinsettias suitable for Valentine's Day and other spring holidays. In 2002, growers reported a wholesale price of $2.50–4.00 per bloom, or "stem" during Christmas, which indicates that cut poinsettias can be a economically viable product.

Figure 13-1. Freshly cut Eckespoint 'Renaissance Red' cut poinsettias for bucket sales (left) and a flower arrangement with stock (*Matthiola*)

Two series of cut poinsettias have a particularly long postharvest life, making them suitable as cut flowers. The Eckespoint 'Renaissance' series has large, striking inflorescences carried on long, strong stems, which makes them easy to use by the floral industry and the general public. 'Renaissance' is a restricted-branching cultivar that produces two to three stems on each shoot when pinched, even if more than three nodes remain. The free-branching 'Winter Rose' series currently used for potted plants can also be used as a cut flower and produces four or more stems per plant if sufficient nodes remain after pinching. However, 'Renaissance' plants produce longer stems and larger inflorescences than do 'Winter Rose' plants. Other series suitable for cut flowers are sure to be introduced in the future.

SCHEDULING

A sample schedule for Christmas flowering is included in table 13-1. For Christmas sales, 22–24" (55–61 cm) stems can be produced by planting rooted cuttings mid-July (week 29) and pinching one and a

TABLE 13-1. SAMPLE PRODUCTION SCHEDULE FOR 'RENAISSANCE RED' CUT POINSETTIAS.

Cultural Step	Date	Production Time (weeks)	Temperature °F (°C)
Receive and plant rooted cutting	July 7[x]		75–80°F (24–27°C) days; 68–72°F (20–22°C) nights
Pinch to 4 nodes/plant	July 21[y]	2	75–80°F (24–27°C) days; 68–72°F (20–22°C) nights
Thin stems to 2–3/plant	August 18[z]	4	75–80°F (24–27°C) days; 68–72°F (20–22°C) nights
Respace to 12" x 12" (30 x 30 cm) if using 2 plants/8" (20 cm) pot.	September 8	3	75–80°F (24–27°C) days; 64–68°F (18–20°C) nights
Flower initiation	September 22–26	2	75–80°F (24–27°C) days; 62–68°F (17–20°C) nights
Flower	December 1–5	10	75–80°F (24–27°C) days; 62–68°F (17–20°C) nights
Total		21	

[x] If using Pro-Gibb, plant two weeks later.
[y] Or when roots are to the edge of the pot.
[z] Or when stems are large enough to thin.

half to two weeks later (figure 13-2). This will provide approximately twenty weeks for a pinched crop, comprising ten weeks from planting rooted cuttings to the start of flower initiation (generally September 25, week 39) and ten weeks from the start of flower initiation to the market date. Plants will typically flower the first week of December (week 49) if grown under natural day lengths. Earlier or later flower dates will require the manipulation of the photoperiod with night-interruption lighting (long days) or blackcloth (short days). The crop schedule must be adjusted accordingly to maintain stem length.

STEM LENGTH

Stem length is determined by the number of weeks that the plants are grown under long days following pinching (figure 13-2). Stem length will increase by approximately 2" (5 cm) for every extra week from pinching to the start of flower initiation (short days). For example, to obtain 24–26" (61–66 cm) stems, add one week of production time, which would mean planting eleven weeks prior to start of flower initiation (ten weeks for 22–24" [56 to 61 cm] long stems plus one week for the extra 2" [5 cm]). 'Winter Rose' plants can produce long stems if plants are kept under long days for a longer duration than are 'Renaissance'. However, the longer the duration of long days, the greater the chance for splitting (see chapter 17). In addition, maintain a positive DIF to encourage stem elongation.

Figure 13-2. Effect of pinching and planting time on stem length

	No Pinch			Pinch (15 days after plant)		
Plant Date	7/16	8/1	8/16	7/16	8/1	8/16
Length (in)	36	33	26	23	22	17

PAUL FISHER

Figure 13-3. Effect of ProGibb (GA3) on stem elongation. From right to left: Control (water) or ProGibb at 10, 25, or 50 ppm. ProGibb increased final stem length by 8–10" (20–25 cm). A delay of several days occurred when plants were treated with the two higher rates of ProGibb.

ProGibb (gibberellic acid) can be used to provide additional height so that production time (the number of long days) can be reduced, or to produce long-stemmed flowers (longer than 24" [61 cm]). ProGibb can be applied weekly at 10–25 ppm (figure 13-3). Start applications three weeks after pinching plants or when the axillary shoots are 1" (2.5 cm) long. Use four to seven applications and continue them until the start of short days. This will provide an additional 8–10" (20–25 cm) of stem length. Do not apply after the start of short days, since gibberellic acid may delay bract coloring.

SPACING

For pinched crops, provide 4 stems/ft.^{2} (43 stems/m^2) of bench or bed space. Planting two rooted cuttings per 8" (20 cm) pot and spacing the pots at 12 x 12" (30 x 30 cm) can provide this spacing. Closer spacing of 6 x 6" inch (15 x 15 cm) can be used with non-pinched plants. If growing in pots, space them pot-to-pot until after leaves overlap to encourage stem elongation and straight stems, which will reduce stem breakage and maximize space usage.

PINCHING AND DISBUDDING

'Renaissance Red' can be pinched one and a half to two weeks after planting rooted cuttings, or when roots are visible at the edge of the medium. If pinched too early, there will be insufficient root growth to support the developing axillary shoots, and the resulting shoots will be weak and slow to develop. Thus, premature pinching may reduce quality. If the crop is behind schedule prior to the pinch, it is best to raise the average daily temperature to 75°F (24°C).

Generally, two marketable stems can be produced from each cutting when pinched to four nodes. Three weeks after pinching, when the leaves are 1" (2.5 cm) long, remove (disbud) all but two or three of the most vigorous axillary stems. Leave two stems per plant on the inner rows and three stems/plant on the outer rows. Extra stems will probably not produce marketable flowers and will make pest control more difficult. Florel has not been effective on 'Renaissance Red' to increase the number of branches per plant.

Non-pinched plants produce larger stems and flowers (figure 13-2). Non-pinched plants elongate 9–12" (23–30 cm) longer for the same planting date as a pinched crop. However, half the number of stems will be produced per square foot, so the cost per stem will be higher. Non-pinched plants will also flower several days earlier than pinched plants.

'Winter Rose' plants can be produced either as non-pinched or as pinched plants. With pinched plants, the number of axillary shoots produced from a pinch is usually equal to or one less than the number of nodes or leaves remaining on the plant. For example, leaving five leaves on a plant after a pinch should result in four to five marketable inflorescences. If weather or plant quality is poor at the time of the pinch, growers may want to leave one additional leaf to ensure a proper number of quality inflorescences. However, if too many axillary shoots are allowed to remain, stems will be weak and inflorescences will be small.

CONTAINERS AND SUPPORT

Cut poinsettias can be grown in large pots, bulb crates, or ground beds. The shoots will need support to reduce stem breakage and to prevent plants from falling over. One or two wires or strings around the perimeter of the bench or bed is sufficient. The use of netting will slow harvesting.

GREENHOUSE ENVIRONMENT

After propagation, cut poinsettias should be grown at 68–72°F (20–21°C) night temperature and 75–85°F (24–29°C) day temperature until stems are thinned or plants are spaced. Grow at 62–68°F (17–20°C) nights and 75–85°F (24–29°C) days until finished. During the last one to two weeks of production, the temperature can be reduced to 55–60°F (13–16°C) to enhance bract color. Cut poinsettias should be grown under a positive DIF to encourage maximum stem elongation. Temperatures cooler than 60°F (16°C) will lead to slow plant development and small bracts. Night temperatures above 72°F (21°C) after start of flower initiation may delay flowering.

High light is necessary for best growth. For crops to be marketed prior to the first week of December, short days may need to be started before September 25. For later crops (second or third week of December), long days will need to be provided after September 5–10 to delay flowering.

INSECTS AND DISEASES

The same insects and diseases will be problems on cut poinsettias as on potted poinsettias; however, there are some unique characteristics of cut poinsettias. Whitefly control will be more difficult due to the lengthy crop time and the difficulty of penetrating the dense foliar canopy for spray applications. The application of systemic pesticides such as Marathon will not last the entire crop cycle. In addition, the woody stems and heavy foliar canopy that develop in the last month will reduce the effectiveness of Marathon. One possible strategy is to apply granular Marathon normally and then follow with spray applications after eight weeks to penetrate the foliage.

Botrytis can be especially prevalent on cut poinsettias due to the lengthy crop time and heavy foliar canopy. The fungus is often found on dead tissue that has fallen at the base of the plant, which can serve as a reservoir of inoculum for disease on living tissue. Removal of fallen foliage would be beneficial but is generally not practical. Do not harvest flowers when water is on the foliage or bracts. During shipping or storage, botrytis may develop on the nectaries or on the bracts, especially if stored warm. Botrytis can cause spotting of the bracts.

PHYSIOLOGICAL DISORDERS

SPLITTING

Splitting is the premature initiation and development of terminal flower buds on vegetative or young reproductive plants (see chapter 17,

Physiological Disorders and Production Problems). If splitting occurs on young plants to be flowered for Christmas, the terminal flower bud may reach anthesis but the inflorescence will be malformed, excessively large, and open. Individual bracts may form in the middle of the flower cluster and grow vertically. In addition, if splitting occurs early in the production schedule, vegetative growth will cease and plants may be too short.

CENTER BUD DROP

Premature abscission of the poinsettia cyathia can make cut stems appear old because normal cyathia drop occurs as the inflorescence matures (see chapter 17). While the vase life of cut stems is not affected by delaying harvest after flowering (pollen is visible on the cyathia), cyathia drop can occur. Premature cyathia drop can also occur if the light level is too low or night temperatures are too high during production. The problem is greatest in low-light areas of the North and coastal areas, but is rare in southern areas. If growing in a chronically cloudy area, maintain a clean glazing to allow as much light transmittance as possible, reduce or eliminate overhead hanging baskets, reduce night temperatures late in the production cycle after bracts have expanded, and avoid water stress.

LEAF DROP

The lengthy crop time and close spacing of cut poinsettias can cause extensive dropping of the lower leaves. While the fallen leaves are a problem due to botrytis, the quality of the cut stem will not be diminished since the lower two-thirds of leaves are typically removed anyway. In fact, the vase life of cut poinsettias is longer with all of the leaves removed than with the leaves remaining on the stem.

STEM BREAKAGE

The long stems and large inflorescences make cut poinsettias prone to stem breakage (see chapter 17). Provide support and avoid moving plants growing in pots.

HARVEST

Cut stems of 'Renaissance Red' when at least two of the cyathia are show-ing pollen. If sufficient stem length is present, cut stems up to 2" inches (5 cm) above the base. The softer tissue at this location will allow easier harvest and improved water uptake. Latex dripping from the cut stem is a nuisance, but no special handling is required. If bracts or leaves crack, beads of latex will appear but will dry clear and will not be noticed.

All foliage can be removed at the time of harvest, or a few leaves can be left on each stem. Remove at least one-third to two-thirds of the foliage for easier handling. Interestingly, removing all foliage increases vase life and delays flower abscission. Florists commonly remove all the foliage for use in arrangements.

For bucket sales, put stems into clean water with a low EC (0.1–0.5 mmhos/cm) and low pH (less than 5.0). For dry shipping, stems can be allowed to wilt slightly to allow more inflorescences to be packed in a box. Slight wilting decreases vase life and time to first leaf abscission, but the vase life is still sixteen days.

POSTHARVEST

Contrary to popular opinion, pretreatments with heated floral solution, alcohol dips, or 10% sucrose either have no effect or are detrimental. Recutting stems every three to five days increases vase life and delays leaf abscission. A 1–2% sucrose concentration in the vase solution produced the longest postharvest life for stems placed in foam but had little effect on stems not placed in foam. As with most cut flowers, the use of floral foam decreases vase life and accelerated leaf yellowing and abscission; however, the vase life in foam is still ten to fourteen days. Commercial floral hydra-tion and holding solutions delay leaf abscission but have no other effect.

Stems can be stored or shipped dry at 34–41°F (1–5°C) for up to twenty-four hours, allowing them to be shipped with most common cut flower species. After shipping, recut and rehydrate. However, for storage of three days or more, they should be in water at 50°F (10°C) or higher to prevent cold damage (but vase life will be decreased). Unfortunately, for long-term storage, cut poinsettias should be stored separately from most other cut flowers, which are stored at 34–41°F (1–5°C), and need to be stored with tropical flowers, which are typically stored at 55–59°F (13–15°C). This special handling may increase the cost of cut poinsettia stems and might limit their importation or distribution through wholesale flower distributors. Stems can be shipped wet or dry.

Acknowledgements: This chapter was written by John Dole, North Carolina State University, and Paul Fisher and Geoffrey Njue, University of New Hampshire.

14

❦

CULTIVAR GUIDE

New poinsettia cultivars are introduced to the market after they have passed extensive trial and evaluation at university and grower sites. These evaluations take place throughout North America and, in many cases, other parts of the world. In order to be commercialized, a poinsettia must be easy to grow under normal conditions, attractive, and durable. Failure in any of these areas usually prevents these plants from being made commercial.

The following information is a summary of the poinsettias sold commercially by the Ecke Ranch at the time of this publication. Cultivars are presented in alphabetical order by early season, mid-season, and late season timing groups. The information presented in this chapter will be helpful as growers develop crop schedules (see chapter 12) and integrate Ecke genetics into production programs. Details such as the response time and plant vigor are used for production scheduling. Information such as the media EC and foliage type help determine the fertilization regimes appropriate to these poinsettias. While more complete details and information can be found on each series or cultivar at the Ecke Web site (www.ecke.com), the information below should be helpful in understanding the key characteristics that influence how they should be grown. Especially important are comments found in the "Cultural Notes" section, as these will assist growers with the fine details that impact performance and finished plant quality.

ECKESPOINT 'AUTUMN RED'

Season	**Early season**
Foliage	Dark green
Bracts	Large, dark red, velvety
Flowering response	7.5 weeks
Natural timing	November 15
Forms	6" (15 cm), 8" (20 cm), 10" (25 cm)
Media EC (mmhos/cm)*	1.5–2.0
Height potential	Medium to tall
Plant growth regulators	May be needed in propagation and on finished plants.
Postproduction	Excellent
Cultural notes	• Avoid heat and light stress on young plants. Provide shade until about two weeks after pinch. • Flowering may be delayed in cool, dark climates. • Florel sprays (500 ppm) applied one week before and after pinching can improve the finished form.

PETER JACOBSEN'S 'PEPRIDE'

Season	**Early season**
Foliage	Dark green, oak-shaped
Bracts	Dark red, white, pink, and white-and-pink marble pattern
Flowering response	7.5–8.0 weeks
Natural timing	November 18; similar timing and flowering schedule as the 'Freedom' family
Forms	2" (5 cm), 4" (10 cm), 6" (15 cm)
Media EC (mmhos/cm)*	1.5–2.0
Height potential	Short
Plant growth regulators	Not typically required unless grown at high density.
Postproduction	Excellent
Cultural notes	• High density planting. • Easy to grow. • Small leaf size results in lower water requirements. • Leave two additional nodes at pinch to produce more bract color at finish. High temperatures and humidity increase bract and leaf size.

* Measured with a saturated media extract test. See chapter 8, Growing Media, for target EC using other testing procedures.

'WINTER ROSE
EARLY RED'

Season	Early season
Foliage	Dark green, incurved
Bracts	Dark red, incurved
Flowering response	7.5–8.0 weeks
Natural timing	November 15–20
Forms	4" (10 cm), 6" (15 cm), 8" (20 cm), Mini trees
Media EC (mmhos/cm)*	1.5–2.0
Height potential	Short to medium
Plant growth regulators	Not required in propagation and minimal on finished plants.
Postproduction	Excellent
Cultural notes	• High density planting. • Same culture as 'Winter Rose', difference is only in early flowering characteristics

ECKESPOINT
'ENDURING
PINK'

Season	Early mid-season
Foliage	Dark green
Bracts	Pink
Flowering response	8.0–8.5 weeks
Natural timing	November 21; similar timing and flowering schedule as the 'Freedom' family
Forms	2" (5 cm), 4" (10 cm), 6" (15 cm)
Media EC (mmhos/cm)*	1.5–2.0
Height potential	Short to medium
Plant growth regulators	Minimal requirements. Can experience late-season stretch if finished at tight spacing.
Postproduction	Outstanding
Cultural notes	• High density planting. • Same culture as 'Freedom'.

* Measured with a saturated media extract test. See chapter 8, Growing Media, for target EC using other testing procedures.

ECKESPOINT 'FREEDOM' FAMILY

Season	**Early mid-season**
Foliage	Dark green
Bracts	Full color series available
Flowering response	8.0–8.5 weeks
Natural timing	November 21; 'Freedom Bright Red', 'Pink', and 'Salmon' will mature 4–5 days later than 'Freedom Red'
Forms	2" (5 cm), 4" (10 cm), 6" (15 cm), 8" (20 cm), 10" (25 cm)
Media EC (mmhos/cm)*	1.5–2.0
Height potential	Medium
Plant growth regulators	Can experience late-season stretch if finished at tight spacing.
Postproduction	Outstanding
Cultural notes	• Easy to grow. • Flowering can be delayed with "mum lighting" starting Sept. 5. For November 25 flowering, lights should be discontinued September 25. • Sensitive to drying or rapid changes in light and temperature conditions, which may result in minor leaf curl and leaf burn. • Bracts sensitive to sunburn if exposed to high light intensities at finish. Provide shade to prevent bract damage. • 'Freedom Bright Red' and 'Salmon' have slightly smaller leaves and bracts and are slightly shorter than 'Freedom Red'. • 'Freedom Rose' grown in warm climates can be used as a dark pink color.

ECKESPOINT 'FREEDOM FIREWORKS'

Season	**Early mid-season**
Foliage	Dark green
Bracts	Novel dark red, narrow but long
Flowering response	8.0–8.5 weeks
Natural timing	November 21–25; similar timing and flowering schedule as the 'Freedom' family
Forms	2" (5 cm), 4" (10 cm), 6" (15 cm), 8" (20 cm), 10" (25 cm)
Media EC (mmhos/cm)*	1.5–2.0
Height potential	Medium

* Measured with a saturated media extract test. See chapter 8, Growing Media, for target EC using other testing procedures.

ECKESPOINT
'FREEDOM
FIREWORKS'
(continued)

Plant growth regulators	Minimal requirements unless grown at high density.
Postproduction	Outstanding
Cultural notes	• High density planting • Same culture as 'Freedom'.

ECKESPOINT
'JESTER' FAMILY

Season	**Early mid-season**
Foliage	Dark green
Bracts	Upright, dark red, red-and-pink jingle bells pattern and white-and-pink marble
Flowering response	8.0 weeks
Natural timing	November 21; timing is similar to 'Freedom'
Forms	2" (5 cm), 4" (10 cm), 6" (15 cm), 8" (20 cm), 10" (25 cm)
Media EC (mmhos/cm)*	1.5–2.0
Height potential	Medium
Plant growth regulators	PGRs are not typically required unless grown at high density.
Postproduction	Excellent
Cultural notes	• High density planting. • Easy to grow. • Small leaf size results in lower water requirements. Provide slightly drier conditions. • Leave two additional nodes at pinch for increased shoot count to maximize bract color and show. • Higher temperatures and humidity produce a flatter bract presentation but enhance bract expansion and size. Cooler, darker climates will emphasize the upright leaves and bracts.

---

* Measured with a saturated media extract test. See chapter 8, Growing Media, for target EC using other testing procedures.

**ECKESPOINT
'JINGLE BELLS
4.0'**

Season	**Early mid-season**
Foliage	Dark green
Bracts	Dark red with bright pink flecks
Flowering response	8.0 weeks
Natural timing	November 21; similar timing and flowering schedule as the 'Freedom' family
Forms	4" (10 cm), 6" (15 cm), 8" (20 cm), 10" (25 cm)
Media EC (mmhos/cm)*	1.5–2.0
Height potential	Short
Plant growth regulators	Minimal requirements.
Postproduction	Outstanding
Cultural notes	• High density planting. • Easy to grow. • Bract sensitive to sunburn if exposed to high light intensities at finish. Provide shade to prevent bract damage. • More stable than other 'Jingle Bell' types, although mutation rates up to 20% may still be observed.

**ECKESPOINT
'PUNCH' FAMILY**

Season	**Early mid-season**
Foliage	Dark green
Bracts	Full color series: red, rose, hot pink, light pink, and white
Flowering response	8.0 weeks
Natural timing	November 21
Forms	2" (5 cm), 4" (10 cm), 6" (15 cm), 8" (20 cm), 10" (25 cm), trees
Media EC (mmhos/cm)*	1.5–2.0
Height potential	Medium
Plant growth regulators	Minimal requirements
Postproduction	Excellent
Cultural notes	• Easy to grow. • Avoid heat and light stress on young plants. Provide shade until about two weeks after pinch. • Bracts and leaves are smaller and more serrated than other cultivars, making them ideal for use in miniature forms.

* Measured with a saturated media extract test. See chapter 8, Growing Media, for target EC using other testing procedures.

ECKESPOINT
'RED
VELVETEEN'

Season	**Early mid-season**
Foliage	Dark green
Bracts	Large, dark red, velvety
Flowering response	8.0 weeks
Natural timing	November 20
Forms	6" (15 cm), 8" (20 cm), 10" (25 cm)
Media EC (mmhos/cm)*	1.5–2.0
Height potential	Medium to tall
Plant growth regulators	May be needed in propagation and on finished plants.
Postproduction	Excellent
Cultural notes	Same culture as 'Autumn Red'.

ECKESPOINT
'STRAWBERRIES
AND CREAM'

Season	**Early mid-season**
Foliage	Dark green
Bracts	Unique cream and dark pink bicolor
Flowering response	8.5 weeks
Natural timing	November 23
Forms	2" (5 cm), 4" (10 cm), 6" (15 cm)
Media EC (mmhos/cm)*	1.5–2.0
Height potential	Short
Plant growth regulators	PGRs not usually required.
Postproduction	Excellent
Cultural notes	• High density planting. • Easy to grow. • Slow-growing. High temperatures and humidity enhance bract expansion and plant size. Provide 2–3 additional weeks of vegetative growth time to enhance finished height. • Similar timing and flowering schedule as the 'Freedom' family. • Small leaf size results in lower water requirements.

* Measured with a saturated media extract test. See chapter 8, Growing Media, for target EC using other testing procedures.

ECKESPOINT 'HOLLY POINT'

Season	**Mid-season**
Foliage	Dark green and gold variegated foliage
Bracts	Dark, ruby red
Flowering response	8.5 weeks
Natural timing	November 25
Forms	2" (5 cm), 4" (10 cm), 6" (15 cm)
Media EC (mmhos/cm)*	1.5–2.0
Height potential	Short to medium
Plant growth regulators	Compact growth habit, so not usually required.
Postproduction	Outstanding
Cultural notes	• High density planting. • FloraStar Winner (1999). • Soft pinch with leaf removal recommended. • Avoid heat and light stress on young plants. • Transplant and pinch 1–2 weeks earlier than other cultivars. • High temperatures can reduce branching. • Not recommended for single-stem production due to early splitting characteristics. • Finish the crop cool to intensify color and minimize bract expansion, allowing for maximum contrast of foliage and bracts.

RAI BEVELANDER'S 'MARBLESTAR'

Season	**Mid-season**
Foliage	Medium green
Bracts	Salmon pink with white edges
Flowering response	8.5 weeks
Natural timing	November 25
Forms	4" (10 cm), 6" (15 cm), 8" (20 cm), 10" (25 cm), hanging baskets, trees
Media EC (mmhos/cm)*	2.0–2.5
Height potential	Medium
Plant growth regulators	May be needed in propagation. Minimal requirements on finished plants.
Postproduction	Very good
Cultural notes	• Group with 'Peterstar' family. • Cuttings root slower than 'Freedom'.

* Measured with a saturated media extract test. See chapter 8, Growing Media, for target EC using other testing procedures.

RAI BEVELANDER'S 'MARBLESTAR'
(continued)

Cultural notes *(continued)*

- Foliage is susceptible to yellowing and burn on margins. Provide additional calcium and molybdenum throughout production to minimize the expression of this characteristic.
- Calcium sprays aid in the prevention of bract edge burn.

RAI BECKMANN'S 'MAREN'

Season	**Mid-season**
Foliage	Medium green
Bracts	Coral pink
Flowering response	8.5 weeks
Natural timing	November 25
Forms	4" (10 cm), 6" (15 cm), 8" (20 cm), 10" (25 cm), hanging baskets, trees
Media EC (mmhos/cm)*	2.0–2.5
Height potential	Medium
Plant growth regulators	May be needed in propagation. Minimal requirements on finished plants.
Postproduction	Very good
Cultural notes	• Group with 'Peterstar' family. • Bracts do not fade in warm temperatures. • Calcium sprays aid in the prevention of bract edge burn.

* Measured with a saturated media extract test. See chapter 8, Growing Media, for target EC using other testing procedures.

ECKESPOINT
'PRESTIGE'

Cultivar	**Mid-season**
Foliage	Dark green
Bracts	Dark red
Flowering response	8.5 weeks
Natural timing	November 25
Forms	2" (5 cm), 4" (10 cm), 6" (15 cm), 8" (20 cm), 10" (25 cm)
Media EC (mmhos/cm)*	1.5–2.0
Height potential	Medium
Plant growth regulators	May be needed in propagation. Minimal requirements on finished plants. No late-season stretch.
Postproduction	Excellent
Cultural notes	• Strong stems and upright growth habit. • Resistant to stem breakage. • Shoot growth is uniform with all bracts visible in the floral display. • Avoid heat and light stress on young plants. Provide shade until about two weeks after pinch.

ECKESPOINT
'SNOWCAP'

Season	**Mid-season**
Foliage	Medium green
Bracts	White
Flowering response	8.5 weeks
Natural timing	November 25
Forms	4" (10 cm), 6" (15 cm), 8" (20 cm), 10" (25 cm), hanging baskets, trees
Media EC (mmhos/cm)*	2.0–2.5
Height potential	Medium to tall
Plant growth regulators	Multiple applications often needed in propagation and on finished plants.
Postproduction	Very good
Cultural notes	• Cuttings root slower than 'Freedom'. • More compact than 'V-17 Angelika'. • To reduce bract damage, avoid drought stress and high salts. • Calcium sprays aid in the prevention of bract edge burn.

* Measured with a saturated media extract test. See chapter 8, Growing Media, for target EC using other testing procedures.

GROSS
'AMAZONE
PEPPERMINT'

Season	**Mid-late season**
Foliage	Medium green
Bracts	Pink with red flecks
Flowering response	9.0 weeks
Natural timing	December 1
Forms	4" (10 cm), 6" (15 cm), 8" (20 cm), 10" (25 cm), hanging baskets, trees
Media EC (mmhos/cm)*	2.0–2.5
Height potential	Medium to tall
Plant growth regulators	May be needed in propagation. Multiple applications usually required.
Postproduction	Very good
Cultural notes	Cuttings prefer warmer temperature during propagation.

ECKESPOINT
'BRIGHT RED
SAILS'

Season	**Mid-late season**
Foliage	Dark green
Bracts	Large, cascading red
Flowering response	9.0 weeks
Natural timing	December 1
Forms	6" (15 cm), 8" (20 cm), 10" (25 cm), hanging baskets
Media EC (mmhos/cm)*	1.5–2.0
Height potential	Medium
Plant growth regulators	Very responsive—half-rates are suggested.
Postproduction	Very good
Cultural notes	• Soft pinching with leaf removal is suggested for best results. • Avoid heat or high light stress on the young plants to assure uniform branching.

* Measured with a saturated media extract test. See chapter 8, Growing Media, for target EC using other testing procedures.

ECKESPOINT 'CHIANTI'

Season	**Mid-late season**
Foliage	Dark green
Bracts	Wine-red bracts and showy cyathia
Flowering response	9.0 weeks
Natural timing	December 1
Forms	2" (5 cm), 4" (10 cm), 6" (15 cm), 8" (20 cm)
Media EC (mmhos/cm)*	1.5–2.0
Height potential	Medium
Plant growth regulators	Compact growth habit, so often not required unless grown at high density.
Postproduction	Excellent
Cultural notes	• High density planting. • For a standard 6" crop, plant and pinch one week earlier than higher vigor cultivars. For larger pot sizes, provide additional vegetative growth time.

GROSS 'HEIRLOOM PEACH'

Season	**Mid-late season**
Foliage	Silvery green with white edges
Bracts	Peach
Flowering response	9.0 weeks
Natural timing	December 1
Forms	4" (10 cm), 6" (15 cm)
Media EC (mmhos/cm)*	2.0–2.5
Height potential	Short
Plant growth regulators	Compact growth habit, so not often required.
Postproduction	Very good
Cultural notes	• High density planting. • Transplant and pinch 10–14 days earlier than other cultivars to attain a similar height. • Avoid heat and light stress on young plants (up to 2 weeks after pinch). • Calcium sprays aid in the prevention of bract edge burn.

---

* Measured with a saturated media extract test. See chapter 8, Growing Media, for target EC using other testing procedures.

ECKESPOINT
'MAX RED'

Season	**Mid-late season**
Foliage	Dark green
Bracts	Large, dark red
Flowering response	9.0 weeks
Natural timing	December 1
Forms	2" (5 cm), 4" (10 cm), 6" (15 cm), 8" (20 cm)
Media EC (mmhos/cm)*	1.5–2.0
Height potential	Short to medium
Plant growth regulators	Compact growth habit, so not often required.
Postproduction	Excellent
Cultural notes	• High density planting. • Transplant and pinch 7–14 days earlier than other cultivars to attain a similar height.

PETER
JACOBSEN'S
'PETOY'

Season	**Mid-late season**
Foliage	Medium green
Bracts	Large red
Flowering response	9.0 weeks
Natural timing	December 1
Forms	6" (15 cm), 8" (20 cm), 10" (25 cm)
Media EC (mmhos/cm)*	2.0–2.5
Height potential	Medium
Plant growth regulators	Multiple applications often needed in propagation and on the finished crop.
Postproduction	Very good
Cultural notes	• Exceptionally thick stems. • Performs well in warm climates. • Large leaves in propagation may require additional space. • Soft pinch and leaf removal recommended to reduce the potential for dominant shoots. • Calcium sprays aid in the prevention of bract edge burn. • The large, fleshy bracts are susceptible to damage during shipping.

---

* Measured with a saturated media extract test. See chapter 8, Growing Media, for target EC using other testing procedures.

ECKESPOINT
'PLUM
PUDDING'

Season	**Mid-late season**
Foliage	Medium green
Bracts	Unique, plum purple
Flowering response	9.0 weeks
Natural timing	December 1
Forms	4" (10 cm), 6" (15 cm), 8" (20 cm), 10" (25 cm)
Media EC (mmhos/cm)*	2.0–2.5
Height potential	Medium
Plant growth regulators	PGRs often beneficial in propagation and on finished plants.
Postproduction	Very good
Cultural notes	• Grows similar to 'Peterstar' family. • Use PGRs more aggressively early in production to control height and avoid bract size reduction. • Susceptible to botrytis, so it will benefit from preventative spray programs. • Calcium sprays help to prevent bract edge burn. • Warm temperatures during finishing enhance bract color and expansion, especially in low light, cool climates.

ECKESPOINT
'RED VELVET'

Season	**Mid-late season**
Foliage	Dark green
Bracts	Large, dark red, velvety
Flowering response	9.0 weeks
Natural timing	December 1
Forms	4" (10 cm), 6" (15 cm), 8" (20 cm)
Media EC (mmhos/cm)*	1.5–2.0
Height potential	Medium to tall
Plant growth regulators	May be needed in propagation and on finished plants.
Postproduction	Excellent
Cultural notes	• Same culture as 'Autumn Red'. • Color and bract expansion are relatively late. Do not cool the greenhouse or shade until full bract maturity is reached.

* Measured with a saturated media extract test. See chapter 8, Growing Media, for target EC using other testing procedures.

GUTBIER 'V-17 ANGELIKA'

Season	**Mid-late season**
Foliage	Medium green
Bracts	Large, red, white, pink, marble
Flowering response	9.0 weeks
Natural timing	December 1
Forms	6" (15 cm), 8" (20 cm), 10" (25 cm), hanging baskets, trees
Media EC (mmhos/cm)*	2.0–2.5
Height potential	Tall
Plant growth regulators	Multiple applications often needed in propagation and on the finished crop.
Postproduction	Very good
Cultural notes	• Cuttings root slower than 'Freedom'. • Calcium sprays aid in the prevention of bract edge burn. • Well suited for warm-temperature and high-light growing conditions. However, provide shade and cool temperatures once bracts have matured to avoid fading.

ECKESPOINT 'JINGLE BELLS 3'

Season	**Late season**
Foliage	Medium green
Bracts	Multicolored red bracts with light pink flecks
Flowering response	9.5 weeks
Natural timing	December 5
Forms	6" (15 cm), 8" (20 cm), 10" (25 cm)
Media EC (mmhos/cm)*	2.0–2.5
Height potential	Medium
Plant growth regulators	Multiple applications usually required.
Postproduction	Very good
Cultural notes	• Ideal to group with 'Success' family and 'Monet Twilight'. • Challenging to root. Prefers warmer temp. • Color and bract expansion are relatively late. Do not cool the greenhouse or shade until full bract maturity is reached. • The most stable 'Jingle Bell' type. Look for dark pigmentation in young leaves and distinct stripe on petioles to select for uniform product when planting. The ability to visually select in the vegetative stage is unique to 'Jingle Bells 3'.

* Measured with a saturated media extract test. See chapter 8, Growing Media, for target EC using other testing procedures.

Season	**Late season**
Foliage	Medium green
Bracts	Unique, multicolored cream and rose
Flowering response	9.5 weeks
Natural timing	December 5
Forms	6" (15 cm), 8" (20 cm), 10" (25 cm), hanging baskets, trees
Media EC (mmhos/cm)*	2.0–2.5
Height potential	Medium to tall
Plant growth regulators	Multiple applications often needed in propagation and on the finished crop.
Postproduction	Excellent
Cultural notes	• Bracts deepen in color as they mature. • Ideal to group with 'Jingle Bells 3' and 'Success'. • Cuttings root slower than 'Freedom'.

ECKESPOINT
'MONET
TWILIGHT'

Season	**Late season**
Foliage	Dark green
Bracts	Dark red
Flowering response	10.0
Natural timing	December 8
Forms	4" (10 cm), 6" (15 cm)
Media EC (mmhos/cm)*	1.5–2.0
Height potential	Medium
Plant growth regulators	Minimal requirements in propagation and on finished plants.
Postproduction	Excellent
Cultural notes	• High density planting. • Performs well in warm climates. • Keep in a warm greenhouse until the bracts have expanded.

'RED
SPLENDOR'

* Measured with a saturated media extract test. See chapter 8, Growing Media, for target EC using other testing procedures.

ECKESPOINT 'SUCCESS' FAMILY

Season	**Late season**
Foliage	Medium green, oak-shaped
Bracts	Smooth, bright red, coral, and light pink
Flowering response	9.5 weeks
Natural timing	December 5
Forms	4" (10 cm), 6" (15 cm), 8" (20 cm), 10" (25 cm), trees
Media EC (mmhos/cm)*	2.0–2.5
Height potential	Medium
Plant growth regulators	Multiple PGR applications usually required in propagation and on the finished plants.
Postproduction	Excellent
Cultural notes	• Cuttings root slower than 'Freedom'. • Ideal to group with 'Jingle Bells 3' and Monet Twilight'. • Bract color expansion is later on 'Success' than other cultivars. Maintain warm greenhouses until bracts are fully expanded. • In northern climates, 'Success' should be grown without shade and with warm temperatures. • Bracts resist fading. • 'Success' should be grown drier than most other cultivars since constant high moisture can cause leaf yellowing or root loss.

* Measured with a saturated media extract test. See chapter 8, Growing Media, for target EC using other testing procedures.

'WINTER ROSE' FAMILY

Season	Late season
Foliage	Dark green, incurved
Bracts	Incurved, full color series: dark red, white, hot pink, pink, marble
Flowering response	9.5
Natural timing	December 5
Forms	4" (10 cm), 6" (15 cm), 8" (20 cm), mini trees
Media EC (mmhos/cm)*	1.5–2.0
Height potential	Short to medium
Plant growth regulators	Not required in propagation and minimal on finished plants.
Postproduction	Excellent
Cultural notes	• High density planting. • Does not branch as freely as most cultivars, but can be grown as a pinched plant. • Florel sprays (500 ppm) applied one week before and after pinching can improve the finished form. • Incurved bracts are difficult to spray for insect control. Use systemic pesticides for good pest control. • Small, incurved leaves result in low water requirement. Grow on a separate bench to help manage water requirements and to avoid overwatering. • Pinched plants require additional cuttings per pot and additional vegetative growth time as container size increases. • Suggested configurations: 3–5" pots: 1 plant per pot. 6–6.5" pots: 2 plants per pot. 7" pots: 3 plants per pot. 8" pots: 4 plants per pot.

* Measured with a saturated media extract test. See chapter 8, Growing Media, for target EC using other testing procedures.

15

PESTS AND PEST MANAGEMENT

Poinsettias are subject to attack by various insect pests under greenhouse conditions. Whiteflies, fungus gnats, and spider mites are the most prevalent pests of poinsettias, although other pests may occasionally cause problems. An integrated pest management (IPM) program employs various control strategies including, sanitation, exclusion, scouting, monitoring, biological control, and chemical control.

EXCLUSION

One of the first lines of defense against insect pests is preventing their entrance into the greenhouse. With increasing regulations and restrictions of chemical pesticide use, screening of all vents and doors may become an effective and economical means of excluding insects from greenhouses, especially in mild climates, where cold conditions are not available to reduce or eliminate insect and mite pressure each year. Consider insect exclusion screen in areas where invasion of whitefly from outside the green-house is heavy. A screen hole size of 462 microns will exclude whiteflies. Visit www.ecke.com for insect screening design considerations (follow the keywords: Poinsettias, Tech Help, Production Guidelines, Pest Control

Figure 15-1. Insect screens are used to exclude pests from entering through greenhouse vents.

193

with Insect Screening). Exclusion practices also include the thorough inspection of all incoming plant material.

SANITATION

Sanitation and cleanliness are also of utmost importance in an effective control program. Weeds and groundcovers in and around greenhouses provide favorable locations for pests that may easily move onto cultivated plants. Growers with the fewest insect problems are usually those with the cleanest operations. Remove debris daily, and cull piles from the greenhouse. Maintaining a host-free period before the poinsettias arrive can be extremely beneficial; overlapping spring flowering annuals with the beginning of the poinsettia season often results in thrips damage on the poinsettias.

CULTURAL PRACTICES

Several cultural factors can be easily implemented to improve pest control. For example, take advantage of chemical control opportunities after pinching the crop, since improved spray coverage can be achieved at this time. Remove mature leaves that have immature whiteflies on them after the new lateral shoots have developed. Proper fertilization can aid in pest management, since excess fertilization is known to increase pest feeding on the plants.

SCOUTING AND MONITORING

Another essential element of pest management is an effective scouting and monitoring program, since early detection is critical for pest control. Frequent (at least once a week) and thorough inspections of plants for the location and identification of insect and mite pests may help prevent an infestation from becoming an unmanageable epidemic. Focus the inspection for immature life stages on the older leaves, and look for the adults on the upper leaves. Tag infested "sentinel plants" for follow-up inspection to determine if control measures are effective or if immature life stages are continuing to develop toward adulthood.

Yellow sticky cards are an effective tool for monitoring flying insect populations. At a minimum, place one yellow sticky card per 1,000 ft.^{2} (93m^2), but one card per 250 ft.^{2} (23 m^2) is more effective. Keep in mind that sticky traps only catch flying pests, thus mites and mealybugs will not be caught. Therefore, plant inspection must also be an essential practice. Crops must be monitored at least weekly. Records should be kept on the number of pests observed and the pesticides applied. These records will help to evaluate the effectiveness of your pest management program. A sample scouting form is provided at the end of this chapter.

Yellow sticky cards are an effective tool for monitoring flying insects, such as whiteflies, thrips, and fungus gnats.

All employees should be involved in pest management. Employees that are involved in the day-to-day greenhouse activities often see more individual plants than scouts or managers do, so it is worthwhile to train all employees how to look for and identify greenhouse pests.

BIOLOGICAL CONTROL

Poinsettias are better candidates for biological control programs than many other greenhouse crops because they are often grown in a monoculture, which reduces the number of different predators or parasites that need to be introduced. Biological controls are not usually considered to be the only control method used on a poinsettia crop, but rather biological control is often a component of an overall IPM program.

Fungi that prey on insects can be used in a poinsettia IPM program. *Beauveria bassiana* is an example of a fungus that is very effective if used when the whitefly populations are low. These fungi are best used in conjunction with conventional pesticides or insect growth regulators.

Natural predators and parasitoids have also been shown to be effective for whitefly control on poinsettias, although higher cost may be an issue in some cases. *Encarsia formosa* has been used for many years for greenhouse whitefly, but is not effective for silverleaf whitefly. *Delphastus pusillus* combined with *Encarsia luteola* has proven to effective in trials against the silverleaf whitefly. *Eretmocerus eremicus* is a parasitic wasp that has been effective against silverleaf whitefly when used in conjunction with insect growth regulators.

Fungus gnat larvae can be controlled with *Bacillus thuringiensis* var. *israelensis, Hypoaspis* (syn. *Geolaelaps*) *miles* predatory mites, and *Steinernema feltiae* nematodes.

CHEMICAL CONTROL

Chemical control is still a major component of most poinsettia IPM programs. A Federally Registered List of Insecticides for Poinsettias is available at www.ecke.com (http://www.ecke.com/html/fastfax/pdfs/ Poin%insect.pdf). In addition to evaluating chemical effectiveness, there are a number of other factors to be considered before making an insecticide application.

PESTICIDE DECISIONS

There are two general approaches to pest control: preventive and curative. The preventive approach assumes that a particular pest will be a problem, so pesticide applications are made regardless of the pest population on the crop. This approach is usually taken for whitefly control on poinsettias since whiteflies are nearly always present during poinsettia production. A curative approach bases a pesticide application on the results of weekly scouting and monitoring rather than calendar dates. This approach can provide the desired pest control while potentially reducing the number of pesticide applications and thus the costs of pest control.

PESTICIDE RATES

The dose of active ingredient applied to a crop depends on the concentration of pesticide mixed in the tank and the volume of solution applied. The standard volume of solution applied for most pesticides is 2 qt. of solution applied per 100 ft.^{2} of bench space (1 gal./ 200 ft.^{2} [2 L/10 m^2]).

A range of recommended concentrations or rates of pesticide is provided on the product label, e.g., 1–2 fl. oz./100 gal. (7.4-14.8 ml/100L). The low end of the range is often considered the preventive rate or the rate that would be applied if the pest population were very low. The high end of the range is often considered the curative rate or the rate that would be applied if the pest population were relatively large.

PESTICIDE PHYTOTOXICITY

Before using an insecticide for the first time or when making an application to a new cultivar, treat a few plants and evaluate for phytotoxicity for three to five days before treating the entire crop. It is desirable to control pests prior to bract development since poinsettia bracts are more sensitive to pesticide injury than green leaves are. Phytotoxicity is more likely to occur on plants that are under water stress or at high temperatures. Also, the potential for phytotoxicity increases with higher rates of chemical and higher volumes of solution. Phytotoxicity may be caused by the adjuvants (surfactants or wetting agents) or carriers mixed with the pesticide by the manufacturer rather than by the active ingredient, so growers must be very cautious when adding their own adjuvants since this may increase the possibility of phytotoxicity.

Figure 15-3. Phytotoxicity on bracts can be caused by pesticides, adjuvants, or carriers.

PESTICIDE APPLICATION FREQUENCY

Pesticide application frequency depends on the pest's life cycle and the chemicals used. At warm temperatures, pests reproduce much faster (table 15-1), thus the pesticide applications must be more frequent. Five-to-seven-day spray intervals may be required during warm weather.

TABLE 15-1.
THE EFFECT OF TEMPERATURE ON THE NUMBER OF DAYS TO MATURE
FROM EGG TO ADULT FOR COMMON PESTS ON POINSETTIAS

	Days to mature from egg to adult	
Pest	Greenhouse temperature 77–86°F (25–30°C)	Greenhouse temperature 50–68°F (10–20°C)
Fungus gnats	12	27
Mealybugs	—	60
Spider mites	8	28
Thrips	10–15	57
Whitefly, greenhouse	21–26	—
Whitefly, silverleaf	16	31

PESTICIDE APPLICATION METHODS

Different application methods can improve pest control. For example:
- High-volume hydraulic sprayers are generally more effective for controlling the immature stages of whiteflies since the underside of the leaves is easier to contact. Both hydraulic sprayers and low-volume sprayers are effective for targeting whitefly adults. Hydraulic sprays to control whitefly adults may be most effective in the early morning, when the adults are least active and therefore easier to contact. Applications of smokes, aerosols, or fogs should be applied in the late afternoon, when whitefly adults are still flying and more likely to come in contact with the airborne pesticide particles.
- Drenches are required for controlling the immature stages (larvae) of fungus gnats since these occur in the growing medium.
- High-volume hydraulic sprays are more effective against spider mites since contact with the undersides of the leaves is required for most miticides to be effective.

PESTICIDE CLASS ROTATION

Rotate pesticide classes to avoid building pesticide resistance in the pest population. The number of sequential applications of a particular pesticide depends on the type of chemical and the label instructions. One chemical or chemical combination can be applied for at least one generation of the pest before rotating to another class of pesticides. For whiteflies, that would be at least two to three weeks of the same material.

PESTICIDE TANK MIXES

In most cases, tank mixes containing two or more pesticides should be avoided since these can increase the rate at which a pest population can develop resistance. One exception occurs when the two materials have a synergistic effect. For example, the application of Orthene mixed with a pyrethroid is more effective than the two products applied separately. A second exception occurs for materials where the insect is not likely to develop resistance. For example, pests are not likely to develop resistance to products such as soaps or oils.

COMMON PESTS OF POINSETTIAS

Following is a review of the biology and control of the most important poinsettia pests.

FUNGUS GNATS (*BRADYSIA* SPP.)

Fungus gnats are small, slender, dark-colored flies that are about 3 mm (¹/₈") long, with long legs and antennae. They resemble miniature mosquitoes. The larvae are slender, legless maggots that are white with black heads. Adults move rapidly over plants and usually congregate in

Figure 15-4. Fungus gnat larvae feed on callus tissue and young roots during propagation.

moist soils or under benches. Fungus gnat adults are often considered only "nuisance pests" that do not warrant any control measures. However, the larvae are capable of invading live plant tissue, feeding on tender roots, and causing cuttings and plants to wither and die. Fungus gnat larvae may transmit fungal diseases to poinsettias. Larvae may be especially active during propagation of poinsettia cuttings. The rooting environment is ideal for fungus gnats, and the rooting medium should be checked frequently for larvae activity.

Development: Eggs are laid in the soil, 30–120 eggs per female. Laid singly or in batches of up to 30, the eggs hatch in about a week. The larvae feed for about two weeks on organic matter in the growing medium, including plant roots, and can be seen when watering or fertilizing. The pupal stage lasts about four to six days prior to adult emergence.

Fungus gnat larvae can be destructive to poinsettia cuttings or potted plants. Larvae will feed on any organic matter in growing media, including tender roots and stem and leaf tissue that contacts media. Affected leaves exhibit holes with brown edges. Feeding on roots and stems can result in poor plant growth and eventual death.

Use of hydrated lime drenches (with or without copper sulfate) on soil surfaces, under benches, and on aisles will control the food source of this pest. In addition, this procedure enhances the cleanliness and aesthetics of the greenhouses. Lime is applied as a slurry (1.5 lb/gal. water [180 g/L]) with copper sulfate (1 lb./gal. water (120 g/L]).

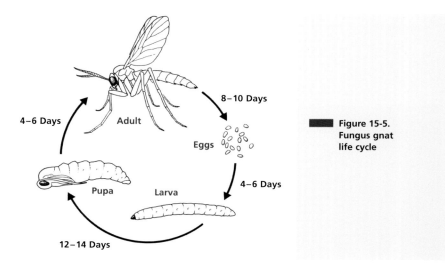

Figure 15-5.
Fungus gnat
life cycle

MEALYBUGS (*PHENACOCCUS, PLANOCOCCUS, PSEUDOCOCCUS*)

Plants infested with mealybugs look unsightly due to the whitish cottony mass of insects and the black sooty mold fungus that develops on honeydew excretions. Four species, citrus mealybug (*Planococcus citri*), Mexican mealybug (*Phenacoccus gossypii*), grape mealybug (*Pseudococcus maritimus*), and longtail mealybug (*Pseudococcus longispinus*), are found on poinsettias. The first three species lay eggs, whereas the longtail mealybug bears living young.

Figure 15-6. Mealybugs can infect poinsettia stems and leaf axils.

Mealybugs are soft-bodied insects that are covered with a whitish powdery wax. They are about 6 mm (¹/₄") in length when mature. Waxy filaments are often formed about the body. Unlike their relatives, the scales, mealybugs retain their legs and move around throughout their life.

Females lay masses of several hundred eggs in white cottony sacs. Egg-laying extends over a period of about ten days, and the eggs commence hatching in about two weeks. Mealybugs reach maturity in six to eight weeks. Immature males form cocoons and develop into flying adults. Adult males use their delicate wings to fly to females for fertilization.

Mealybugs injure plants by sucking the sap with their needlelike mouthparts. Cottony masses of wax form from their bodies, and their cottony egg sacs render the plants unsightly. Mealybugs excrete excess sugars, called honeydew. This honeydew attracts ants and serves as a growing medium for sooty mold.

Pesticide spraying appears to be the most economical way to control mealybugs. However, their waxy coating makes it difficult for pesticide sprays to penetrate and kill the insects. Repeated spray applications may be necessary.

MITES (*EOTETRANYCHUS* AND *TETRANYCHUS*)

Mites are not insects, since they have eight legs instead of six. The effectiveness of Marathon on whiteflies has resulted in fewer pesticide applications than growers used in the past. As a result, spider mites have become a more serious pest on poinsettias in recent years. Mites are very small; therefore, plant damage may occur before they are detected. Several species of mites have been reported to infest poinsettias. Two of the more common species, the two-spotted spider mite and the Lewis mite, are described below.

Two-spotted spider mite (Tetranychus urticae)

The adult female is less than 0.5 mm in length and very difficult to see without a 10x hand lens. They are greenish, yellowish, or reddish in color and often have dark spots on each side. The eggs are globular and pearly, amber, or red in color. Fine strands of silk are spun by the spider mites. When the infestation is very severe, parts of the plants may become completely webbed and masses of mites may hang from the tips of the leaves.

Figure 15-7. Two-spotted spider mites cause poinsettias leaves to have a silvery, speckled appearance.

Eggs are laid singly, and an adult female may lay from fifty to one hundred eggs. An entire generation may be completed in seven days when greenhouse temperatures are 80°F (27°C) and in fourteen days at 70°F (21°C), but under cooler conditions a period of two or more months may be required.

Mites are most active on the underside of leaves. On most plants, their presence becomes apparent by a fine mottling of the upper leaf surface caused by the puncturing of leaf cells. The cells immediately adjacent to these punctures collapse and dry so that the leaves become hard and almost parchment-like.

Currently, most spider mite control is by pesticide applications. However, there are several cultural practices that can help reduce mite problems. Eliminate weeds and rogue out infested plants. Mites are often carried into the greenhouses on employees' clothes; therefore, it is important not to handle infested plants before working with clean plants. Mites are not usually found on yellow sticky cards, so plants must be scouted to observed infestation.

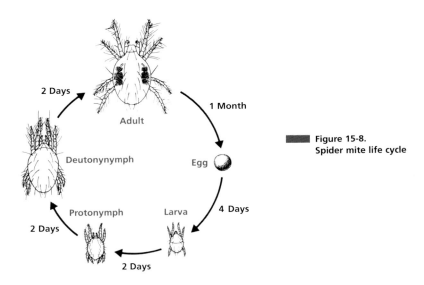

Figure 15-8.
Spider mite life cycle

Lewis mite (Eotetranychus lewisi)

Lewis mite adults are smaller than the two-spotted spider mite and they are yellowish in color. Injury to the leaf surface is very similar to that caused by the two-spotted spider mite. Very fine stippling of the upper leaf surface is the first indication of the presence of the mites. Follow the same procedures as for the control of the two-spotted spider mite.

NEMATODES

Roots of poinsettias grown outdoors or in native soil may show evidence of root-knot nematodes. These wormlike organisms are soilborne and cause damage by feeding on roots and/or transmitting disease. Root-knot nematodes create galls in poinsettia roots. Aboveground symptoms are similar to those caused by other root diseases, including stunting, chlorosis, and wilting.

Figure 15-9. Nematodes feed on roots and cause stunted growth, leaf chlorosis, and wilting.

SHORE FLIES (*SCATELLA STAGNALIS*)

Shore fly adults are similar in size to fungus gnats. They live in the same environment as fungus gnats and are often seen in great numbers in greenhouses. Shore flies resemble miniature house flies, while fungus gnats resemble miniature mosquitoes. Shore flies—in both the adult and larval stages—are not known to feed on plants. They are considered a nuisance pest, but shore fly larvae are capable of transmitting diseases to plants, and their presence indicates the conditions that are also attractive to fungus gnats. Dark, wet environments, standing water, and algae create ideal habitats. Yellow sticky traps attract shore flies in great numbers, making the identification of other insect pests difficult. Control measures are similar to those for fungus gnats.

Figure 15-10. Comparison of shore flies (left) and fungus gnats (right).

SNAILS AND SLUGS (*HELIX, MILAX, ZONOTOIDES*)

Slugs and snails can be very destructive pests in the greenhouse. Although they are primarily leaf feeders, they have been known to chew on the stems and roots. Both pests have soft bodies covered with slime and leave a slime trail as they move about. Snails form a hard shell for protection. Primarily night feeders, they hide during the day under pots or benches. They lay their eggs in the soil and reach maturity in a period of several months to two years. Control can be achieved by placing granular baits under the benches or on the growing medium surface.

THRIPS (*FRANKLINIELLA, HELIOTHRIPS, TAENIOTHRIPS, THRIPS*)

The poinsettia is not a preferred host for thrips. It is unusual to find thrips feeding on poinsettias, unless there is a large thrips population in the greenhouse. Thrips damage on poinsettias is most often observed during the summer, when the greenhouse is shared with flowering plants.

Thrips are slender, very small insects about 1–2 mm ($^1/_{25}$–$^1/_{12}$") in length. Adults are usually brown or yellowish in color. Immature stages are white or yellow with red eyes. Females may lay as many as 200 eggs. These eggs hatch in two to four days and the two larval stages last from three to seven days at 80°F (27°C). The resting pupal stages are spent in the growing medium and last from two to five days at 80°F (27°C). The adults live up to two months.

Adults and larvae feed by imbibing cell contents after piercing plant cells with their mouthparts. Affected cells fill with air giving leaves or flowers a silver-flecked appearance. Adults may fly into the greenhouse as early as mid-February during a mild winter, although this invasion usually

Figure 15-11. Thrips can be difficult to observe on poinsettias, however the damage cause by thrips is evident. Leaves appear scarred and deformed as they expand.

occurs when outdoor weeds and crops start to flower. Thrips can be difficult to find on vegetative tissue, so yellow or blue sticky traps are often used to monitor thrips populations.

WHITEFLY (*BEMISIA* AND *TRIALEURODES*)

Whitefly is the most serious insect pest of poinsettias. Greenhouse whitefly (GHWF) was the predominate species of whitefly attacking poinsettias prior to 1986. The silverleaf whitefly (SLWF) has also become a serious pest of poinsettias. SLWF is considered by many to be more difficult to control than GHWF. Neither whitefly is known to overwinter outside the greenhouse in northern areas, and they do not develop at temperatures below 50°F (10°C). There are subtle differences in the appearance of the two species, but their biology and control are similar. Several other species of whitefly have been reported on poinsettia although they aren't currently considered pests. Three such insects include the ash whitefly, *Siphoninus phillyreae*; the bandedwinged whitefly, *Trialeurodes abutilonea*; and the cloudywinged whitefly, *Dialeurodes citrifolii*.

*Greenhouse whitefly (*Trialeurodes vaporariorum*)*

Greenhouse whitefly (GHWF) adults are covered with white, waxy powder. They are about 2 mm (¹/₁₂") long, and cluster on the undersides of leaves.

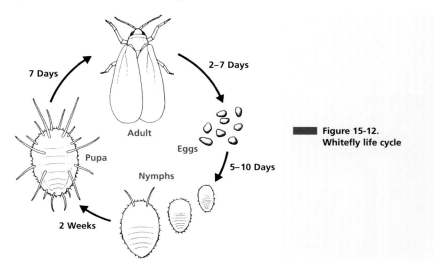

7 Days

2–7 Days

Adult

Eggs

Pupa

Nymphs

5–10 Days

2 Weeks

Figure 15-12.
Whitefly life cycle

The immature stages are oval, light in color, and have a fringe of white wax threads or filaments. Pupae have a translucent marginal fringe that is elevated in profile with sides perpendicular to the leaf.

Elongated eggs are attached to the leaves by a short stalk. The eggs are often laid in a circular pattern. Hatching takes place in five to ten days, and the young crawl a short distance and settle down. After feeding for about two weeks, a transformation stage (pre-pupa and pupa) is formed that lasts about a week. The adult female lives about one month, laying from 50 to 150 eggs. At temperature of 64–76°F (18–24°C), GHWF require approximately thirty-two days to mature from eggs to adult. The average lifespan of an adult GHWF is six days.

The adult feeds by inserting its mouthparts into a leaf and withdrawing sap from the phloem. Heavy feeding may result in a mottled or chlorotic appearance of infested leaves. In addition, honeydew excreted by the whiteflies is an excellent growing medium for sooty mold. As affected foliage becomes chlorotic or dies, infested plants lose color and generally deteriorate.

Yellow sticky traps should be used to determine and monitor the presence of whiteflies in greenhouses. Control measures should be taken with the first sign of infestation. When spraying plants, care should be taken to thoroughly cover the lower surfaces of the leaves.

*Silverleaf whitefly (*Bemisia argentifolii, *also known as strain B of the sweetpotato whitefly,* B. tabaci)

Silverleaf whitefly (SLWF) adults are smaller and tend to be more active than the GHWF. Silverleaf whitefly has less white wax on its body and usually appears more yellow. The easiest and most consistent way to identify this species is to examine the later-stage larvae or pupae. These immatures have a distinctive yellow color, while GHWF has a whitish or translucent appearance. SLWF immatures are ellipsoidal and appear to have a "waist" (an indentation or otherwise irregular shaped margin). No spires or fringes of hair or setae are present. The pupal stage of SLWF is convex or flattened in shape, whereas GHWF has a strong transparent marginal fringe and is elevated in profile with perpendicular sides. The average lifespan of an adult SLWF is around twenty-two days, during which time they produce seven times more eggs than GHWF. Adult females begin to lay eggs about four days after emerging. A female can lay as many as ten eggs per day.

Figure 15-13.
Silverleaf whitefly adult

High levels of SLWF feeding on poinsettias can cause white stems to develop and may also lighten bract color. If both SLWF and GHWF are present in a poinsettia crop, the SLWF will out-compete and eventually exclude the GHWF. Control measures are similar to control of the GHWF.

Figure 15-14. Silverleaf whiteflies cause poinsettia stems to turn white.

WORMS (LEPIDOPTERAE)

There are many types of lepidopterous larvae ("worms") that attack greenhouse plants. One of the most difficult to control is the cutworm group. This group attacks all parts of the plant, especially the growing tips and flowers. Cutworms are fat, shiny larvae, ranging in color from darker hues of gray and brown to yellow or green with various colored markings and striations. The adults are amber-colored, medium-sized moths. They are often seen flying around the lights at night. As adults, they feed only on nectar from the flowers and do not damage plants. The adult female lays several hundred eggs, usually on the foliage or below the flower heads. The larvae feed on plant tissue upon hatching from the egg.

The omnivorous looper, also called the tortrix, is another worm that feeds on poinsettias. The adults are tan, and the wings have an oblique, dark band across the middle. They are 10 mm ($^2/_5$") long when at rest. The wings fold along the back to give a bell-shaped appearance. The larvae are yellow or pale green with a light brown to black head. They are about 13 mm ($^1/_2$") long when mature. When disturbed, they wriggle violently, escaping backwards into their shelter or dropping by a silken thread.

Lepidoptera lay eggs in overlapping masses that resemble fish scales. Larvae emerge in one to three weeks. Newly hatched larvae feed on leaves or enter cut ends of poinsettia stems after cuttings are taken. The larvae curl the leaves over or web them together for protection. Feeding lasts for three to four weeks and is followed by a two-week pupal stage. An adult female may lay several hundred eggs.

Infestations can be expected as early as March with mild winter conditions, although heavy infestations usually occur when the night temperature starts to average above 50°F (10°C). Injury begins to be seen a week or two after the adult moths are observed flying around in the greenhouse. Pesticide applications have been the most economical and efficient way to control the larva and adults. Hand picking infested leaves and growing tips is not economically feasible if there is a heavy infestation.

16

❦

DISEASES AND DISEASE MANAGEMENT

Three factors are essential to the occurrence of a disease. There must be:
- a susceptible host (weak or damaged plants are the most susceptible)
- a pathogenic organism (fungi, bacteria, or virus)
- a favorable environment for the development of the disease.

Therefore, proper disease management is not simply applying preventative fungicide applications. Disease management integrates a range of techniques and procedures to reduce the susceptibility of the host, reduce the population or presence of the pathogen, and to avoid favorable environments for the disease.

Disease management can be achieved with a combination of:
- proper sanitation and handling
- excluding the pathogen from contact with the plants
- avoiding environments that are conducive to pathogen infection and/or cause a weakening of the host plants
- scouting, monitoring, and proper disease identification
- strategic application of biological and/or chemical products.

SANITATION & HANDLING

Consistent and rigorous sanitation practices are essential for avoiding or minimizing disease problems. Sanitation procedures should begin *before* the poinsettias arrive and continue throughout the crop. The following is a list of sanitation practices that should be used as a first line of defense against poinsettia diseases.
- Keep hose ends off the floor.
- Remove growing media and plant debris on and under benches.
- Eliminate weeds inside and outside the greenhouse since they can

211

harbor diseases and insects.

- Clean and disinfect everything the poinsettia crop encounters, such as hands, knives, and benches.
- Never re-use old pots without thoroughly washing and disinfecting them.
- Keep feet and shoes off of benches.
- Discard cuttings that have fallen on the floor.
- Immediately remove any disease-infected material from the greenhouse.
- Test your water source for the presence of pathogens. Water purification systems such as ultraviolet light, ozonation, or chlorination may be required if the source has significant pathogen levels.

Proper sanitation of materials, such as pots, flats, benches, and knives can be achieved with the use of quaternary ammonium compounds, bleach, TSP (sodium hypochlorite), and hydrogen peroxide products (ZeroTol).

ENVIRONMENT

Plant pathogens have specific environmental requirements and growers can reduce the risk of disease problems with good environmental control. Poinsettias that are under excessive stress—whether temperature, moisture, or fertility—are more susceptible to disease. Most of the fungi and bacteria that attack poinsettias are favored by high relative humidity and free water in contact with the plants. Cultural practices such as watering in the morning, avoiding water applications over the foliage, good air circulation, and the use of venting plus heat at night will help to reduce humidity levels around the crop and therefore reduce disease potential. For some diseases, such as botrytis blight, poinsettia cultivars differ in their susceptibility. In this case, choosing less susceptible cultivars will help avoid infection.

SCOUTING, MONITORING, AND IDENTIFICATION

Frequent monitoring is an important component of an integrated disease management program. Be aware of which diseases are most likely to occur at each stage of crop development, and monitor the crop at least once a week. Proper identification of the disease is necessary for the appropriate selection of chemicals. Fungicides work best on a preventative basis. To insure proper application of chemicals, monitor after fungicide applications as a regular follow-up procedure.

Periodically check the greenhouse water for disease-causing organisms, especially if the water comes from a nontreated source, such as a pond. Some water sources harbor plant pathogens such as *Erwinia, Phytophthora,* and *Pythium.* By putting all available tools together in an integrated program, growers can minimize the impact of diseases on their poinsettia crops.

BIOLOGICAL CONTROL

Biological controls are not yet widely available for poinsettia diseases. Growing media that suppress *Pythium* and rhizoctonia are currently available. Other examples of biological control include microbial fungicides to protect against some root and stem rots or foliar diseases and a bacterium to protect against crown gall.

CHEMICAL CONTROL

Most poinsettia growers use chemical controls to treat their crops. Fungicides are most successful when combined with the proper sanitation, environmental, and cultural practices. Pesticides work best when used on a preventative basis or early in the disease development. Rotation of different types of fungicides will help delay the development of resistance. Tank mixes with two different types of fungicides can potentially improve disease control.

Where chemicals are to be used, limited trials should be employed before treating an entire crop, unless there has been adequate prior experience. Fungicide sprays are not generally recommended on blooming poinsettias. Fungicide registrations may vary from state to state; therefore, it is the grower's responsibility to read and follow the label rates approved for his or her state.

For the most current information on chemicals with federal registration for use on specific diseases of poinsettias go to The Poinsettia Federal Disease Chart at www.ecke.com/html/fastfax/pdfs/Poin%20disease.pdf.

DISEASES OF POINSETTIAS

The following descriptions include pertinent information on the ecology of pathogens. This provides an important basis for planning control measures and preventing infection.

FUNGAL PATHOGENS

Alternaria blight (Alternaria euphorbiicola)

Symptoms

Leaf infections begin as small spots (1–3 mm in diameter) with tan centers, dark thin margins, and chlorotic halos. Spots enlarge to form irregular, necrotic lesions and leaves may be distorted, chlorotic, and abscise. Stem lesions appear light to dark brown and sunken.

Figure 16-1. Alternaria blight

Pathogen characteristics

Spores of *Alternaria euphorbiicola* are airborne and can survive dry periods before infecting the plant during extended periods of wetness. *Alternaria* has primarily occurred on poinsettia crops grown outdoors in Florida and Hawaii during warm, rainy weather.

Suppression

Minimizing leaf wetness and removing diseased plants will help control this disease. See the Poinsettia Federal Disease Control Chart for a list of pesticides registered for *Alternaria* control on poinsettias.

Black root rot (Thielaviopsis basicola*)*

Symptoms

Symptoms of this disease include black roots and black chlamydospores (resting spores) in the pith of stems and in roots. Lower leaves may become chlorotic, necrotic, and defoliate. Other symptoms include stunting, lesions and cracks at the base of the stem, and sudden plant collapse, especially when exposed to temperatures below 60°F (15°C).

Figure 16-2. Black root rot or *Thielaviopsis*

Pathogen characteristics

At one time this was a very common disease of poinsettias, but it occurs less frequently with soilless media. *Thielaviopsis basicola* is a soilborne fungus, and its chlamydospores can survive in growing media for long periods of time. Cool temperatures, excessively wet growing media, and high pH encourage development of black root rot.

Suppression

Rogue infected plants, avoid low growing media temperatures, and lower the growing media pH below 5.5. Fungus gnats and shore flies may spread this fungus. Drench with fungicides. This pathogen is less commonly observed on poinsettias since using soilless growing media has become a standard practice. See the Poinsettia Federal Disease Control Chart for a list of pesticides registered for *Thielaviopsis* control on poinsettias.

*Botrytis blight or gray mold (*Botrytis cinerea*)*

Symptoms

Botrytis blight is the most prevalent disease of poinsettias. It can occur during all stages of development and attacks all above ground plant parts. The rot begins as a water-soaked area with tan-to-brown lesions, regardless of the tissue infected. Under humid conditions, a gray fuzzy mold composed of mycelia and spores form on the rotting tissue. Botrytis quickly infects leaves during propagation. On young stems, the disease may begin at a wound or where the fungus grows down the petiole into the stem. On mature stems, dry, tan cankers may form. The cankers may eventually girdle the stem, resulting in chlorosis and wilting of leaves above the canker. Red bracts develop a purplish color in infected areas.

Figure 16-3. Botrytis blight, or gray mold

Pathogen characteristics

Gray mold is spread through airborne fungal spores that can be assumed to be present everywhere at all times. The fungus thrives on dead or decaying organic matter and plant debris, but it will also infect healthy leaves and bracts when the environmental conditions are ideal. The same fungus can attack hundreds of different plant species, so botrytis from other crops can spread to poinsettias, and vice versa. Botrytis blight is most common on poinsettias during propagation and again at the end of the blooming cycle. This fungus can grow at temperatures ranging from 32–96°F (0–36°C), so temperature control will not eliminate this disease. Botrytis spores require free moisture on the plant surface for a minimum of four hours to germinate and infect plant tissues. The sporulation stage of gray mold requires high relative humidity (90–100%); therefore, cultural practices that reduce relative humidity and eliminate moisture condensation on the plants will help to control botrytis blight.

Suppression

The first line of defense is control of the greenhouse environment. For finished plants, maintain constant air circulation with horizontal airflow fans. Water plants in the morning, and exhaust humid air out of the greenhouse before closing the greenhouse up for the night. Do not get foliage and bracts wet while irrigating. During cold weather, you can heat the greenhouse to allow water to evaporate, then exhaust the humid air while bringing cold, drier air into the greenhouse. This technique can help reduce greenhouse humidity so that less condensation occurs inside the greenhouse and the leaves stay drier during the night. Space plants to allow for air movement through the plant canopy. Keep temperatures above 60°F (16°C) and remove all dead plant material. The propagation environment is ideal for botrytis infection, so daily cleaning of infected leaves is necessary. Fungicides may be applied for reduced botrytis infection. Thorough coverage is important, and frequent treatment is necessary to provide protection to newly developing plant tissue. See the Poinsettia Federal Disease Control Chart for a list of pesticides registered for botrytis control on poinsettias.

Choanephora *wet rot* (Choanephora cucurbitarum)

Symptoms

The fungus *Choanephora cucurbitarum* causes a soft, wet rot of poinsettias. The symptoms can be similar to botrytis and rhizopus blight. This disease is most prevalent under the hot, humid conditions of propagation and is not active below 58°F (14°C). The symptoms include a soft, wet, mushy rot of leaves, petioles, and stems. If conditions remain hot and moist, this disease can continue to develop during the blooming season. On woody stems, the fungus may only cause necrotic lesions rather than a mushy rot. *Choanephora* has primarily been observed in very warm climates, such as Florida.

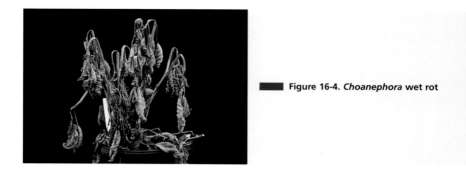

Figure 16-4. *Choanephora* wet rot

Suppression

Avoid leaf wetness and provide good air circulation.

Corynespora *bract and leaf spot (*Corynespora cassiicola*)*

Symptoms

The fungus *Corynespora cassiicola* can cause brown-to-black spots up to 3 cm (1") in diameter along the margins of poinsettia bracts or leaves. Chlorotic halos may surround the spots on the leaves of an infected plant. Tissue infected from this disease can look similar to botrytis, but *Corynespora* produces brown conidia, unlike the gray ones produced by botrytis. This disease was first found in Florida in 1982. It has primarily been a problem in Florida during the winter but has also been reported in Louisiana.

Figure 16-5. *Corynespora* bract and leaf spot

Suppression

Reduce relative humidity and leaf wetness. See the Poinsettia Federal Disease Control Chart for a list of pesticides registered for *Corynespora* control.

Fusarium *stem rot (*Fusarium *spp.)*

Symptoms

Stem rots and cankers on poinsettias may occasionally show evidence of *Fusarium* spp. The symptoms of the disease include a brown-to-black rot on the base of the stem, usually beginning just above the soil line. The infected tissue may become a shrunken canker with distinct margins. Internal discoloration may extend beyond the canker margins. Infected plants will wilt and may eventually die.

Figure 16-6. *Fusarium* stem rot

Suppression

See the Poinsettia Federal Disease Control Chart for a list of pesticides registered for *Fusarium* control.

Phytophthora *crown and stem rot (*Phytophthora *spp.)*

Symptoms

Phytophthora generally causes stem rot, but this fungus can attack all parts of the poinsettia plant. Gray-to-brown or black lesions and basal cankers develop on poinsettia stems. Under warm, wet conditions the disease continues to develop. Black streaks may appear on the stem, and the infected branch or entire plant will wilt and die. Under less-than-optimum conditions (low moisture and cool temperatures) a brown stem canker will form and the pith cavity and vascular area will also turn brown. The internal discoloration may extend above and below the visible canker. Leaf symptoms begin as small tan-to-grayish-brown spots, and eventually the entire leaf turns brown to black. On bracts the lesions will appear purple or brown. Black lesions can also develop on cyathia. The disease can spread quickly on leaf, bract, and cyathia tissue, resulting in extensive blighted areas.

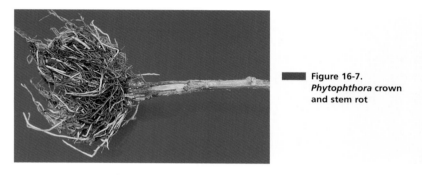

Figure 16-7.
Phytophthora **crown and stem rot**

Pathogen characteristics

This disease may be caused by several species of water mold fungi.
It is readily spread in water, and the fungi are favored by high moisture availability, low oxygen, and high salt levels.

Suppression

Rogue infected plants and avoid scattering debris from infected plants. Drench the medium with fungicides. Avoid overwatering—proper watering practices are essential to reduce losses. See the Poinsettia Federal Disease Control Chart for a list of pesticides registered for *Phytophthora* control on poinsettias.

*Powdery mildew (*Oidium *spp.,* Leveillula clavata*)*

Symptoms

All aboveground portions of the poinsettia are susceptible to powdery mildew. During the early stages of infection, the white spots can look much like pesticide residue. If the foliage is constantly moist, as in propagation conditions, the powdery mildew fungus may begin to grow on the undersides of leaves, making detection more difficult. When a powdery mildew colony is well established on the undersurface of a leaf, a chlorotic patch may appear on the upper surface. Tissue infected with powdery mildew can become necrotic.

Figure 16-8. Powdery mildew

Pathogen characteristics

Powdery mildew can occur during any phase of poinsettia production, but is most likely to develop in the spring or late fall, when the environmental conditions are most favorable and there is a greater fluctuation between day and night temperatures. High humidity is a necessity for powdery mildew development.

Suppression

Scout both the upper and lower leaf surfaces for infected leaves. Increase air movement around the crop to reduce relative humidity. See the Poinsettia Federal Disease Control Chart for a list of pesticides registered for powdery mildew control on poinsettias.

Pythium *root rot* (Pythium *spp.)*

Symptoms

This fungal disease begins as a brown root rot that may progress up the stem. The outer surface of roots infected with *Pythium* will easily slough off, leaving only a threadlike root. As the disease progresses, a brown or black canker may form at the soil line, especially on infected cuttings. Other symptoms include chlorosis of the lower foliage, stunting, wilting, and plant death. Fungus gnat larvae often appear together with *Pythium*. Fungus gnats and shore flies can contribute to the spread of this disease. *Pythium* root and stem rot may appear during propagation, but this is more commonly a problem toward the end of the blooming season, as low temperatures prevail and roots become less active. Poorly drained, excessively wet potting media are conducive to this disease development.

JIM FAUST

■ **Figure 16-9.** *Pythium* **root rot**

Pathogen characteristics

Several water mold fungi that are easily spread in water may cause *Pythium* root rot. There are no airborne spores, but the fungi may be carried on dust particles. The fungi are favored by high moisture availability. Different species of *Pythium* are prevalent under warm and cool temperatures.

Suppression

Rogue infected plants and avoid scattering debris from infected plants. Preventative fungicide drenches are commonly used due to the relatively high frequency of occurrence. Proper watering practices are essential to reduce losses due to *Pythium.* See the Poinsettia Federal Disease Control Chart for a list of pesticides registered for *Pythium* control on poinsettias.

Rhizoctonia *stem and root rot (*Rhizoctonia solani*)*

Symptoms

Rhizoctonia solani is the most frequent cause of stem rot on poinsettias. This disease begins with an oval, reddish brown lesion on the stem near the soil line and proceeds to encompass the entire stem. This disease may progress up the stem as well as down into the roots. *Rhizoctonia* is most likely to occur in the early stages of poinsettia production, in propagation or on recently transplanted cuttings. Under propagation conditions the leaves may rot and the stems become mushy. On mature plants, a stem canker may form. The brown-to-black canker begins at or below the soil line and is sunken. Lower leaves may become chlorotic and then fall off. Stem cankers may kill or stunt the growth of an infected plant.

■ **Figure 16-10.** *Rhizoctonia* **stem and root rot**

Pathogen characteristics

Rhizoctonia stem rot is caused by a fungus that is easily spread by water. There are no airborne spores, but the fungus may be carried on dust particles. Warm temperatures and environmental conditions that cause plant stress, such as high salts and improper watering practices, favor this disease.

Suppression

Rogue infected plants and avoid scattering debris from infected plants. Preventative fungicide drenches are commonly used due to the relatively high frequency of occurrence. See the Poinsettia Federal Disease Control Chart for a list of pesticides registered for *Rhizoctonia* control on poinsettias.

Rhizopus blight (Rhizopus stolonifera)

Symptoms

Rhizopus is relatively uncommon on poinsettias, but it can be very destructive under favorable conditions in propagation. In Florida, rhizopus has also affected the leaves, bracts, and stems of blooming poinsettias. The symptoms consist of a soft, mushy brown rot. The black spores of rhizopus make it easily distinguishable from the gray botrytis spores. The abundant mycelia give the disease a "bearded" appearance. It is necessary to use a hand lens or microscope to distinguish rhizopus from *Choanephora* wet rot since both have grayish mycelia and dark, round sporangia. Once the sporangia are mature, they split open to expose dark-colored spores. Rhizopus spores are round and attached around a central enlarged stalk. In contrast, *Choanephora* spores are football-shaped and found in several clusters rather than all attached to one stalk.

Figure 6-11. Rhizopus blight

Pathogen characteristics

The spores are airborne and may be spread by water. *Rhizopus stolonifera* requires high temperatures, 80–90°F (26–32°C), high relative humidity (above 75%), and wounded or weakened host tissue to attack. The mode of attack is similar to bacterial soft rot, with an enzyme being released to cause cell deterioration. When wounds callus or heal rapidly, the fungus does not become established. It could be referred to as a "high temperature botrytis."

Suppression

Sanitation and careful handling of cuttings to avoid injury are the best methods of preventing rhizopus. No fungicides are currently registered to control rhizopus on poinsettias.

Scab *(Sphaceloma poinsettiae)*

Symptoms

On stems and leaf petioles, the symptoms include scablike or raised lesions with tan centers often surrounded by white, red, or purple margins, sometimes completely encircling the stem, causing dieback above the infected area. Heavily infected branches may exhibit a gibberellin-like effect and grow twice as long as other branches. On leaves, the symptoms include brown, round-to-angular spots with purple margins. A yellow or bleached out area develops near the leaf spots and the leaves with spots are often distorted or puckered.

Figure 16-12. Scab

Pathogen characteristics

Poinsettia scab is not a common disease on greenhouse-grown poinsettias, although it is regularly found outdoors in Florida, Hawaii, Puerto Rico, and other areas of outdoor production. It was originally discovered in Florida in 1940. Hot, wet conditions favor development of this disease. The fungus is primarily spread by splashing water. Leaf scarring, odema, *Alternaria* leaf spot and environmental disorders can produce similar symptoms to poinsettia scab.

Suppression

This disease has been occasionally seen in greenhouses in North America, but with early detection, rouging and fungicide treatment, it can be eliminated quickly. See the Poinsettia Federal Disease Control Chart for a list of pesticides registered for *Sphaceloma* control on poinsettias.

BACTERIAL PATHOGENS

Bacterial soft rot (Erwinia carotovora)

Symptoms

Bacterial soft rot primarily occurs in propagation. Cuttings develop a soft, mushy rot beginning at the basal end within three to five days of sticking. The rot may continue to move up the stem, destroying the entire cutting.

JAN HALL

**Figure 16-13.
Bacterial soft rot (*Erwinia*)**

Pathogen characteristics

The bacterium is prevalent on dead plant material and can be carried on windblown dust, unsterilized tools, and the hands of workers. It spreads readily in water and may be found in pond water. Wounded tissue, waterlogging of the rooting medium, high temperatures, and other stress factors encourage the development of this disease.

Suppression

Avoid waterlogging the rooting medium. Keep propagation temperatures below 90°F (32°C). See the Poinsettia Federal Disease Control Chart for a list of pesticides registered for *Erwinia* control on poinsettias.

Bacterial stem rot (Erwinia chrysanthemi)

This species of *Erwinia* is much less common than *E. carotovora*. *E. chrysanthemi* will occasionally cause a stem rot on poinsettias. The infected stems will darken in color, wilt, and then collapse. This disease occurs near the end of the poinsettia crop cycle. Warm, humid conditions and soft, succulent growth encourage the development of bacterial stem rot.

Bacterial canker (Curtobacterium flaccumfaciens *pv.* poinsettiae [previously Corynebacterium flaccumfaciens *pv.* poinsettiae])

Symptoms

Stem symptoms of this disease include water-soaked stems, stem cankers, stem dieback, and black streaks in the stem. The black streaks usually start

■ Figure 16-14. Bacterial canker

at the apex of the plant and do not extend to the soil line. Infected stems can crack open, and bacteria may ooze out. Brown spots with chlorotic halos form on the leaves of infected plants, and the leaves may become distorted. This bacterium can also cause small brown angular leaf spots surrounded by chlorotic halos. In these cases, bacterial ooze may be present on the undersides of leaf spots.

Pathogen characteristics

This disease may occur anytime during the production cycle. Warm, wet, humid conditions favor disease development. Under dry conditions, infected plants may produce new growth and lateral branches. It is unusual to find bacterial canker on poinsettias.

Suppression

Rogue infected plants. Avoid overhead irrigation and syringing. Keep humidity as low as practical, and avoid excessively high temperatures. Plants should be protected from wind and/or rain, and good sanitation practices must be followed.

Bacterial leaf spot (Xanthomonas campestris *pv.* poinsettiaecola)

Symptoms

This pathogen affects the leaves of poinsettias, producing dull, gray-to-brown, water-soaked lesions several millimeters in diameter. The spots are first visible on the undersides of the leaves. The lesions become dark

**Figure 16-15.
Bacterial leaf spot**

brown with age and develop yellow halos . Heavily infected leaves may drop prematurely. This disease is most often seen on outdoor-grown poinsettias in warm, humid climates, such as Florida. Although this bacterium is named *poinsettiaecola,* it has infected other *Euphorbia* species such as the crown-of-thorns and can be transmitted from one species to another. Two additional pathovars—*Xanthomonas campestris* pv. *euphorbiae,* and pv. *manihotis*—have been reported to cause leaf spots on poinsettias.

Suppression

Avoid leaf wetness. See the Poinsettia Federal Disease Control Chart for a list of pesticides registered for *Xanthomonas* control on poinsettias.

*Greasy canker (*Pseudomonas viridiflava*)*

Symptoms

An oily or greasy canker that occurs primarily at the site of a wound on the stem is a prominent characteristic of this disease. The canker will dry out with age, becoming tan to brown with a papery texture. This bacterium does not cause a soft rot. It can also cause water-soaked spots on leaves, with a chlorotic halo, and blight of the bracts and cyathia. Symptoms of the blight include a rapidly spreading necrosis with bacteria oozing out of the infected tissue. Infected cyathia may drop prematurely. Hot (80–90°F [26–32°C]), humid conditions favor development of this disease in California trials, while tests in Florida showed severe disease at 50–60°F (10–15°C) with less disease development at 81°F (27°C). Under low

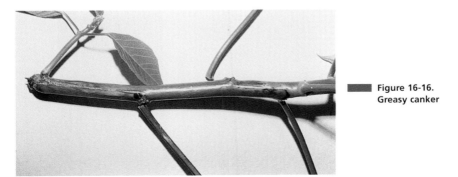

Figure 16-16.
Greasy canker

humidity, the disease will stop developing and infected stem cankers will dry out.

Suppression

See the Poinsettia Federal Disease Control Chart for a list of pesticides registered for *pseudomonas* control.

VIRUSES

Several viral diseases have been identified on poinsettias, although none of them are of major importance. Poinsettia mosaic virus was-first described in 1977. This virus may cause a mild mottling or no symptoms at all. Poinsettia cryptic virus was reported in Germany in 1980, but this virus does not cause any symptoms on poinsettias. Crinkle mosaic has also been reported on poinsettias.

17

PHYSIOLOGICAL DISORDERS AND PRODUCTION PROBLEMS

Like most crops, poinsettias are subject to a range of disorders that do not have a singular factor as the source point, such as nutrition, pesticide phytotoxicity, or specific actions. In many cases, these disorders result from multiple layers of influences and may not be expressed uniformly in the crop or even within a specific cultivar. Growers are constantly challenged to avoid these problems, as they reduce the value of the finished plants and can even result in significant losses. Fortunately, with good crop management practices and the improvements in genetics we have experienced in the past ten to fifteen years, it is possible to prevent most of the problems identified in this chapter.

BILATERAL BRACT SPOTS

Often called "rabbit tracks," this condition is characterized by breakdown of the tissues between the veins located on either side of the midrib. It occurs in later stages of bract expansion. The condition can effectively

Figure 17-1. Rabbit tracks are characterized by the breakdown of the tissues between the veins located on either side of the midrib.

lower plant quality, rendering it unsalable. Modern cultivars are relatively resistant to this phenomenon, so it not commonly seen today.

Bilateral bract spots seem to be associated with high relative humidity or changing humidity levels. High temperatures, above 70°F (21°C), especially high night temperatures during the bract development phase, cause a greater incidence of bilateral bract spots. High levels of nitrogen fertilization near the end of the crop or high nitrogen content in the plants also cause a higher frequency of bilateral bract spots.

BRACT EDGE BURN

Bract edge burn, or bract necrosis, describes a disorder in which the bract margins develop necrotic spots as the bracts are reaching full expansion. As cells along the edges of the bracts die, small, brown necrotic spots appear on the largest, most mature bracts. The spots may enhance a secondary botrytis infection in which the germinating spores easily invade the soft dying tissues and spread to adjoining bract tissue, thus increasing the problem. As the condition worsens, the entire bract edge may die and turn brown, giving a "burned" appearance.

Symptoms often first appear in the greenhouse and then worsen during shipping or after the plants have reached their market destination. Most susceptible are excessively mature plants that are sent to the market in less than prime condition. Fortunately, the dry environment in the average consumer's home is not conducive to bract edge burn.

Calcium seems to be the most important nutrient associated with bract

Figure 17-2. Initial (left) and advanced (right) bract edge burn symptoms.

edge burn. There is also information suggesting silica may be a key factor; however, this theory is less accepted in the grower community. Plants use calcium to build strong cell walls that are resistant to environmental stresses and pathogens. Calcium is a unique plant nutrient in that it relies on the flow of water to be transported throughout the plant. Since bracts lack functioning stomata, less water and less calcium are transported into the bracts. The result is that the margins of large bracts may experience a localized calcium deficiency. Plenty of calcium may be present in the growing medium, yet insufficient calcium may be transported to the bract margins as a result of root loss, high humidity, low light levels, low temperatures in the medium, or excess salts in the growing medium.

Foliar applications of calcium can be used to help prevent bract edge burn. The standard practice is to apply 200–400 ppm calcium (with calcium chloride) weekly from the time of first color to the market date. Use a laboratory- or reagent-grade calcium chloride, since fertilizer-grade salts may have impurities that may cause bract damage. Apply the calcium as a fine, low-pressure mist, and apply only enough to wet the bracts without run-off.

Bract edge burn was particularly problematic in the 1980s and early 1990s on cultivars such as Gutbier 'V-14 Glory' and Gross 'Supjibi'. It is less common today due to the introduction of less-susceptible cultivars and now that many growers use foliar calcium sprays as a preventive measure.

CHLORINE INJURY

Improper use of bleach or other chlorine-containing disinfectants can result in the development of black streaks, blotches, or ring patterns on the

Figure 17-3. Chlorine injury resulting from the improper use of bleach.

lower stems and petioles. Black veins sometimes develop on the underside of the leaves. These symptoms occur most commonly when poinsettias are placed on benches without first rinsing the disinfectant or allowing the benches to fully dry. The symptoms are most noticeable on white cultivars, but other cultivars are also susceptible.

Black streaks and blotches are general symptoms on poinsettias that can occur whenever the latex-producing system becomes injured or plugged. The streaks or blotches generally begin near the soil line and may progress up the stem. Excessive stem injury when taking cuttings can cause black streaks. Symptoms of stem rots on poinsettias caused by fungi such as *Rhizoctonia solani, Pythium* spp., and *Fusarium* spp. can include black streaks on the stems; however, the streaks would not be the primary or most obvious symptoms.

ENATIONS

Enations are ruffled leaf tissue that appear on the interveinal leaf tissue on the underside of leaves. These symptoms most often appear during periods of heat stress when use of airflow across the crop results in constant movement of the foliage or bracts. The symptoms have also been attributed to exposure to asphalt fumes. Although the exact cause is still unknown, this disorder does not usually impact flowering plant quality.

JOHN DOLE

Figure 17-4. Enations result from heat stress.

EPINASTY

Epinasty refers to the wilted appearance of leaves and bracts in reaction to ethylene. Historically, epinasty was observed on poinsettias after having spent a couple of days in a box or sleeve during shipping. Also, retailers have always been warned against placing poinsettias in the produce section of grocery stores where ethylene from the various fruits or vegetables might result in epinasty. Eckespoint 'Lilo' was the first cultivar to be highly resistant to epinasty, and since its introduction most modern cultivars have proven to be resistant to epinasty.

Figure 17-5.
Epinasty describes the wilted appearance of poinsettia bracts and leaves in reaction to ethylene (on left) compared with an unaffected plant.

HEAT DELAY

Poinsettia flowering can be delayed by high night temperatures (above 74°F [23°C]) that occur during flower initiation (fig. 10-2). High night temperatures are common during late September in many parts of North America. At this time, poinsettias are less susceptible to heat delay if short days (less than eleven hours) are provided (natural photoperiod is approximately twelve hours); however, the process of providing short days with black curtains can actually increase night temperatures due to heat buildup under the curtains. Growers faced with this problem often opt to wait to pull blackcloth until early in the morning (prior to sunrise) so that an appropriate dark period is still provided, but during the cooler morning hours instead of the warm, afternoon period when heat buildup under the cloth is a problem.

LATE STRETCH

Late stretch refers to the tendency for certain cultivars to achieve a significant portion of their overall height during the last few weeks of production. The result is an excessively tall plant with uneven heights of the flowering shoots. Several factors contribute to late stretch.

Certain cultivars, such as Eckespoint 'Freedom', elongate relatively slowly (0.5" [1.3 cm] internodes) when grown at wide spacing; however, they elongate very rapidly (larger than 2" [5 cm] internodes) when placed at tight spacing. As a result, little growth regulator may be used in September and early October. Then the canopy closes together in mid-October, and the elongation rate increases rapidly. Late stretch is less common with some cultivars because plant growth regulator is regularly applied to these cultivars during the early season. As a result, there is some residual growth regulation when the canopy closes together and the elongation rate doesn't dramatically increase.

The transitional bracts, not the true bracts, generate the initial color display of 'Freedom'; therefore, 'Freedom' is still elongating (expanding internodes between the transitional bracts) while it is close to being marketable. In contrast, the true bracts generate the initial color display of many cultivars. As a result, these cultivars are nearly finished elongating as the plant approaches marketability.

Another potential cause of late stretch in certain cultivars (such as 'Freedom') has been in reaction to fertilization programs and higher EC levels in the growing medium than may be desirable. For example, dark-leaf poinsettias generally require about 25% less fertilizer than do medium-green-leaf types such as 'Peterstar'. Under the fertilizer program required for 'Peterstar', water uptake for 'Freedom' may be less than optimum due to the higher medium EC. Once growers reduce fertilizer levels as color is forming in late October to early November, the lower EC levels promote better water uptake and can result in late stretch. Current recommendations for poinsettia nutrition suggest that acceptable EC level (based on a saturated media extract test) for dark-leaf poinsettias is between $1.5-2.0$ mmhos/cm^2, while medium-green-leaf poinsettias should be maintained between $2.0-2.5$ mmhos/cm^2. Close monitoring and adherence to these levels can help minimize the risk of late stretch due to fertilizer levels and water uptake potential.

Paclobutrazol (Bonzi or Piccolo) drenches applied one to three weeks prior to the market date will reduce late-season stem elongation (see chapter 5, Height Control, for further details). Some growers will use a "late-season graphical tracking curve" to help anticipate late stretch.

LATEX ERUPTION

Plants belonging to the *Euphorbia* genus contain latex, which is exuded upon cell injury. This became a problem in poinsettia production as far back as when the cultivar 'Paul Mikkelsen' and its sports first became popular. The malady is sometimes termed "crud." The mechanism is one of bursting cells with latex spilling over the tissue resulting from high turgor pressure. Upon drying, the latex hardens, creating a growth-restricting layer. When this occurs at developing stem tips, distortion or stunting of growth results. The exuding of latex has also been observed on fully expanded leaves, sometimes giving the appearance of mealybug infestation due to the white splotches scattered over the leaf surface.

Figure 17-6. Latex eruption

All contributing factors have not been clearly defined, but several obvious ones include high moisture availability and high humidity, both of which result in high fluid pressure within the cells. Low temperature is also a contributing factor. Mechanical injury from rough handling or from excessively vigorous air movement may also increase injury to cells.

Control is best attained by using a growing medium that dries out in a reasonable length of time and by avoiding extremes of high humidity, particularly during the night. Moderate shading in extremely bright weather might also be helpful. Sudden lowering of temperature can trigger the reaction. Fortunately, latex eruption is rarely seen on modern cultivars.

LEAF CRIPPLING, DISTORTION, PUCKERING

Various forms of leaf deformity are commonly observed. The symptoms are extremely variable. Most often the damage begins when the leaf is very young. Cells that are physically damaged or ruptured cause the leaf to become distorted as the leaf expands. The physical damage may be due to environmental stress, foliar contact with phosphorous fertilizer, botrytis, thrips, abrasion, or improper handling. In most cases, the damage does not persist on many leaves and does not become economically important.

Figure 17-7. Leaf distortion

Leaf distortion frequently occurs in late September and early October after the plants have been moved from propagation to the finishing area. Branches that develop after pinching may have two or three misshapen and distorted leaves. Close observation of the symptoms can help lead to a logical conclusion as to the cause of the problem and, therefore, how to prevent it from getting worse.

Changes in the temperature and humidity levels contribute to leaf distortion, so growers should help plants transition to the new environment through staged reduction in shade and humidity levels rather than the dramatic change in conditions usually experienced. Misting during the hottest part of the day can help reduce stress and cool tender new leaves as they adjust to the harsh new environment. Avoid overhead application of fertilizers that contain phosphorous and result in damage to the young leaves. Monitor for pest problems, such as thrips, and treat as appropriate if found on the crop. In most instances, these leaves remain distorted, and the leaves that expand later are usually normal and hide the damaged leaves by market time. However, if symptoms continue into October, it is important to reevaluate factors that may be contributing to the problem and correct them before significant damage to the crop results.

POOR CYATHIA DEVELOPMENT

The number of cyathia that develop per stem can be relatively low on some crops. Although this does not usually cause any marketing problems, the final presentation is not optimal. This phenomenon is most often observed on large-bracted cultivars, such as 'Freedom', that are grown under relatively low light levels. The low light does not provide sufficient energy to support a lot of flowers (cyathia). Large-bracted cultivars are more susceptible to poor cyathia development because the bracts have a large demand on the plant's resources (carbohydrates). This has been demonstrated by removing the bracts as they develop; these plants will produce very high cyathia counts. This suggests that conditions that limit, or tone, bract expansion will allow for more cyathia development. Cooler finishing temperatures and plant growth regulators can produce a small, but desirable, reduction in bract size on large-bracted cultivars that will also allow for better cyathia development.

POOR LATERAL BRANCHING

Excessively high temperatures on the stock plant cause the lack of lateral shoot development following pinching. Stock plants that are exposed to average daily temperatures above 75°F (24°C) will produce axillary buds that do not develop properly or may fail to develop at all. These buds will appear blackened or be completely absent from the leaf axil. Cuttings taken from these stock plants will not branch after being pinched. Most poinsettia cultivars in the market today are not susceptible to reduced branching unless prolonged exposure to extreme heat and stress conditions is ongoing. It is still advisable for growers to evaluate cutting sources based

Figure 17-8. Poor branching following pinching results from the stock plants being exposed to high temperatures, which cause the axillary buds to not develop properly in the leaf axils.

on temperatures and conditions impacting stock plants and to avoid sources that have less ability to manage the environmental factors.

POOR ROOT GROWTH

Poor root growth can be caused by several factors. Pathogens, such as *Pythium* root rot, can suppress root growth throughout the production cycle, then plant death may occur in November when the growing conditions are even poorer. *Pythium* is often a problem where the growing medium has been kept excessively wet. Also, irrigation systems that continually recirculate water appear to have chronic disease pressure that makes it difficult to produce an extensive, healthy root system.

Figure 17-9. Poor root growth

In general, plants will place their resources where there is the greatest need. As a result, if luxury amounts of nutrients and water are continually available, then there is no need for plants to expend energy to produce and maintain an extensive root system. There is not a link between the amount of roots and the appearance of the top growth, so limited root growth may not indicate a problem.

PREMATURE CYATHIA DROP

When the cyathia (true flowers) drop off the plants before the flowers reach maturity, this is referred to as premature cyathia abscission, or drop. This may occur before the plants are ready for market, particularly in northern climates under low-light conditions. Because this detracts from the appearance of the poinsettias and makes them appear to be overly mature, it also reduces their economic value. Premature cyathia drop is primarily caused by low light levels and/or high forcing temperatures. Water stress aggravates the problem. These conditions allow the food reserves (carbohydrates) of the plant to become depleted. As the food reserves become low, the plant reacts by dropping the cyathia.

Cloudy weather can be common during late October and November in northern states. If poinsettias are grown at lower than optimum temperatures during the early part of the production period, flower development may be delayed when the cloudy weather begins. It then becomes necessary to raise greenhouse temperatures to speed up the rate of flower development. As temperatures increase, the plants' food reserves are used at a faster rate (high respiration rate) and the plants are more susceptible to premature cyathia drop. It is important to maintain optimum greenhouse temperatures for rapid poinsettia development during the early part of the production period so that when cloudy weather begins, it may then be possible to start lowering greenhouse temperatures and slow the depletion of food reserves.

STEM SPLITTING

Stem splitting occurs when a single flower (cyathium) is initiated in the terminal of a shoot, but that flower fails to develop. Three lateral shoots then develop below the terminal flower. The flowering stimulus can occur even when poinsettias are grown under non-inductive photoperiods (long days). The probability of flower initiation during long days increases as a stem produces leaves and is not pinched. The number of leaves that are produced prior to the terminal flower developing is referred to as the *long*

Figure 17-10. Splitting produces a terminal flower (cyathium) that fails to develop (left, center), resulting in three stems branching below the flower (right).

day leaf number. Cultivars that are most susceptible to splitting may produce twelve to fifteen leaves before a flower initiates in the shoot tip, while more resistant cultivars require more than thirty leaves.

Whenever a shoot is pinched, the lateral shoots that emerge from the leaf axils restart the leaf count. For example, the lowest leaf on a new shoot is leaf #1. After six weeks, that shoot may have ten leaves. If a cutting is removed from the shoot, the cutting may contain leaves #8, 9, and 10. The leaves do not forget their leaf number while the cuttings are in propagation. Following propagation, this shoot continues to develop and produce leaves #11, 12, etc. If the shoot is not pinched and it reaches the long day leaf number, then stem splitting may occur.

Stem splitting is most likely to be observed on cuttings that have been harvested from stock plants in which the shoots are overly mature, i.e., the stems have high leaf numbers due to infrequent cutting harvesting. Cultivars that are susceptible to stem splitting are not recommended for poinsettia tree forms or for straight-ups (non-pinched forms) (see chapter 14, Cultivar Guide). Stem splitting is occasionally observed on poinsettias that have been placed under inductive photoperiods (short days) for a long enough time to initiate flowers but then placed under non-inductive photoperiods (long days), which inhibits further flower development. Stem splitting may also be observed where cool night temperatures (less than 60°F [15°C]) occur under non-inductive photoperiods, inducing flowering, followed by a return to conditions more conducive to vegetative growth.

STEM BREAKAGE

Stem breakage can occur during shipping and handling of finished poinsettias, resulting in reduced quality or unsalable plants and is one of the biggest challenges to poinsettia growers today. Low light levels early in blooming schedule contribute to weakened lateral shoots. In particular, the time prior to the start of short days has been shown to influence stem strength. Light levels above 3,000 f.c. (32 klux) are recommended at this time. Also, plant rings, or supports, have been a practical solution and an insurance policy against stem breakage. Cultivars such as Eckespoint 'Prestige' are highly resistant to stem breakage because of the genetically thick stems and upright branch position.

Figure 17-11. Stem breakage can result from low light conditions early in the production schedule.

There are several other factors that can contribute to stem breakage. Plants that are grown on the edge of a bench are more likely to have lower shoots that grow horizontally so they may intercept more light. These shoots often break off while the plant is placed in a sleeve. Pinching too high and leaving excess nodes can result in too many shoots and leaves growing on individual plants. The result is that the lowest shoots lack adequate light to develop well, and these shoots are more likely to break off.

POOR BRANCHING

The number of stems in the flowering canopy is a crop specification for some markets. Often, pinched 6" (15 cm) crops will only produce two or three main stems, while the remaining stems do not contribute to the flower display. There is not a single cause for this problem. Several of the contributing factors include:

Figure 17-12. Poor branching resulting in low flower count in the flowering canopy.

DAVID HARTLEY

As the poinsettia grew in popularity and volume, the Ecke Ranch soon recognized the need to find solutions to crop problems that could cause economic losses to growers around the world. As our research director, Dr. David Hartley took on the challenge of finding solutions to crop problems through targeted research and investigation into the cause of each disorder. By evaluating significant problems—such as bract edge burn—through coordinated research with scientists at universities and private companies, David was able to help growers understand how to prevent disorders through good production practices. His background in plant physiology and nutrition and his role as an extension agent and educator made for the perfect blending of disciplines.

The ability to take complex problems and find easy to implement solutions is a true testimony to the talent David has shared with growers throughout his years in the industry, a talent he continues to share today in his role with Colorado State University at the W. D. Holly Research Center.

- *Excessively hardened cuttings.* If the axillary buds and stem tissue are restricted during the end of propagation, these buds will not branch as vigorously as the buds associated with leaves that developed after propagation.
- *Low light.* Inadequate light does not allow the plant to support all the possible shoots that initially develop following pinch.
- *Tight spacing.* When poinsettias are tightly spaced for too long, the top two or three shoots become dominant because all the lower shoots do not receive adequate light.
- *No growth regulator.* Poinsettias grown without growth regulators often have a more uneven canopy than do plants that have received some growth regulation. The proper application of growth regulators will produce toned plants, even shoot growth, and improve final plant display. Spray applications target the uppermost shoots, which can allow the lower shoots to "catch up." Growth regulators will usually cause a slight reduction in bract size that can allow more shoots to finish in top of the canopy.
- *Tall primary stem after pinch, and high pinches.* Cuttings that are allowed to stretch in propagation or transplanted cuttings that stretch prior to pinch can have a high pinch height. After pinching, the upper nodes can

be several inches above the lowest nodes. The result is that several inches exist between the upper and the lower nodes on the mother stem. The top shoots become dominant, and the lowest nodes may not catch up to the height of the top shoots.

• *Warm finishing temperatures.* Plants grown warm (above 68°F [20°C]) create very large bracts, which can crowd out smaller shoots. The result is that only two or three flowering shoots can be easily seen. Cooler finishing temperatures (65–68°F [18–20°C]) create smaller bracts so the fourth and fifth shoots are visible in the final canopy.

Even branching can be achieved with proper pinch timing and technique, proper growth regulation, proper timing of plant spacing, and cool finishing temperatures. In addition, Florel applied before and after pinch can improve lateral shoot uniformity (see chapter 5, Height Control, for more on Florel).

18

❦

POSTPRODUCTION CARE
AND HANDLING

Today's poinsettias are genetically improved to last longer and give greater satisfaction to the customer. However, even with superior keeping qualities, poinsettias cannot withstand mishandling or exposure to adverse environmental conditions without suffering a decrease in quality. Special attention to care and handling during shipping and at the retail level is necessary to insure customers receive the best plants possible.

TEMPERATURE

The best temperature range for transporting poinsettias from the greenhouse to the store is 50–55°F (10–13°C). Avoid shipping temperatures below 50°F (10°C), since poinsettias are susceptible to chilling damage. Indicators of chilling injury include bluing or whitening of bracts on red plants. Chilling damage is usually not immediately apparent, but appears one to two days after exposure. Warm temperatures (above 65°F [18°C]) during transport can cause epinasty on susceptible cultivars.

Once a customer has purchased a poinsettia, protection from cold, snow, and frost is very important. Exposure to just a few seconds of freezing temperatures or chilling winds may destroy a beautiful plant. Placing the poinsettia in a sleeve or large, roomy shopping bag to keep the cold air off the bracts will usually give it the protection needed.

WATERING

Poinsettias should be watered thoroughly before being placed on display.

The medium should feel moist at all times; however, overwatering poinsettias on display can be just as detrimental as underwatering the plants. Check the plants daily and water only when the potting mix feels dry to the touch. No fertilizer is needed in the postproduction environment.

When watering the plants, allow excess water to drain through the holes in the bottom of the pot. It is important to discard the excess water, as poinsettias left sitting in water may suffer from permanent root-rot damage. This can be a concern especially when the pots are foil-wrapped or placed in preformed pot covers. If this is the case, be careful to apply just enough water to wet the medium without water coming out the bottom of the pot, or discard the trapped water inside the pot covers.

SLEEVES

The proper care during transit will prevent bruising and mechanical damage to the leaves and bracts. The sleeves should extend 2–3" (5–8 cm) above the tips of the bracts to provide complete protection. The first step in preserving quality is to unbox and unsleeve poinsettias immediately upon arrival. Ideally, poinsettias should not be sleeved for more than twenty-four hours. Prolonged storage of poinsettias in any type of sleeve (paper, plastic, or mesh) may result in epinasty. Poinsettias should never be displayed in their sleeves.

POSTPRODUCTION PROBLEMS

BRACT ABRASION

Poinsettia bracts are very fragile and bruise easily. During shipping they

Figure 18-1. Bract abrasion can be caused by rubbing of the bract against the inside of the shipping containers or in the greenhouse due to close proximity to horizontal airflow fans.

may rub against the plant sleeve, the box, or against each other. Bract abrasion may not be apparent when the plants are first unpacked. To help prevent bract abrasion, use plant sleeves that are taller than the plants and boxes that are taller than the sleeves.

CHILLING INJURY

Poinsettias may be damaged by exposure to temperatures between 32–50°F (0–10°C) without the plant tissue being frozen. The longer plants are exposed, the greater the damage. Chilling injury may not be apparent when the plants are first unpacked, but the damaged bracts develop over time as the plants return to warmer temperatures.

Figure 18-2. Chilling injury results from exposing poinsettias to temperatures below 50°F (10°C).

EPINASTY

Epinasty is a condition characterized by the droopy appearance of the plant. The upward bending of leaf and bract petioles during sleeving causes the plant to produce ethylene. The exposure to the ethylene gas may result in droopy bracts and leaves after the removal of the sleeves (see fig. 17-5). The length of time the plants are sleeved affects the severity of the epinasty.

Newer cultivars tend to be much more resistant to this condition. Generally, recovery from moderate epinasty is possible after forty-eight hours of proper care in a well-lit environment (minimum 100 f.c. [1.1 klux]) with temperatures of 65–75°F (18–24°C). However, plants may be slow to recover or may not recover at all if they have been sleeved for an extended length of time.

There is a link between epinasty and ethylene. See below for an explanation of ethylene and ethylene damage.

ETHYLENE

Ethylene is a gas generated by heaters, gas engines, and poinsettias themselves when sleeved. When poinsettias are exposed to ethylene, the leaves and bracts appear droopy and twisted (see Epinasty above). With extended exposure the leaves may turn yellow and drop. Avoid placing poinsettias in poorly vented areas and remove plants from the shipping boxes and sleeves upon arrival. Don't store or ship poinsettias with bananas or other ethylene-producing fruits. Warn supermarket retailers to keep the plants away from the banana-ripening room and coolers.

FREEZING DAMAGE

Poinsettias are killed by momentary exposure to freezing temperatures. The risk of freezing can be reduced by sleeving and boxing the plants and transporting them in heated trucks.

19

❦

MARKETING POINSETTIAS

PAUL ECKE SR., BUILDING THE FOUNDATION
Paul Ecke Sr. is the person credited with making the poinsettia "the Christmas flower." Paul was born in Magdeburg, Germany, in 1895 and immigrated to the U.S. with his family in 1902. The family settled in Los Angeles and began growing vegetables and cut flowers that they sold in the local markets and from their flower stand on Sunset Boulevard. On a December day in 1906, Paul was walking in the hills above their small farm and noticed a field of bright red wildflowers. Thinking he would display them at the flower stand, he gathered as many as he could carry and brought them home. The brilliant red and green foliage was an instant success with their customers. Overwhelmed by the demand, the Eckes eventually abandoned their other crops and focused their full attention on growing poinsettias.

By 1920, Paul Sr. had developed the first poinsettia that could be grown as a potted plant. The yearly blooming cycle during the winter, near the holiday season, gave him the notion that the poinsettia would make an ideal official holiday flower. But how to promote and market a plant that most people had never heard of or even seen, let alone associate it with the holiday season?

He packed dormant plants in a suitcase and during the 1920s and 30s began to travel the country by train and in his Model T car. He visited growers, teaching them what he had learned and selling them on the idea that poinsettias could be grown indoors anywhere in the country. He encouraged them to grow and market the plant as "*the* Christmas flower." In the years that followed, Paul Ecke Sr. pioneered the techniques for breeding and hybridization of poinsettias in the United States, and in his lifetime saw the poinsettia become universally acknowledged as an icon of the Christmas season.

251

PAUL ECKE JR. AND THE GENIUS OF PRODUCT PLACEMENT

When Paul Ecke Jr. took over the reins of the Ecke Ranch from his father in the early 1960s, he decided that the best way to grow the company was to expose more consumers to poinsettias as a holiday decorating tradition. Television, having become a fixture in most American homes, was the perfect tool. Rather than pay for expensive magazine advertising or television commercials, Paul Jr. devised a very effective public relations strategy to get national television exposure for the poinsettia.

Blooming poinsettia plants were sent free of charge to the set decorators of dozens of televised Christmas specials during the early 1970s. Paul was careful to only place product on shows that would create a visual perception of poinsettias as the perfect way to decorate for Christmas. Holiday shows hosted by Andy Williams, Pat Boone, and Dinah Shore are only a few examples. *The Tonight Show,* hosted by Johnny Carson and now Jay Leno, has for many years featured Paul Ecke poinsettias on the set during December. For a number of years, Johnny and Doc Severinsen kept up a running joke about the proper way to pronounce "poinsettia." This repeated television exposure helped to insure the poinsettia a place in every home at Christmas.

Paul then supported these efforts by getting the "poinsettia story" into hundreds of daily newspapers and family magazines. He diligently communicated with garden writers and editors by sending slides of new poinsettia varieties, decorating ideas, and concepts for interesting poinsettia stories. Examples of story ideas sent to magazines and newspapers include: "History of the Poinsettia Plant," "How to Care for Poinsettias in the Home," and "How to Decorate Using Poinsettias." By making it easy to write about poinsettias, Paul got massive free story placement in every major lifestyle magazine in the country. The Ranch still uses many of the same stories—distributed by e-mail and using digital images.

Today, product placement on television and movies is a major part of consumer marketing. From ET's famous eating of Reese's Pieces to James Bond driving a BMW, we know that product marketing works—and we can thank Paul Ecke Jr. for using product placement and public relations to grow the poinsettia market into what it is today and creating the poinsettia as an American decorating tradition.

MARKETING 101

As greenhouse product marketers, we have a series of hurdles to climb. A good way to start a discussion on marketing is to start with some marketing basics.

Most definitions of marketing start with the overall concept of matching a product or service to a consumer need. As an example, say you are driving and suddenly notice you are thirsty. Your choices are:

- Stop the car at a gas station or convenience store and buy a bottled beverage.
- Stop at a rest area, park, and use a drinking fountain.
- Drive through a fast-food drive-up window and buy a soda.

A marketer's role is to connect your need (thirst) with a product (beverage) or service (drive-through).

All overviews of marketing require the telling of the "Four Ps"—the tools a marketer uses to connect product to need. A marketer would pick some or all of these tools as the marketing program is shaped to support sales.

PRODUCT

The marketer should look at the product as a piece of clay waiting to be shaped into a necessity. Water in a hose is different than water in a small bottle with an Evian label—and has a different price point. Take amoment and reflect—how is your product different from others? Be specific in your examples.

PRICE

The marketer may change the perception of the product just by changing the price. Keeping with the bottled water example—had Evian been priced at 20¢ a bottle versus $2.00 a bottle, the consumer may never have accepted the idea of a "premium" grade of water. It could still be a commodity. Perfume, cosmetics, house paint, and many clothing lines often use price to set consumer expectation. Is your pricing strategy in line with the image you want to maintain in your market?

PROMOTION

Using either purchased promotions such as magazine ads or television commercials or by using promotions driven by public relations activity, a marketer can influence consumers' feelings toward products. How do you use promotion in your business?

PLACE

Place, or distribution, is where and how a product or service is made available. Selling only to high-end clothing boutiques versus making clothing available to a discount store is an example of how much of a product's "value" is determined by where the product is sold. You might expect to see expensive perfume at a department store or boutique, but not at a discount drug store. Much of the product value is set by your choice of distribution. Is your distribution in alignment with the price and value of your product?

MARKETING POINSETTIAS

STARTING WITH THE PRODUCT

Poinsettias have much to offer for the budding marketer. There are few floricultural products that have as elastic a range of product form as the poinsettia. Growers are able to grow poinsettias from small containers up to gigantic tubs. Add the wide range of colors and patterns, and a marketer can easily create the right product for the right customer need. Much has been written over the years that a poinsettia will grow to fill any space in the greenhouse—tight spacing equals promotion priced-plants, and generous spacing equates to high-value, higher quality plants. This very variable quality gives you many choices in matching product to customer needs.

Some of our favorite examples are the Texas Sized tubs grown at Ellison Greenhouses in Brenham, Texas. These gigantic plants have graced both the Texas governor's mansion and the White House. With a total height of over 6' (1.8 m), these are wholesaled at over $100 per plant. Why grow plants of this size? According to P. J. Ellison-Kalil, "Our Texas Sized plants help set our customers expectations of product quality. With our top-of-the-line plants going to the White House, and clearly worth hundreds of dollars, it allows our retailers to ask for premium prices on the rest of our line."

GREENHOUSE GROWER

Figure 19-1. P. J. Ellison-Kalil surrounded by Ellison's renowned poinsettias. Notice the Texas Sized poinsettias in the background.

Small 2" (5 cm) pots of poinsettias sold in self-watering wells are an example of product form at the other end of the poinsettia size scale. By adding a self-watering container to a nice retail display tray, retailers have very successfully marketed mini poinsettias.

Adding the well gives the product a longer shelf life and strategic placement at the checkout stand, where they are not competing for space with other plants, giving retailers a "high turnover" location to display. This is a high-margin crop for both the grower and the retailer, and a fast turnover rate for the retailer is essential for a seasonal plant such as a poinsettia.

At the Ecke Ranch, we have been experimenting with different product forms for many years. Topiary trees and straight-up single-stem plants are two good examples of how to widen a product offering. The Ecke Ranch's blooming crop is sold in Southern California, primarily to upscale retail florists, with high-end product forms commanding good wholesale prices. The core items in the Ecke local program are straight-up plants with dinner plate–sized bracts. These single-stem, multi-cutting per pot plants include three plants to a $6^1/_2$" (17 cm) pot, four plants to a 7" (18 cm) pot, etc. By growing at wide spacing, the Ecke Ranch is able to deliver a high-grade, florist-quality plant and allow our florist customers a product "weapon" to battle promotion-priced plants sold by mass marketers. As of this writing, Ecke charges $8.00 per plant wholesale for a $6^1/_2$" (17 cm) pot, three plants per pot, straight-up.

Growing a high-end crop for a small, high-end florist market is fairly easy to understand and execute. The larger challenge is how to come up with unique product ideas if you grow for the larger market of big-box stores or supermarkets.

Again, the product and product form can help a marketer succeed. Focusing on supermarkets, the typical supermarket plant buyer is in a tight place at Christmas. How do the supermarkets offer good quality poinsettias that match up to other quality products sold year round in the floral section without being overpriced compared to big-box competitors or other supermarket chains? If the buyer guesses wrong, either their sales dollars are too low (bad) or their margin dollars are too low (also bad). To help a supermarket buyer find the right value, balance is critical for long-term success and creative use of product form concepts can be invaluable. Ideas to this group may include:

- Ship "named" varieties. Everyone else is selling red poinsettias—offer your buyers 'Prestige' or 'Jester Red', not just generic red.
- Ship newer novelties to support the upper-end floral department need of a supermarket. Some of the savvy supermarket buyers were the first to embrace the 'Winter Rose' family as a fun new novelty.
- Consider multiplant-per-pot configurations. Three plants pinched in a 6" (15 cm) pot gives a full bush look, very different from what is commonly sold
- Consider different product forms such as mini 'Winter Rose' or 'Jester' trees. Both look great in a 6½" (17 cm) pot with a short stem. How about a square terra-cotta clay pot? It is harder to ship, but it fits the need of being different for a buyer faced with margin and sales issues.

Product packaging can dramatically change the product's consumer value. Packaging can be anything from the pot to the tag to the wrap or pot cover. Poinsettias have traditionally been poorly packaged, with the majority of plants sold in a 6" (15 cm) pot with a red or green pot cover. While maybe novel at some point, it is generic today.

Starting with the pot, a marketer would consider options to differentiate the poinsettia. If everyone else's is in a green plastic pot, should your pot color be different? A different type, shape, or material? If everyone is growing poinsettias in 6" (15 cm) pots, should the pot size be different to help shift into a better-packaged product?

On the outside of the pot, the marketer has many choices. If "all" poinsettias are sold with shiny red and shiny green pot covers, should you consider any of the new Mylar covers and foils as way to reposition a poinsettia for your buyers? What about bows and ribbon? Should you sell the plants "bare" and let the customers decorate their own plants with material sold by the store? All of the above add cost, but they also add value, and if your job is to help the retailer shift away from a generic poinsettia sold "cheap," it is your role as a marketer to offer the retailer choices.

Tags and signs are another method to allow the poinsettia a different look at retail. One technique the Ecke Ranch has used for our local crop has been to use tags with an old-fashioned look to them. If everyone else is using shiny white plastic tags, the Ecke Ranch product has an almost sepia-colored paper tag. Tag companies offer wonderful services to customize a tag to fit your customer requirements. Many recent marketing studies show that a well-packaged plant with a large tag is a more attractive consumer product than the generic plant—even if the plants themselves are identical. Studies note that better packaged plants sell more quickly and at a higher price.

Hanging tags work well with poinsettias, as the tag is above any pot cover. Large hanging tags can convey any one of a number of unique messages:
- Holiday wishes
- Holiday decorating suggestions
- Showcase new varieties
- Plant care
- Space for a co-promotion

Larger tags are more expensive than smaller tags, but larger tags give you space to convey a value-added message and thus allow you to shift consumer perception. Remember: Higher price and faster sales are music to the ears of any retailer.

PRICE AS A TOOL

We see the same plant and pot size selling five pots for $10 at a big-box store; for $7.99 in a supermarket with a nicer wrap, and finally for $17.00 in a high-end florist with a cache pot, ribbon, and gift card.

Clearly we have a series of issues in the market, with the end result being that consumers are often unable to determine any value or quality statement. As consumers, we often default to a quality standard of good, better, best. For example, let's say we have three choices for a power drill at a hardware store—three drills at three different prices. Assuming the consumer knows nothing about drills, the logical thought is that the most expensive one must be best. The drill purchase is then based on how much the consumer is prepared to spend that day, not on the actual quality of the drill!

We force this choice on consumers in most cases and often let the poinsettia's selling price be the single largest factor to establish quality in the customer's mind.

Knowing that price can set quality, a marketer can use price as a tool. Should you offer to your retailers two different 6" (15 cm) products, one with more features and at a higher price? While this can create confusion at the checkout stand, the grower can use this combination of price/package to easily allow the retailer to turn more dollars of sales. This is especially critical when you factor in that at least half of the poinsettias sold are purchased as a gift for someone. When buying a gift, the consumer always wants a quality/value choice. She may ask herself, Just how much is Aunt Martha worth to me this Christmas?

Another opportunity with price is to give the product sizes a name and then price the name. At the Ecke Ranch we do sell 6½" (17 cm) pots of pinched poinsettias, but we call them Holiday Specials, not 6½" pinched poinsettias. Our catalog does list the pot size, as labeling laws are very clear on the topic, but we can market and promote the Holiday Special as the special bundle of plant, tag, promotion that it is—and then price the product accordingly. Other Ranch names include calling a 4" (10 cm) pot a "Pixie"; our 2" (5 cm) mini is a "Mini Star"; and our huge tub is a "Presidential Bouquet."

PROMOTION

Promotion in poinsettias can take many forms, with purchased ad space usually looked at as the most common type of promotion and public-relations-driven story placement a more specialized type of promotion activity. Trade shows, open houses, direct mail, and magazine ads are all types of promotion we frequently see in the poinsettia business.

Most poinsettia promotion is done by retailers to get consumers to look for the product at retail, and most today seem to be priced based, selling a 6" (15 cm) at $4.99, or less! We do see some retailers trying to shift away from price point ads and talk about the latest variety. Many retail ads in the past few years highlight 'Winter Rose' and 'Plum Pudding' as "new" varieties, with the implication being that customers should come to their store, as they have the newest/best quality. Retailers are using a "new" poinsettia to help establish a value not only of the plant, but of their entire store! We also see promotion programs that talk about quality, greenhouse freshness, unique product forms such as trees or mini trees, and novelty colors.

As mentioned earlier, Paul Ecke Jr. was the energy behind much of the initial efforts to use public relations as a tool to get more exposure to poinsettias. Paul was able to get placement on TV specials nationally plus such shows as *The Tonight Show.*

One of his less-talked-about efforts in the local San Diego market is a great example of using public relations to support retailers and price points. The Ecke Ranch has for many years sent *all* the local San Diego television stations free poinsettias to use as decorations for their newsroom sets. Each year in early December a staff member at the Ecke Ranch calls to the local ABC, NBC, CBS, FOX, and WB stations to arrange the delivery. We do not have to give away too many plants—about forty-eight per TV station—but it does take some time to coordinate the deliveries. We then follow up with calls to offer any support we can to tell the story of poinsettias, how to decorate at Christmas, facts and figures, etc. In return, most stations invite someone from the Ecke Ranch to talk about poinsettias, will send out a remote crew to film a story about poinsettias, or will frequently send out the local weather crew to do their location shot from the Encinitas Ranch.

The results are that we get a chance to support our local florists by telling people where they can buy our poinsettias, we can showcase new varieties, and we can show our product quality. This program gives us the chance to support all the poinsettia growers in the area, as consumers will buy plants at all retail outlets. Additionally, we get a chance to add a little more value to the overall crop and keep both growers and retailers happy. Giving away a small number of poinsettias is a cost-effective way to keep a lot of people very happy.

The Ecke Ranch has also used magazine advertising to support our retailers. By using lifestyle magazines such as *San Diego Magazine*—a

typical color glossy magazine full of restaurant review and fancy homes—
we have been able to list all of our florist retailers as places where our
high-quality poinsettias may be purchased.

Ecke also uses the Internet to support the poinsettia sales locally. We
have a consumer Web site (www.pauleckepoinsettias.com) that is full of
easy to find care and history about poinsettias. This is a safe site to send all
local media for more information. It showcases pictures from our library,
and it also lists where one may buy in the local market.

Finally, we do some very traditional public relations every year in
our local market. We will e-mail out a series of stories about poinsettias
to all the local newspapers, addressed to the garden editor of each city
and suburban paper. We also invite them in for a sneak peak at what we
are trialing for next year. Each year we have to keep the story fresh, so
one year we will talk more about care at home, the next year will talk more
about how we select new product for the coming season, then in another
year we will talk more about how to decorate using poinsettias. We help
the garden editors with story ideas, and they in turn help us by writing
about the product and getting more consumers excited about using
poinsettias. A win-win.

PLACE

The last marketing tool we think about is place, or product distribution.
This tool deals with where you choose to sell your plants. Do you sell them
retail out of your own store? Do you sell exclusively to big-box stores? Or
are your poinsettia customers a blend of large and small retailers?

Frequently, we hear from growers that their only choice is to be a
price taker from a big-box store and that the grower's marketing options
are minimal. Changing whom you sell to is a large and important under-
taking. We do see a number of trends in our customer profile. More
wholesale growers are looking at ways to sell retail. More growers are looking to alternate channels such as fund-raisers as a way to diversify their
customer base.

The fund-raising market is an excellent example of how many growers
have shifted their customer base. We understand that over 5% of the
total U.S. poinsettia crop is sold to fund-raisers. Schools, church groups,
scouts, and service organizations are just a few of the outlets for this type

of activity. The service requirements that a grower must provide fund-raiser groups are very different from traditional retailers. Orders are pooled by the group, then plants are drop-shipped to one or more locations. Growers must frequently put more work into how plants are packed and staged so the charity's volunteers can distribute the poinsettias to customers.

One example of a successful fund-raising program uses a mini 'Winter Rose' plant in a self-watering well that is sold in a gift box. By offering schools a better than 30% margin on this gift item and giving the schools something different to sell, program administrators have found many schools like the idea of giving up candy as a fund-raising tool. This makes flowers a great choice, with poinsettias being an easy program to explain and execute. The Ecke Web site, www.pauleckepoinsettias.com, is a great resource to order or download free POP material for fund-raisers.

BARTRAM'S GARDEN

Bartram's Garden in Philadelphia has a long history of firsts. In 1728, botanist John Bartram established the first botanic garden devoted to the collection and study of North American plants, and in 1783, his sons issued the first printed plant catalog in America. Robert Carr, husband of Bartram's granddaughter Ann Bartram Carr, received some of the earliest poinsettia cuttings and seeds sent by Joel Poinsett and others from Mexico in 1828–29. So impressed by its extraordinary color, Carr submitted a "A new euphorbia with bright scarlet bracteas or floral leaves" to the First Semi-Annual Exhibition of Fruits, Flowers and Plants of the Pennsylvania Horticultural Society," held June 6, 1829, an event now known as the Philadelphia Flower Show.

From the time of this first public appearance in 1829, the poinsettia captured the hearts of all who saw it, and the link to the richness of Christmas holiday tradition was established.

While shifting the customer base to a retail or fund-raiser base is not suitable for many growers, the approach of treating current customers differently often is a solution. For example, we see many supermarket customers looking to have products and services shifted either up to a more traditional retail florist package or going the other way and trying to take on mass merchants with low-priced product. The growers' role in helping current customers make key decisions is vital.

Being a marketer today is not all that different than when Paul Ecke Jr. set the stage back in the 1970s. We have a few more tools with CDs and the Internet, and there is a very different retail landscape, but overall the tenets have not changed; the four Ps—**p**roduct, **p**rice, **p**romotion and **p**lace—still work as an overall template for a marketer to make decisions. And, the poinsettia still has many opportunities to allow the grower and retailer great success.

SUGGESTED READING

Some books to read on overall marketing include:

Why We Buy: The Science of Shopping by Paco Underhill (Simon & Schuster, 1999).

Purple Cow: Transform Your Business by Being Remarkable by Seth Godin (Portfolio Publishing, 2003).

The 22 Immutable Laws of Marketing by Al Ries and Jack Trout (Harper Business, 1993).

Just Ask a Woman: Cracking the Code of What Women Want and How They Buy by Mary Lou Quinlan (Wiley, 2003).

GLOSSARY

abscission. The dropping of leaves or cyathia resulting from a lack of carbohydrates or exposure to an environmental stress.

abiotic. Not caused or produced by living organisms.

alkalinity. A measure of the bicarbonates and carbonates in the irrigation water. High alkalinity water causes the growing media pH to increase over time, while low alkalinity water causes the growing media pH to decrease over time.

anthesis. The stage of flower development when the male flower part (the anther) first sheds pollen. Anthesis is often used as an indicator of a poinsettia's maturity.

apex. The tip of a plant organ; that portion of a root or shoot containing the apical meristem.

auxin. A naturally occurring plant hormone. Auxins are used as rooting hormones to stimulate rooting in propagation.

axillary bud. Meristem positioned in the leaf axil between the leaf petiole and the main stem that develops into a lateral shoot when the shoot apex is removed (pinched).

bacterium (*pl.* bacteria). A unicellular microscopic organism that lacks chlorophyll and multiplies by dividing in two.

biotic. Caused or produced by living organisms.

blight. A disease that results in sudden, conspicuous damage that is not limited to small spots. Symptoms of blight may include withering, cessation of growth, and death of part or all the plant.

bracts. Modified leaves often associated with flowers. On poinsettias, bracts are the brightly colored part of the plant immediately below the cyathia. *True bracts* refer to the three bracts immediately below the cyathia and emerge red colored. *Transitional bracts* refer to the bracts that appear on the stem below the true bracts and are initially green, turning red color as they mature.

callus. A mass of undifferentiated cells. Callus cells form at the base of a poinsettia cutting prior to rooting.

canopy closure. The time when the leaves of neighboring plants begin to overlap. At this point stem elongation begins to increase rapidly.

canker. A localized necrotic area on a plant generally occurring on woody tissue. The infected tissue becomes shrunken, and the stem may become girdled, causing a wilt or blight of the tissue above the canker.

chlamydospore. A thick-walled spore resistant to temperature and moisture extremes.

chlorotic. Yellowing of normally green tissue.

conidium (*pl.* conidia). An asexual fungal spore.

cultivar. A cultivated variety.

cyathium (*pl.* cyathia). The true flower structure of the poinsettia. The cyathia are not as conspicuous as the brightly colored bracts that surround the cyathia.

daily light integral (DLI). The sum of the light delivered throughout the course of a day. The unit for DLI is mol·m^{-2}·day^{-1}, or moles/day.

DIF. The difference between the day and the night temperature (day temperature − night temperature = DIF). Stem elongation increases as the DIF increases.

electrical conductivity (EC). A measure of the soluble salt content of a solution. This provides a measure of the amount of salts (or fertilizer) present in a fertigation solution or in the growing media.

enation. Ruffled leaf tissue that appears on the interveinal leaf tissue on the underside of the leaf.

epinasty. The wilted appearance of leaves and bracts that have been exposed to ethylene.

fasciation. Multiple stems that are fused together side-by-side on poinsettias grown in excessively high temperatures.

feathering. The appearance of flowers (cyathia) in the leaf axils down the stem below the primary flowers that appear at the top of the shoot.

fungus (*pl.* fungi). Saprophytic and parasitic lower plants that lack chlorophyll.

gibberellic acid. A naturally occurring plant hormone that stimulates cell elongation. Plant growth regulators that inhibit stem elongation are actually inhibiting the synthesis of gibberellic acid.

graphical tracking. The process of weekly measuring plant height and comparing the actual height to an ideal height. This provides a tool for aiding growers in making height management decisions.

integrated pest management (IPM). Employs various pest control strategies, including sanitation, exclusion, scouting, monitoring, biological control, and chemical control.

late stretch. Rapid stem elongation that occurs during the last three weeks prior to flowering.

latex. A milky fluid of mixed composition found in some herbaceous plants and trees. Its function is not clear but it may assist in protecting wounds.

lesion. A localized area of discolored, diseased tissue.

mycelium (*pl.* mycelia). The stringlike tissue that makes up the body of a fungus.

necrotic. Dead and discolored.

nematode. Wormlike animal, generally microscopic, that lives saprophytically in water or soil or as a parasite of plants and animals.

night-interruption lighting. Low light intensity lighting (~10 foot-candles) provided in the middle of the night (typically 10 p.m. to 2 a.m.) to provide long day (short night) conditions which keep poinsettias growing in a vegetative state. Different light sources can be used, such as incandescent, fluorescent, and high-pressure sodium lamps.

parasite. An organism living on or in another living organism, usually causing it harm.

pathogen. Disease-causing organism.

pH. A measure of the concentration of hydrogen ions in a solution. The growing media pH influences the availability of nutrients to the plant.

phytotoxicity. Damage appearing on leaves or bracts due to the application of a pesticide, wetting agent, etc.

pith. A usually continuous central strand of spongy tissue in plant stems that functions chiefly in storage.

saprophyte. An organism that uses dead organic material for food.

senescence. The aging process of a plant part, such as a leaf, that usually terminates with abscission of that plant part.

splitting. The premature initiation and development of terminal flower buds on vegetative plants.

sporangium (*pl.* sporangia). A reproductive structure that produces asexual spores.

spore. The reproductive unit of fungi, comparable to a seed.

APPENDIX A

POINSETTIA RESOURCES ON THE INTERNET

ECKE RANCH WEB SITE

WWW.ECKE.COM

Crop Information and Fastfax Cultivar Information Sheets: Download information sheets for all Ecke cultivars.

Disease and Insect Control Charts: Useful charts containing a list of the federally registered pesticides and fungicides for use on poinsettias.

Graphical Tracking Software: Download software to produce your own graphical tracking charts.

Poinsettia Diagnostic Key: The key walks you through a step-by-step process from initial diagnosis to potential causes and solutions for your particular production problem.

Production Guidelines: A list of Technical Information Bulletins on cultural and production issues

Tech Help Bulletin Board and Poinsettia Forum: Interactive bulletin board for discussing poinsettia issues with experts

Tech Updates: Technical documents, archived Eckefresh newsletter, and Ecke E-Letters

Product Catalog: View the latest listing of poinsettia cultivars from the Ecke Ranch

Consumer information support: Poinsettia history, care, support information and re-blooming instructions available at **www.pauleckepoinsettias.com.**

CALCULATORS FOR PLANT GROWTH REGULATORS, FERTILIZER, AND ACID INJECTION

From North Carolina State University, these spreadsheets can be downloaded to aid in making greenhouse calculations:
http://www.floricultureinfo.com

COST ACCOUNTING

These two sites provide guidelines for getting started doing cost analysis and budgeting while using poinsettia as an example crop.

From the University of Maryland:
http://www.agnr.umd.edu/MCE/Publications/Publication.cfm?ID=165

From Michigan State University:
http://www.hrt.msu.edu/HortLinks/pdf_files/Production_Costs_Article.pdf

MARKETING

A unique European cause marketing program:
http://www.stars-for-europe.de/english/

NATIONAL POINSETTIA CULTIVAR TRIALS

Results of annual trials conducted at Purdue University, North Carolina State University, and the University of Florida:
http://www.poinsettiatrial.org

NATIONAL POINSETTIA DAY

December 12 is National Poinsettia Day:
http://www.ecke.com/html/h_corp/corp_pntday.html

POINSETTIA CAM

See poinsettias grown from start to finish at Purdue University (during poinsettia season only): http://128.210.161.164/view/view.shtml

POINSETTIA FLOWER DEVELOPMENT

From the University of New Hampshire, the weekly growth and development of forty poinsettia cultivars: **http://www.ceinfo.unh.edu/poinseta.htm**

POINSETTIA HEIGHT CONTROL AND GRAPHICAL TRACKING

From the University of Florida, weekly height reports during the poinsettia season: **http://hort.ifas.ufl.edu/floriculture/height2003/index.htm**

POINSETTIA PRODUCERS GUIDE

From Texas A&M University: **http://aggie-horticulture.tamu.edu/ greenhouse/nursery/guides/poinsettia/history.html**

POURTHRU GUIDELINES FOR POINSETTIAS

From North Carolina State University, growing media testing guidelines for the PourThru method. Includes charts for recording measurements: **http://www.ces.ncsu.edu/depts/hort/floriculture/hils/HIL590c.pdf2OK http://www.ces.ncsu.edu/depts/hort/floriculture/crop/crop_poinsettia.htm**

APPENDIX B

CONVERSION TABLES

LIQUID MEASURES

1 tablespoon = 3 teaspoons = 0.5 fluid ounces = 14.8 milliliters
1 fluid ounce = 2 tablespoons = 29.57 milliliters
1 cup = 8 fluid ounces = 16 tablespoons = 236.6 milliliters
1 pint = 2 cups = 16 fluid ounces = 473.2 milliliters
1 quart = 4 cups = 2 pints = 32 fluid ounces = 0.946 liters
1 gallon = 4 quarts = 8 pints = 128 fluid ounces = 3.785 liters
1 liter = 2.114 pints = 1.057 quarts = 1000 milliliters
1 cubic foot of water = 7.5 gallons = 62.4 pounds = 28.3 liters
1 acre inch of water = 27,154 gallons = 3,630 cubic feet

VOLUME

1 cubic inch = 0.00058 cubic feet = 16.4 cubic centimeters
1 cubic foot = 1,728 cubic inches = 0.037 cubic yards = 0.028 cubic meters
1 cubic yard = 27 cubic feet = 0.765 cubic meters
1 cubic centimeter = 1 milliliter

LENGTH/DISTANCE

1 inch = 2.54 centimeters = 25.4 millimeters
1 foot = 12 inches = 0.3048 meters = 30.48 centimeters
1 meter = 3.28 feet = 39.38 inches
1 mile = 1,760 yards = 5,280 feet = 1.61 kilometers = 1,609 meters
1 kilometer = 1,093 yards = 3,281 feet = 0.6214 miles

WEIGHT

1 gram = 1,000 milligram
1 kilogram = 1,000 grams = 2.205 pounds = 35.27 ounces
1 ounce = 28.3 grams
1 pound = 16 ounces = 454 grams
1 ton = 2,000 pounds = 907.2 kilograms = 0.907 metric tons

AREA

1 square inch = 6.45 square centimeters
1 square foot = 144 square inches = 929 square centimeters
1 square yard = 9 square feet = 0.836 square meters
1 square meter = 10,000 square centimeters = 10.76 square feet
1 square mile = 640 acres = 2.59 square kilometers
1 acre = 0.405 hectare = 4,840 square yards = 4,047 square meters = 43,560 square feet
1 hectare = 2.47 acres = 107,635 square feet = 10,000 square meters

CONCENTRATION

1% = 10,000 ppm
1 ppm = 1 milligram per liter

ELECTRICAL CONDUCTIVITY (EC)

1 millimho per centimeter (mmhos/cm) = 1 milliSiemen per centimeter (mS/cm) = 1 deciSiemen per meter (dS/m)

ALKALINITY (BICARBONATES)

1 milliequivalent (meq.) = 50 ppm

TEMPERATURE

$°F = °C \times 1.8 + 32$
$°C = (°F - 32) \times 0.56$

°F	32°	41°	50°	59°	68°	77°	86°	95°	104°
°C	0°	5°	10°	15°	20°	25°	30°	35°	40°

LIGHT

1 foot-candle = 1 lumen/square foot = 10.76 lux = 0.01076 kilolux
1 foot-candle = 0.192 µmol m^{-2} s^{-1} = 0.928 W m^{-2} (for sunlight*)

*These conversion factors are unique for sunlight. Artificial light sources will use different conversions. See the following table.

Light Source	Visible light (foot-candles)	Photosynthetically active radiation (PAR) (µmol m^{-2} s^{-1})	Solar radiation (W m^{-2})
Sun	1,000	192	93
High-pressure sodium	1,000	127	56
Metal halide	1,000	152	73
Incandescent	1,000	215	104
Fluorescent (cool white)	1,000	145	65

Note: As an approximation, full sunlight during the summer at noon = ~10,000 foot-candles = ~2,000 µmol m^{-2} s^{-1} = ~1,000 W m^{-2} = ~100,000 lux = ~100 klux

Light intensity* (foot-candles at noon)	Estimated** daily light integral (DLI) (moles/day)		
	Winter (8–10 hours)	Spring/Fall (11–13 hours)	Summer (14–16 hours)
1,000	4	5	6
2,000	7	9	11
3,000	10	13	16
4,000	13	17	21
5,000	15***	21	26
6,000		25	31
7,000		29	36
8,000			41
9,000			46
10,000			

* Measured at noon on a sunny day
** This is not a direct conversion since the day length impacts the calculation. The lower number is more typical of winter day lengths, while the higher number is typical for summer day lengths. The northern U.S. will have slightly lower numbers during the winter.
*** Shaded areas: These numbers are rarely achieved inside of greenhouses due to shading from the greenhouse infrastructure and shade cloth.

APPENDIX C

DESIGNING LIGHTING SYSTEMS
FOR NIGHT-INTERRUPTION LIGHTING

INCANDESCENT LAMPS

CALCULATING INCANDESCENT BULB REQUIREMENTS
FOR NIGHT INTERRUPTION LIGHTING

Input	Unit
Desired light intensity	foot-candles
Greenhouse area	ft^2
Lamp flux*	lumens/bulb

Calculated values**	Equation
Number of fixtures	Desired light intensity x greenhouse area / lamp flux
Estimated height above crop (ft.)	$\sqrt{\text{lamp flux}}/(4.2 \times \text{desired light intensity})$
Area per bulb	Greenhouse area/number of fixtures

* Check manufacturer's specifications, since lamp type (wattage) and the reflector will affect this number. See examples listed below.
** Actual measurements should be made to verify the calculations

Incandescent lamp examples:

Bulb (W)	Lamp flux (lumens/bulb)
40W	430
100W	1,630
200W	3,500

275

HIGH-PRESSURE SODIUM LAMPS

One 400W HPS lamp mounted 15' ft. above a canopy will deliver a minimum of 10 foot-candles to a 1,200 ft.^{2} area (30' x 40'). The maximum light intensity in that area will be 42 f.c., while the average light intensity is 22 f.c.

The addition of an oscillating reflector will allow one 400W HPS lamp to deliver a minimum of 10 f.c. to a 30' x 90' area (2,700 ft.^{2}) when mounted 12–14' above the canopy.

INDEX

* Italic page numbers indicate figures; page numbers with an italic *t* indicate tables.

277

C

'C-1', 6, *6*, 8
Calcium (Ca), 30, 75, 77, 92, 103–105, *104*
    bract edge burn and, 232–233
    foliar applications of, 233
Calcium nitrate, 91
Callus formations, 21–22, 25, *25*, 32
Callus tissue, 21–22, 24, 43
Canopy closure, 64–65
CapSil, 28–29, 50
Carbohydrate partitioning, 105
Cathey, H. Marc, 61
Center bud drop, 171
Chelated nutrients, 106
Chemical control
    in disease management, 213
    in pest management, 196–199
Chemical properties
    media pH, *92,* 92–93, *93*
    media soluble salts, 93–96
'Chianti', *10,* 11, *134,* 141, 149, 149*t*, 186
Chilling injury, 247, 249, *249*
Chlorination, 78
Chlorine (Cl), 111
    injury from, *233,* 233–234
Chlorosis, 93, 107, 109, 110
Choanephora wet rot, 217–218, *218*
Christmas flowering, schedule for, 166*t,*
    166–167
Color series concept, 6–7, 7
Compound 111, 106
Constant liquid fertilization (CLF), 116
Copper (Cu), 74, 91, 92, 110
Copper-based products, 36
Copper sulfate, 26
Corynespora bract and leaf spot, *218,* 218–219
Crinkle mosaic virus, 230
Critical pinch, 16
Crop spacing, 63–65, *63t, 64*
Crud, 237
Cuetlaxochitl, 2
Cultivation, 3–5
Cultural practices
    in disease management, 212
    in pest management, 194
Curative approach to pest control, 196

Cut poinsettias, 165–173
    containers and support in, 169
    disbudding in, 168–169
    greenhouse environment in, 169–170
    harvest in, 172
    insects and diseases in, 170
    physiological disorders in, 170–171
    pinching in, 168–169
    postharvest in, 172–173
    scheduling in, 166*t,* 166–167
    spacing in, 168
    stem-length in, 167–168
Cutting disorders, 37. *See also* Physiological
    disorders
    brown callus, 37
    hard growth, *37,* 37–38
    leaf scarring, 38
    yellow leaves, 38–39, *39*
Cuttings. *See also* Rooted cuttings
    callused, 22
    handling unrooted, *23,* 23–24
    hard, 37–38
    harvesting of, 13
    length of stem, 19
    maturity of stock plants, 18–19
    offshore, 39
    precooling, 36
    size of stock plants, 19, *19*
Cutworms, 208–209
Cyathium, 1, 129, *129*
    poor development of, 239
    premature drop, 240–241
Cyclic lighting, 18
Cycocel (chlormequat), 33, 49, 51, 52, *53,*
    54–55, *55,* 59, 60, 61, 157, 163

D

Daily light integral (DLI), 123
'Dark Indianapolis Red', 5, 7
Day-length extension lighting, 18, 137–138
Delayed flowering, *56*
Delphastus pusillus, 196
Dialeurodes citrifolii, 206
DIF, *62,* 62–63, 120–121
    negative, 62